MEMORY STONES

A History of Welsh-Americans

in Central New York

and Their Churches

Memory Stones

A History of Welsh-Americans in Central New York and Their Churches

by Jay G. Williams III

PURPLE MOUNTAIN PRESS
Fleischmanns, New York

BR
555
.N7
W55
1993

First Edition
1993

Published by
PURPLE MOUNTAIN PRESS, LTD.
Main Street, P.O. Box E3
Fleischmanns, New York 12430

Copyright © 1993 by Jay G. Williams III

All rights reserved under International and
Pan-American Copyright Conventions

Library of Congress Cataloging-in-Publication Data

Williams, Jay G. (Jay Gomer), 1961-
   Memory stones : a history of Welsh-Americans in central New York and their churches / by Jay G. Williams III. -- 1st ed.
      p.   cm.
   Includes bibliographical references (p.   ) and index.
   ISBN 0-935796-43-6 (alk. paper)
   1. Protestant churches--New York--History--19th century. 2. New York (State)--Church history--19th century. 3. Welsh Americans--New York--History--19th century. I. Title.
BR555.N7W55   1993
280'.4'089916607476--dc20   93-27303
                                                                                              CIP

Manufactured in the United States of America

Printed on acid-free paper

To Lilly

Memory Stones

WHEN THE WHOLE NATION had finished crossing the Jordan, Yahweh spoke to Joshua. "Choose out twelve men from the people, one man from each tribe, and give them the command: 'Take from here, from mid-Jordan, twelve stones; carry them with you and set them down in the camp where you pass the night.' " Joshua called the twelve men he had marked out from the Israelites, one man from each tribe, and told them, "Pass on before the Ark of Yahweh your God into the mid-Jordan, and each of you take one stone on his shoulder, matching the number of the tribes of Israel, to make a memorial of this in your midst; for when in days to come your children ask you, 'What do those stones mean for you?', you will tell them, 'The waters of the Jordan separated in front of the ark of the covenant of Yahweh, and when it crossed the Jordan, the waters of the river vanished. These stones are an everlasting reminder of this to the Israelites.' " The Israelites did as Joshua told them; they took twelve stones from the mid-Jordan to match the number of the tribes of Israel, as Yahweh had told Joshua; they carried them over to the camp and set them down there. Then Joshua set up twelve stones in mid-Jordan in the spot where the feet of the priests who carried the ark had rested; they are there even now.

Joshua 4:1-9
The Jerusalem Bible

Contents

Table of Photographs 13
Acknowledgments 15
Foreword 17
Introduction 21

Chapter I: Remsen-Steuben 23
Baron de Steuben. 24
First Settlers 26
Congregational Churches:
Capel Ucha 27
Penymynydd 34
Bethel 37
Peniel 41
Ninety-Six (Congregational) 43
Baptist Churches:
Capel Isaf 44
Third Baptist Church 47
First Baptist Church of Remsen 49
Bardwell Mill 50
Capel Bont 52
Calvinistic Methodist Churches:
Penycaerau 53
Penygraig 60
Nant-Cobin 63
French Road-Hebron 66
Capel Cerrig 69
Enlli 77
Ninety-Six (Calvinistic Methodist) 80
Wesleyan Churches:
Sixty Corners 81
Ninety-Six (Wesleyan) 82

Chapter II: Neighboring Towns 83
Trenton:
Prospect 83
Baptist Church 84
Moriah 84
Calvinistic Methodist Church 86
Holland Patent 87
Baptist Church 87
Zion 88
Congregational Church 89
Barneveld 91

South Trenton 92
Baptist Church 93
Wesleyan Church 95
Deerfield-Marcy:
Salem 96
Bryn Mawr 100
Marcy Baptist .101
Bethania 101
Rehobeth 103
Newport:
Bryn Seion 104
Salem 105
Salisbury 107

Chapter III: Utica **108**
First (Welsh) Baptist 109
Bethesda 113
Moriah 119
Coke Memorial 130
Welsh Episcopal Church 132

Chapter IV: Utica's Suburbs **133**
New York Mills 133
New Hartford 136
Frankfort Hill 138
Ilion 139
Clinton 141

Chapter V: Southern Oneida County **143**
Waterville 143
Paris 145
Bridgewater .147
Plainfield 148
Calvinistic Methodist Church 149
Shiloh 151

Chapter VI: Madison County **155**
Nelson 155
Capel Bach 156
Peniel Church 158
West Eaton 162

Chapter VII: Rome and Vicinity **163**
Camroden 164
Congregational Church 164

Calvinistic Methodist Church 165
Rome:
Bethel 170
Rehobeth 175
Delta 177
Oriskany 177
Quaker Hill .179
Webster Hill .181
Mullen Hill .182
Western Hill .183

Chapter VIII: Lewis County and Beyond 184
Gomer Flats .185
Collinsville .185
Constableville 188
Turin 189
Welsh Hill 190
Nebo 191
Seion 192
The Valley Church 194
Lowville 194
Port Leyden .194
Boonville 195
Sandy Creek .195
Richville 196

Postscript 201
Afterword 204
Sources 205
Index 215
Appendix 238

Table of Photographs

Chapter I

Steuben Cabin 25
Ty Cerrig 28
Capel Ucha Cemetery 30
Penymynydd Monument 36
District 9 School 38
Bethel 40
Peniel 42
Capel Isaf Cemetery 47
First Baptist Church 49
Bardwell Baptist Church 51
Capel Bont Cemetery 52
Home of James Owen 55
Penycaerau Cemetery 57
Penycaerau Monument 59
Penygraig Monument 63
Cobin Cemetery 64
French Road Church 67
Capel Cerrig 70
Enlli 77
Sixty Corners 81

Chapter II

Moriah 85
Calvinistic Methodist Church 86
Congregational Church 90
Trenton Congregational Church 92
South Trenton Baptist Cemetery 94
South Trenton Wesleyan Cemetery 96
Salem 98
East Davis Road 100
Bethania Cemetery 102
Bryn Seion Cemetery 105
Salem Cemetery 106

Chapter III

Plymouth-Bethesda 116
Seneca Street Church 121
Peniel School 124
Moriah-Olivet 125

Coke Memorial 131

Chapter IV

Salem 134
Zion 137
"Y Capel Cymraig"* 140

Chapter V

Congregational Church 144
Rowland Morris Farmhouse 145
Lincoln Davies Store* 147
Plainfield Cemetery* 149
Parsonage 152
Shiloh Monument 153

Chapter VI

Capel Bach 156
Peniel Church 159

Chapter VII

Original Calvinistic Methodist Church 166
Camroden Presbyterian Church 169
Bethel Presbyterian Church 171
Rehobeth 176
Oriskany Welsh Church 178
Quaker Hill Cemetery 180
Webster Hill Church 181
Roberts Farm 182

Chapter VIII

Collinsville Union Church 186
Turin Welsh Church 190
Welsh Hill Cemetery* 191
Welsh Hill School* 193
Ty Cerrig* 197
Richville Welsh Church* 198
Historical Marker* 199

Cover: Capel Cerrig, Prospect Street, Remsen.

All photographs are by Jay G. Williams, except those with an asterisk which were taken by the author.

Acknowledgments

OVER THE COURSE OF THE PAST YEAR OR TWO, I have had the opportunity to speak with many people who have first hand memories of the Welsh churches in Central New York. Many of the people with whom I spoke either attended a Welsh church or had relatives who attended. Some were local historians while others own or maintain former Welsh churches or their cemeteries. The recollections of these people have given life to this book and I am, therefore, deeply indebted to them for taking time to share their memories with me.

Baron de Steuben	Lorena Jersen
Capel Ucha	Ola Griffith Shufelt
Penymynydd	Ray Davis, Lorena Jersen
Bethel	Bernard Williams, Norman Williams
Capel Isaf	Ola Griffith Shufelt
First Baptist-Remsen	Emogene Walter
Penycaerau	Margaret Davies Jones
Penygraig	Nadine Thomas, Leola Thomas
Nant-Cobin	Spencer Evans
French Road	Rev. Paul Creedel
Capel Cerrig	Leonard Wynne, Dorothy Wynne
Enlli	Oliver Jones
Holland Patent	Virginia Kelly
Barneveld	Rev. Derwent Suthers

South Trenton Baptist	Joyce Schweinsberg, Gertrude Reynolds
South Trenton Wesleyen	Mr & Mrs. John L. Sullivan
Salem-Deerfield	David Winston, Gail Lepper, John T. Dizer
Bryn Mawr-Deerfield	Alice Folts
Marcy	Raymond Ball
Salem-Newport	Caroline Canary
Seion-Newport	Ross Corpy
First Baptist-Utica	Rev. Craig Davis-Johnson
Bethesda	Irene Jones
Moriah	David Ellis, Norman Williams, Gwyndaf Roberts, Mair Lloyd
Coke Memorial	Ceinwen Davies Wall
New York Mills	Paula Killian, David Humphrey, Sara Schol
New Hartford	George Humphreys
Ilion	Elizabeth Williams Gorney
Clinton	Phillip Munson
Plainfield	Rose Jones, Deborah Davis, Elizabeth Russell, Ellen Price, Donald Davies, Floyd Armstrong
Camroden	Edwin Evans, Emlyn Griffith
Rome	Mary Downing, Rev. Robert O'Meara
Quaker Hill	Mary Craig Olson
Webster Hill	Robert Williams, Roger Williams
Lewis County	Robert Williams
Richville	Helen Reed
Sandy Creek	Margaret Kestler

I would also like to thank the St. David's Society of Utica for providing a grant for the typing of this book, and Joanne Grower for typing the first draft. I am very greatful for the map of the Welsh settlements which was designed and drawn by Jessica Loy. My mother, Hermine Williams, was very helpful in reviewing the manuscript and in reviewing and preparing the index. Also, my father, Jay G. Williams, has been a great source of help, both in photographing sites and in proofreading. Finally, my wife has been a constant source of encouragement since I began researching this project. Without her love and patience this book would not have been possible.

Jay G. Williams III
Clinton, New York,
May 1, 1993

Forword

IT WAS A WARM AUGUST SUNDAY MORNING. My wife and I had arrived at Plymouth-Bethesda Church just before the start of the service. As the Welsh are well known for arriving early, the sanctuary had probably been nearly full for half an hour. After finding a parking space on State Street, we ran to the thick front doors, where we caught our breath before entering.

Inside, the ushers directed us to a pew in the middle of the congregation. The parishioners seemed at first to be an indistinguishable blur, but soon the sea of faces took shape. From behind bulletins and hymnbooks emerged the Robertses, the Williamses, the Hugheses and the Joneses, lots of Joneses.

Women fanned themselves in the heat of a warm summer morning; the organist played a Welsh hymn as the congregation chatted. Friends gave nods of acknowledgement across the room, and the ushers counted heads for the church's records. This would be a good Sunday for attendance because many people from other churches had come to hear a prominent Welsh preacher, Rev. D. Ben Rees, give the morning sermon.

Rev. Rees was known throughout Wales for his radio broadcasts which originated from his church in Liverpool, England. When he took the pulpit at Plymouth-Bethesda that warm August morning in 1987, the hearts of those in attendance were filled with excitement and anticipation that, through the preacher's words, the hearers would be able to feel the spirit of their homeland, if only for a brief moment.

Rev. Rees preached both in English and Welsh, switching back and forth from one to the other, with considerable frequency. His text was Joshua 4:1-9, which recounts how the Israelites erected stones at the edge of the Jordan to forever remind those who came after where they had come from. He called these monuments "memory stones." "Memory stones." "Memory stones." Again and again he repeated the phrase as his deep voice boomed to every corner of the church.

The previous day Rev. Rees, and the group of Welsh tourists he was leading, had been given a tour of the Welsh "capels," which dot Oneida County's landscape. He had seen Capels Cerrig, Bethel and Enlli. He had seen the cemeteries where the Welsh pioneers rest at Ucha, Isaf, Nant, Sixty and Bont. He had seen the stone markers erected where Penycaerau, Penygraig and the Bardwell church once stood. He had entered the French Road church, opened the old Welsh Bible to Psalm 121 and read, "I will lift up my eyes to the hills." He had walked to Penymynydd on the top of the hill where many of the early Welsh settlers had lived. He had seen there the overgrown foundations and the well-maintained cemetery.

"These places, these capels, these monuments are our memory stones," he said. "These stones serve to remind us of the common heritage of faith which we share."

The preacher's voice rose and the room was filled with a spirit I had never felt before. This was the "hwyl" I had heard so much about. This was the spirit and fervor which swept over Wales in the nineteenth century and led many Welsh to seek a new home in America.

As I sat mesmerized by the preacher's words, my eyes fell on the large stained-glass window behind the pulpit. It depicts an American "memory stone," Plymouth Rock. This scene of the Pilgrims' arrival in America has become a common memory for every American school child, whether they are descended from those first settlers or not. The actual Plymouth Rock is not impressive; it is a rock like a thousand others along the Atlantic, distinguished only by the "memorial shrine" which surrounds it. Its importance is that it marks where the Pilgrims passed into a new land. It is a memory stone for all Americans.

A few blocks away at Moriah-Olivet, the window behind the altar presents another memory stone, the rock upon which Jesus prayed in the Garden of Gethsemane. While that stone is no different from the thousands of stones in the Kidron Valley outside Jerusalem, it is the focus of the church's sanctuary because it marks the journey of Christ. It is a memory stone for all Christians.

In Wales, "standing stones," similar to those at Stonehenge, were possibly erected to mark some important event. While the monuments are impressive, their meaning has been lost over time. The memories those stones were intended to invoke have slipped away. Images of all these "memory stones" filled my head as Rev. Rees continued.

As the preacher captivated the congregation, the significance of the Welsh capels, monuments, and cemeteries which he had visited became clear. Those structures and stones, while not grand in appearance, are significant in that they mark the passage of the Welsh into a new land. Furthermore, they are not only the memory stones of Welsh-Americans but also of all residents of Central New York. They are physical reminders of the reasons our forebears came to this country, of the hopes and dreams of the new immigrants, and of the transformation of a community of immigrants into a community of Americans.

This book is intended to allow the reader to discover the many memory stones of the Welsh in Central New York which often lie forgotton in our now fast-paced world. It is hoped that the information which it contains will allow future generations to know the stories behind these many landmarks, so that our memorials do not become like the standing stones of Wales, impressive reminders of forgotten events.

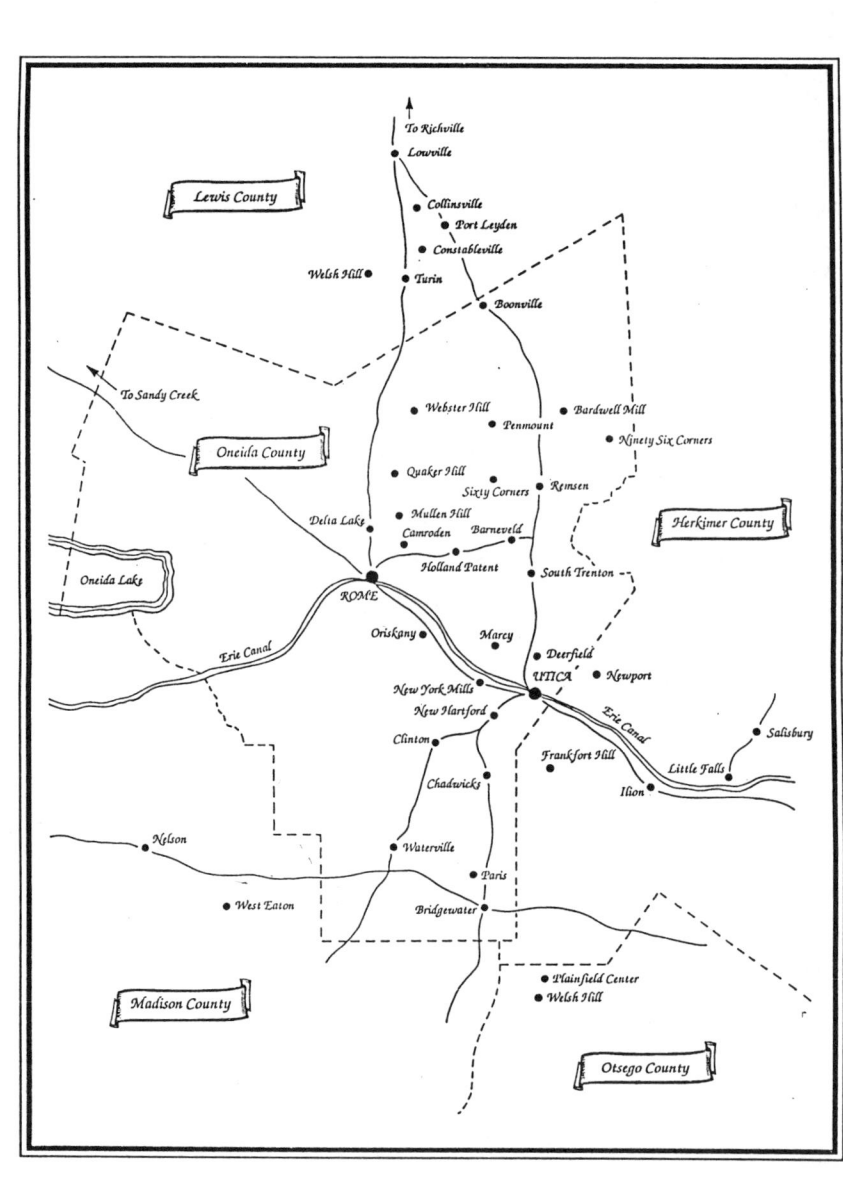

Introduction

OVER THE LAST YEAR I HAVE SEARCHED for the physical reminders of the Welsh in Central New York. More often than not I found myself squinting at empty fields imagining where a church once stood, or pulling back branches in an overgrown thicket while looking for tombstones.

This book tells the stories behind those empty fields and overgrown thickets as well as the churches and cemeteries which still exist. It is a comprehensive study of the Welsh settlements in the Central New York counties of Oneida, Herkimer, Madison, Otsego, Lewis, Oswego and St. Lawrence. I have not discussed the Welsh settlements in Cattaragus or Washington counties or in New York City. Those areas of the state deserve their own books.

I have focused on churches because religion was central to the lives of most nineteenth-century Welsh Americans. A history of the Welsh could not be written without discussing their religious commitment and fervor. A Welsh immigrant's week would frequently be consumed by attending various worship services, singing festivals, Bible study classes, and other events at the local chapel.

When the Welsh first came to Central New York they frequently settled in close-knit communities. This allowed them to live where neighbors spoke the same language and where Welsh chapels were within walking distance. Residing in close proximity to a Welsh church was important, for in the early nineteenth century many Welsh did not believe it was appropriate to drive their horses on the Sabbath. Also at that time, road conditions were not conducive to long rides. Therefore the Welsh established many small chapels instead of a few large and centrally located ones.

In most settlements, no matter how small, there were at least two churches. The Welsh passion for religion often led to heated debates about minute points of doctrine. These disagreements frequently led chapels to split over theological issues.

Welsh churches were generally affiliated with one of four denominations, namely, Congregational, Calvinistic Methodist, Baptist, and Wesleyan Methodist. To confuse matters, many of the early Congregational churches were referred to as being Presbyterian while the Calvinistic Methodists later merged with the Presbyterian church. Other points of confusion will be discussed later in the text.

In as much as the church was the center of Welsh life, I have arranged this book as a series of church histories. Each section locates the church, provides the names of its ministers and important elders, and gives the recollections of those who remember the church when it was active. Finally, pictures are provided so that curious readers can find the site themselves.

As for the photographs, I am greatly indebted to my father who has taken the majority of them. He has spent a great deal of time and effort in following my directions to many out-of-the-way sites.

One of the biggest decisions I had to make in compiling this book was whether or not to include pictures of churches which had been demolished or altered since they were last used. I have resisted the temptation of including those pictures because I would not have been able to present a picture of each church and this might have offended some. Also, some societies had multiple structures or made many significant alterations to their church over time. As such, I would have had to choose between trying to include all the various structures or omitting some. I have therefore pictured the sites only as they exist today. These are the "memory stones" as they have been left to us, and this is what will be shown.

I have also included my recollections, my observations, and my relatives. It is not that my relatives were any more important than the next person's. In fact, in the history of the Welsh they were relatively insignificant. That is why I mention them. Perhaps their experiences will evoke similar memories about the reader's family and friends.

Finally, this book is intended to honor the spirit of those Welsh immigrants who came to Central New York. Their deep commitment to God and country have enriched this area and their legacy continues in the institutions they established.

Chapter I

Remsen-Steuben

As ONE TRAVELS NORTHWARD FROM UTICA on Route 12, there appears to be little to see of Welsh-related interest, even when one passes through the towns of Remsen and Steuben. Along either side of the highway are rolling rocky hills, small farms, and a few scattered businesses. At first glance there appears to be nothing, save a large Draig Goch (Red Dragon) on a barn just south of Remsen, to tell visitors that they are entering what was once the heart of the largest Welsh settlement in New York State.

If one looks closely, however, one will see evidence of the Welsh presence all along the highway. Route 12 passes Pritchard, Evans and Llewellyn Roads. There is also the Penn Mountain Inn, Bethel Church and a sign directing curious travelers to the home of the man who indirectly caused the immigration of the Welsh to Oneida County: Baron de Steuben.

Although Oneida County's first Welsh immigrants did not settle in the town of Steuben, Steuben became the county's first truly Welsh settlement. Willard Scott termed Steuben a lovely "city" when announcing the township's bicentennial on the *Today* show; yet it is one of the smallest "towns" in Oneida County. It has no school, no fire department, no post office and only one business, the Siop Fellon bed and breakfast owned by Leonard and Dorothy Wynne.

Over time Remsen usurped Steuben's position as the center of Welsh activities in Central New York. The placement of the north-south turnpike through Remsen in the mid-nineteenth century caused Steuben's businesses to relocate, its churches to close and its population to move. Nevertheless, while "Remsen" has become synonymous with the Welsh of Central New York, it is in Steuben that our story begins.

Baron de Steuben*

Welsh immigration to Oneida County and to the Remsen-Steuben area was an indirect result of a land grant to Baron Frederick William Augustus Henry Ferdinand de Steuben. Steuben had come to America during the Revolutionary War to organize the undisciplined volunteer troops which made up the Continental Army. His work entitled him to repayment from the new nation's government.

After the war, the Baron waited for the United States to honor its commitment to compensate him for his services. When the Federal Government failed to meet its commitment, the New York State Legislature recognized his contributions and on May 5, 1786 presented him with 16,000 acres of land. On June 27, 1786 Steuben was issued a patent for that land, much of which was located in the present town of Steuben.

In 1787 the Baron's property was surveyed by James Cockburn into 160 lots of 100 acres each. The Baron did not settle in the town until three years later, in 1790. After his arrival, the Baron cleared sixty acres for a farm and built a log house on what is now Starr Hill Road. It was here that the Baron died and was buried in 1794. A large stone monument marks his grave.

One of the Baron's aides during the Revolution, Col. Benjamin Walker, became the executor of his estate. In order to realize a financial reward from the estate, of which Walker and another former aide, William North, were the sole beneficiaries, the previously surveyed lots either had to be sold or leased. At that time, leasing was the option of choice for the cash poor immigrants.

Walker had been appointed as a collector with the immigration department at the Port Authority in New York City by George Washington. In that position he was responsible for immigration policies at that point of entry. He therefore had a unique opportunity to direct new immigrants to the land in Steuben. His solicitation of a group of Welsh families in 1795 helped start the flow of Welsh immigration to Oneida County, a flow which lasted for decades. By the time of Col. Walker's death in 1818, Steuben was the destination of a large percentage of Welsh immigrants.

In 1804 Col. Walker, as executor of the Baron's estate, deeded fifty acres of the Baron's farm, including the "sacred grove" surrounding the Baron's

* The Baron preferred the French "De Steuben" to the more familiar German "Von Steuben."

grave, to Capel Isaf, a Welsh Baptist church. In consideration of this grant, the church agreed to maintain the fence which enclosed the five acres around the Baron's grave and to keep the area "fenced and uncleared for all time."

Steuben Cabin.
This is a reconstruction of the Baron's cabin erected by the State of New York. The original was constructed in 1790 and was occupied by Steuben until 1794.

When Capel Isaf was dissolved in 1892 the fifty acre parcel was transferred to the First Baptist Church of Remsen. Ola Schufelt recalls her father, a member of the church, walking the property to make sure that no animals had gotten through the fence and that the grave site was undisturbed.

In 1930 the State of New York purchased the five acres surrounding the grave from the church and cleared the entrance to the grave site. The Baron's log house was reconstructed by the Park Service, using some of the original stones for the new cabin's foundation.

For the next 60 years the site served as a picnic area and the cabin was opened upon request. Then in 1991, with the State facing budget problems, the log cabin was closed to the public, the furnishings put in storage, and the park and picnic area closed. Through the efforts of volunteers the park has been reopened.

First Settlers

From 1798 to 1802 Wales suffered an unbroken succession of bad harvests. The consequent economic hardships, when combined with the English government's religious persecution of those who opposed the established church, made life in Wales unbearable for many. The Welsh looked to America as a land where they could not only enjoy economic prosperity but also practice their religion and preserve their culture. The rise during the eighteenth century of denominations such as the Calvinistic Methodists, Congregationalists or Independents, Baptists, and Wesleyan Methodists made many Welsh long for a country where there was no established church.

Large waves of immigration from Wales took place in 1794, 1795, and 1796. Many of those arriving in those years settled in Pennsylvania because their port of entry was Philadelphia. Some ships, however, made New York City their destination.

In March of 1795 a group of twelve families left Wales and embarked on a fourteen-week journey to New York City. Upon arrival, two of these new immigrants, William P. Jones and William Davies, made an expedition to upstate New York. They traveled to Trenton for the purpose of examining the area's suitability for settlement. Their report must have been favorable because in September of that year five of the families headed north on the Hudson by sloop to Albany. They then traveled west on the Mohawk River to Fort Schuyler which is now the city of Utica. There were 18 persons in the party. The five listed as "heads" of family were Griffith Rowlands, Captain William Williams, Evan Davies, Hugh Roberts, and Owen Griffith.

The trip from Fort Schuyler to Steuben took four days because the area was heavily wooded. The settlers packed their possessions and children into a hired wagon pulled by four oxen and a horse. On the first night the party reached Deerfield Hill. Here there were no accommodations to shield the families from the driving rain which fell through the night. Each made do as best as he or she could, sleeping under a tree or whatever else could be found for cover. The second night they reached a log shanty one-half mile north of what is now South Trenton. On the third day they arrived at a small settlement now known as Barneveld. Finally, on September 15, 1795 they reached Steuben, where they joined five or six other families which had been living in the vicinity of the Baron's farm for about a year.

The early Welsh settled in the "Siop Fellon" area of Steuben, that is, near the present intersection of Starr Hill and Fuller Roads. They spent those first years clearing the land and making the area habitable. From this nucleus of five families grew Central New York's Welsh community which by 1812 numbered 700 and by 1838, 7000.

Congregational Churches

Capel Ucha

In 1798 more Welsh families joined the settlers in Steuben. Some of these new settlers included Robert Griffith, David Jones, Deacon William C. Jones, and Rhys and Walter Griffith, all from the mostly agricultural Lleyn Peninsula in North Wales.

In the summer of 1798 the first Welsh prayer meeting in the area was held. Rev. James Harris, a Baptist minister, preached the first Welsh sermon in Steuben in 1798 at the barn of Ebenezer Weeks near Ty Goch Corners, the intersection of Pritchard and Starr Hill Roads. An historical marker has recently been erected at the site of Week's farm. So desperate were the Welsh for religious services that the first meeting was attended by one woman who had walked nine miles carrying a four-month-old baby. Prayer meetings were conducted twice each Sunday in various cabins. A fellowship meeting or "seiat" was held once during the week. Since the seiat was peculiar to the Calvinistic Methodists, the early settlers were probably of that denomination.

In 1800 at least twelve persons were regularly attending prayer meetings. By the next year this number increased substantially for there were now 60 Welsh families living in the area. In that year John G. Roberts of Ebensburg, Pennsylvania came to the district and began preaching. In 1802 he was ordained and became the area's first pastor. Rev. Roberts had traveled to America with William C. Jones and Walter A. Griffith but had chosen to settle in Pennsylvania. He was induced by Messrs. Jones and Griffith to come to Steuben to minister to a Calvinistic Methodist church.

The "society" continued to meet in the homes of members. Ty Cerrig, the stone house constructed by John Lewis in 1800, two miles south of Remsen, was a frequent site of these gatherings.

Ty Cerrig.
Here in this house, constructed by John Lewis in 1800, worship services were held by the early settlers. Today its barn is adorned by a large Welsh Dragon which welcomes Route 12 travelers to Remsen.

In 1802 Rev. John G. Roberts presided over the organization of a union church, officially known as the "First Welsh Methodist Society of Steuben." As the name implies, the majority of that first church's congregation was Calvinistic Methodist. Arguably, this was the first church of that denomination in this country; however, the sequence of events which followed its founding preclude its being recognized as such.

In November 1804 the newly formed society erected a log structure which was to have served as both a schoolhouse and church. Sadly, it burned to the ground on Christmas night less than one month after opening. What anguish those first settlers must have felt to see their new church destroyed on Christmas!

While members waited to have a new building constructed, changes were occurring within the society. The Congregationalists, who had worshiped with the Calvinistic Methodists but had not joined the society, met with the leaders of the Congregational church in Utica. The group from Steuben, led by Nicodemus Griffith, decided to form a new Congregational society in the town. Rev. Daniel Morris, the pastor in Utica, invited the Methodists to join the new society. Seeing themselves outnumbered, the

Methodists joined the newly reorganized church and Rev. Roberts was invited to remain as pastor. This "new" church was officially organized at the home of William C. Jones. While it adopted a Congregational form of worship and governmental structure, the name of the society remained unchanged and the Calvinistic Methodists continued to worship at the church until 1826.

The official name of the chapel was Ebenezer, but it was more commonly known as Capel Ucha or Upper Chapel. This distinguished it from the Welsh Baptist church, Capel Isaf, or Lower Chapel, which was constructed in a hollow below the first church in 1806. It is unclear why the name Ebenezer was chosen, although it was a popular name for chapels in Wales at that time. The hymnist Thomas J. Williams titled his famous hymn tune Ebenezer (Ton-Y-Botel) after his chapel in Rhos, Wales.

The Biblical reference to Ebenezer comes in I Samuel 7:12, where Samuel erects a stone which he calls Ebenezer or "Stone of Help." The stone was erected so that future generations would know "hitherto the Lord has helped us." Perhaps such feelings of gratitude for divine help in surviving those first years in the wilderness of upstate New York inspired the selection of the name.

The period from 1801 to 1828 was a prosperous one in the life of the church. During that time membership continued to grow, as did the Welsh population. The Calvinistic Methodists, although a minority within the church, were influential in charting its course. In fact, the society's first two ministers were Methodists. The first, John G. Roberts, served from 1801 until his death in 1817 at the age of 48. The second, Rev. William G. Pierce, served from 1807 until 1828.

Rev. Pierce had been born in Aberdaron, North Wales, in 1768. He arrived in America in 1795 and in Steuben in 1800. Pierce became an elder of Capel Ucha soon after arriving in Steuben and in 1807 was ordained. At first he served as a co-pastor with Rev. Roberts. After Rev. John G. Roberts' death he served as senior pastor from 1820 to 1828, assisted by Rev. Evan Roberts.

The area's Welsh population had grown steadily during Rev. Pierce's pastorate and reached 700 by 1812. Most of the new immigrants were from North Wales and, in particular, from the area then known as Caernarvonshire. The first frame church had been erected on Starr Hill Road near the present cemetery, but the large influx of immigrants in 1818 made the structure too small to adequately accommodate the growing community's needs. Therefore, in 1820 the original frame church was moved down Starr Hill Road to the intersection with Fuller Road. Here it was converted into a private residence.

The first burial in Capel Ucha's cemetery took place in 1798 when Gwen Jones, the 19-year-old daughter of Deacon William C. Jones, died. Twenty-two years later, when the frame church was removed, her body had to be exhumed and reburied so that the new stone structure could be built over her grave's original location.

Capel Ucha Cemetery.
This cemetery's first burial was in 1798. It was the site of four Congregationalist chapels from 1804 until 1948.

As the Steuben settlement grew, the need for the Congregationalists and the Calvinistic Methodists to worship together decreased. One of the new immigrants in 1818 was James Owen. He had been a strong supporter of the Methodist movement in Wales and quickly became embroiled in doctrinal controversies at the union church. In particular, his opinions favoring religious education classes on the Sabbath brought him into conflict with the church elders and the associate pastor.

Rev. Evan Roberts, who had left Oneida County in 1818 to assume charge of the Welsh Union Church in New York City, returned to Steuben in 1820 and became associated with Capel Ucha. He was known for being very methodical and exacting. He, unlike John Roberts and William Pierce, was a firm Congregationalist, and this attitude led to friction between the

Calvinistic Methodists within the church and himself. Rev. Roberts continued to serve Capel Ucha until September 10, 1836 when, while visiting Albany, New York, he was robbed and murdered.

In 1824 many of the Calvinistic Methodists, especially those living near Remsen, removed themselves from Capel Ucha and established their own church, Penycaerau. Four years later the Calvinistic Methodists in Steuben also withdrew to form their own church in the southern portion of the township. Upon their removal the official name of Capel Ucha was changed to "The First Welsh Congregational Society of the Town of Steuben." The name "First Calvinistic Methodist Society of Steuben" was thereafter given to Nant, the church formed by the Methodists who had departed in 1828. When the Calvinistic Methodists left, Rev. Pierce left as well to become the first pastor of the Nant Church.

Rev. Pierce was succeeded at Capel Ucha by his associate, Evan Roberts (1820-1836). Rev. William D. Williams (1835-1838) followed Evan Roberts in the pulpit. Williams, ordained at the Salem Church in Deerfield (Marcy), served both Salem and Capel Ucha for two and a half years. Capel Ucha was filled to capacity while he was pastor and on the last day of his tenure, 97 new members joined the church.

Rev. Williams was assisted in the pulpit by Rev. Morris Roberts in 1837. Other ministers who assisted during this time were Rev. Morris Jones, Rev. James Davies of Ohio, Rev. Evan Evans, later of Pottsville, Pennsylvania, and Rev. Jenkin Jenkins. Rev. Jenkins had been pastor of the New York City Welsh church and went on to the Welsh Hill Church in Clifford, Pennsylvania as well as to churches in Ohio and Minnesota.

In 1838 the church began a new era as the Rev. Dr. Robert Everett commenced his ministry in Steuben. Dr. Everett was born in Flintshire, North Wales in 1791 and began preaching at the age of 18. He emigrated in 1823 and started his career in America at the Welsh Congregational Church in Utica. He then served the Second Presbyterian Church in Utica, the English-speaking Congregational Church in West Winfield and the Presbyterian Church in Westernville before settling in Steuben.

Dr. Everett was a pillar of the local Welsh community and supplied many of the other Welsh Congregational pulpits. He was as influential as a printer and publisher as he was a preacher. Trained as a printer in Wales prior to emigrating, he is credited with publishing the first book setting forth a system of Welsh shorthand. He also published *Uncle Tom's Cabin* in Welsh to sway the Welsh to support the cause of abolition.

Dr. Everett gained national prominence among the Welsh in this country as the editor of *Y Cenhadwr* (*The Messenger*), which was the Welsh Congregationalists' periodical for the entire United States. He published the monthly magazine from 1840 until his death in 1875. His position as editor gave him a unique opportunity to express his views on the issues of the day. In particular he used his pulpit and printing press to argue for the abolition of both slavery and the sale of strong drink.

When Dr. Everett arrived in America in 1823, slavery was still permitted in New York State and continued to be allowed until 1827. On his first trip from New York City to Utica his coachman was a slave who told the newly arrived minister much about the slave system. Even after the abolition of slavery in New York there were many anti-abolitionists in the upstate region who often criticized Everett. Despite this, Dr. Everett was never deterred from voicing his opinions and he became influential in the anti-slavery movement. In 1842 he put his views into practice and was instrumental in forming "The Welsh Anti-Slavery Society of Steuben, Remsen, Trenton, and Vicinities." It is rumored that Dr. Everett's home was a stop on the underground railroad.

Dr. Everett took an equally strong stand in regard to alcohol. His temperance beliefs led to the removal of fermented wine from the communion tables at both Capel Ucha and Penymynydd and his preaching on the subject led to the formation of the Welsh Temperance Society in Utica in 1830.

With Dr. Everett at the helm, Capel Ucha continued to grow and prosper. Between 1839 and 1840 the church was refurbished and enlarged. At that time "an artistic balcony supported by cylindrical columns" was installed. The seating for the congregation on a sloping floor allowed everyone to have a good view. The pulpit was elevated so the minister could look down on the entire congregation which at that time numbered 200 members. Doors were at the side of the pulpit "as if to shut in the eloquence, that it might pour forth with more power from above." The fervent sermons preached from Capel Ucha's pulpit often focused on the political aspects of slavery. In 1844 Dr. Everett began actively supporting the Liberty (an anti-slavery) Party and its presidential candidate James W. Birney. His endorsements were set forth in both his sermons and in *Y Cenhadwr*. Preaching politics from the pulpit did not sit well with many parishioners and some made an effort to oust him as pastor. While their attempts to remove him failed, Dr. Everett did not win many votes for Mr. Birney, who only garnered 37 votes in Steuben and 31 in Remsen, barely five percent of the total from these two townships. Four years later Dr. Everett again preached politics and urged support for the Free Soil Party. Unfortunately his preaching fell on deaf ears and few votes in the township were cast for his candidate, Martin Van Buren.

It would be inaccurate to conclude that Dr. Everett's efforts as a preacher and printer were confined to politics and the support of abolition and temperance. Dr. Everett also made many contributions to the Welsh Congregationalist church. For example, in 1846, Dr. Everett, in conjunction with Rev. Morris Roberts and Griffith W. Roberts published *Caniadau y Cysegr* (*Songs of the Sanctuary*). This was known as the "Everett Hymnal" and a copy of the hymnal was on the organ at a recent service at Enlli Chapel.

Dr. Everett was to have retired in 1867 but the congregation clamored for him to remain. He did so with the assistance of Rev. Sem Phillips from 1866 until 1872. Although Everett had increasing trouble with his voice, he continued to preach until a week before his death at the age of 84 in 1875.

Meanwhile, the church had seriously declined in numbers. In 1867 Capel Ucha, which could accommodate 500 to 600 persons, saw only 100 on a typical Sunday. The church's official membership declined from 200 in 1840 to 70. This decline was not Dr. Everett's fault. During this period the Town of Steuben's population dropped as well, falling from 2,094 in 1830 to 1,261 in 1870. By 1950 Steuben's population would be only 540.

Rev. E. R. Hughes succeeded Dr. Everett as pastor and served for the next ten years. He, in turn, was followed by Rev. Thomas T. Davies who served from 1887 until 1889. He became the pastor of the Welsh Congregational Church in Richville, New York. From 1889 to 1898, Rev. Edward Davies served both Capel Ucha and Bethel and, from 1901 to 1903, Rev. Thomas Jenkins served both Capel Ucha and Peniel.

Capel Ucha's stone church stood until 1902. Unfortunately, the annual thawing of a spring, located under the northwest corner of the church, caused the foundation to crack. Efforts were made to save the church by placing iron rods through the structure, but to no avail. The old stone church was demolished and a new smaller wooden structure was built on the same site. It was made smaller to reflect more accurately the needs of a dwindling congregation. The new wooden church was known for its stained-glass windows which had a beautiful blue hue.

During the years following the construction of the new church, membership continued to decline. Worship at the church was always in Welsh. In fact, Capel Ucha was one of the last churches in that area to use the old language exclusively in its services.

Dr. Mary H. Everett, the daughter of the former pastor, was the heart of the church during this time. She had been instrumental both in attempting to save the old church and in the construction of the new building. Unfortunately membership dwindled to the point where the church would only be opened when Mary Everett was able to attend. The minister of the Peniel Church in Remsen would come and preach in the Welsh language to her and a handful of others. After her passing in 1916 the church fell into disuse, services were held irregularly and the structure was eventually abandoned.

In 1948 one final service was held in the church. Former members, neighbors and old-timers joined in a farewell to the mother of all of Remsen's and Steuben's Welsh churches. Shortly thereafter, the church and its contents were auctioned off. The lumber was sold for $300 and the church was torn down. The pews were sold to a bowling alley for $7.20 a piece. Even the pulpit was sold and is rumored to have been used as a bar.

Many generations of the Everett family, including Dr. Everett's parents, are buried in the Capel Ucha cemetery. A large monument in honor of Dr. & Mrs. Robert Everett has also been erected in the cemetery. While there is no longer any church for the Everetts to attend, the grandchildren and great-grandchildren continue to come back to the area, to bury family members, and to care for the monuments to their family's rich heritage. The story is told of Everett grandchildren caring for and visiting an elderly Welsh man in a Washington, D. C. nursing home, merely because they knew him to be from Remsen.

Today there remains a large cemetery with as many as 700 graves. A white picket fence has replaced the old stone one. Recently, the Remsen-Steuben Historical Society undertook the project of cleaning up the cemetery. While the men cut away brush and trees, the women took down the names on the graves and fixed lemonade for all to enjoy. Ola Schufelt, whose father, Owen Griffith had been a local undertaker, has taken a great interest in Capel Ucha's cemetery and has helped motivate people to care for it. The Historical Society, through the assistance of the late Senator James Donovan, has utilized local prison inmates to keep up the cemetery.

Like the Ebenezer erected by Samuel, Capel Ucha's cemetery stands as a memorial to God's help in bringing so many Welsh immigrants to the area and in sustaining them through years of growth and decline.

A tablet from the original stone church is still set in the southwest corner of the cemetery. It is Capel Ucha's memory stone to remind future generations of how the spirit of those early settlers was sustained. Its message is simple: Ebenezer Adeiladwyd 1820 Gwrandewch a bydd byw (Ebenezer: Built 1820, Hear and Live).

Penymynydd

Penymynydd means top of the mountain and that is where the Congregationalists erected their second chapel in the town of Steuben. Penymynydd or Pen Mount is located in the northwestern portion of Steuben, just west of French Road. Before the heavy woods covered the hill it had one of the most beautiful views of Oneida County, overlooking the town of Western, Delta Lake and beyond. At 1,730 feet it is the highest point in the township. Today it is the site of one of Oneida County's most remote Welsh cemeteries.

Since many members of Capel Ucha resided in the area of Pen Mount, the congregation resolved on February 11, 1832 that the next communion service for the church would be held at Penymynydd. One month later, under the direction of Rev. Evan Roberts, 29 charter members formed a new church to meet on the hill.

At first, the congregation met in a schoolhouse which stood near the eventual site of the church. When the society took its turn to host other area churches for a Gymanfa, a window had to be removed from the schoolhouse so the crowd assembled outside could hear the speaker within.

Soon the congregation had outgrown the school and subsequently, during the pastorate of William D. Williams (1836-1837), a wood frame church was erected. Although the church was bigger than the schoolhouse, it was still a small structure. Likewise, the congregation was never very large and never fully supported its own pastor.

Over the course of the church's history, Penymynydd always shared its ministers with Capel Ucha. Therefore, Dr. Everett preached at the church for many years. By the time of his death in 1875 the church was already in decline and had only 50 members. In 1898 it discontinued regular services. Thereafter, services were held only during the summer months, with the sermons preached in English.

Finally, during the second decade of this century the church was closed and the structure sold. It was purchased by a Mr. Meredith who used the lumber to construct a barn on the road leading to the church. A cemetery association was formed to tend the graves in the small chapel's cemetery. Even though the church has been gone for 75 years many descendants of those early settlers still reside in the area.

In 1975, John Davis, treasurer of the Pen Mount Cemetery Association, oversaw the erection of a plaque on a large stone in memory of the church. The drive to fund the monument, located at the Penymynydd cemetery, was initiated by Margaret Davies, author of the Remsen-Steuben history *Honey Out of the Rafters*. Lorena Jersen of Remsen, whose family first settled in the Penymynydd area in 1807, also worked to restore the cemetery where her ancestors are buried. A small ceremony was held at the time the plaque was placed.

In the years following the erection of the stone and plaque a project was undertaken to clear the cemetery of brush and trees which had grown up.

The brush was cut down and burned off. The cemetery stones were repaired and straightened.

Penymynydd Monument.
This plaque was placed in 1975 to commemorate the Pen Mount church and cemetery. The church stood on this site from 1836 to 1915.

Among those who worked on the cemetery were Howard Coleman and Myron Senchyna. While Mr Senchyna was not Welsh, and his family had moved to the area long after the church had been dismantled, he worked tirelessly in repairing the old cemetery. He not only worked at Penymynydd, but also at Cobin, Ucha, and other Welsh sites.

Today, John Davis' son, Ray Davis, continues as the secretary/treasurer of the cemetery association, having assumed the duty upon his father's death. He attempted to convey the cemetery and its assets to the Remsen-Steuben Historical Society. The Historical Society however did not want to assume the liability associated with owning the property. The Town of Steuben now maintains the cemetery through a grant provided by the State of New York for the care of abandoned cemeteries. As the Town now takes care of the site, the cemetery association is said to have gone underground.

The care of the cemetery is a constant battle. The area is remote and thus a prime location for teenagers' parties. Vandals frequently tip over stones or leave litter behind. In 1989 the Steuben highway department filled in the church's foundation for safety reasons.

The small cemetery serves as a reminder to the heartiness of the early settlers on that remote hill. The road to the cemetery is only passable in the summer for it is too muddy in the spring. It is in the middle of a New York State Forest Preserve and the roads to the hill are designed more for four-wheel-drive vehicles than for standard cars. Recently one of the roads was covered by a small lake which had been created by a beaver dam.

Bethel

At a revival meeting conducted by Rev. Morris Roberts at Penymynydd, those in attendance resolved to establish a church from which Rev. Roberts could serve the rural Welsh population in the northern part of the Remsen township. Thus, in 1838 Bethel was founded.

When the church was first organized, the congregation met in a school on what is now the west side of Route 12. The schoolhouse sat across from Route 12's intersection with Dustin Road, near the Boonville town line. This little school served the area for many years. When it closed, it was sold at auction and moved across the road further north on Route 12, next to the present Kayuta Drive-In. In the 1980s a small Welsh gift shop was located in the old school. Today it is a real estate office.

A few years after its organization the present church building was erected at the corner of Route 12 and Bethel Road. This intersection is located six miles north of Remsen, just south of Alder Creek. The land on which it was built was conveyed to the church by Oneida County historian Pomroy Jones.

On September 5, 1842 the church was officially incorporated as the "Second Independent Congregational Church of Remsen." It appears that although Bethel was formed before the Peniel Church in Remsen it was incorporated later. That is why it bears the name "Second."

The church's first minister was Morris Roberts. He remained until about 1872. In that year the church had 76 members. The following year Rev. Robert Evans (Togwy) succeeded Rev. Roberts. In 1882, Edward Davies, the last editor of *Y Cenhadwr*, replaced Rev. Evans. Prior to 1889 Bethel had always been linked with Peniel Church in Remsen. Davies discontinued this association and instead yoked Bethel with Capel Ucha. He served both congregartions until 1898. It was during this period that the church was remodeled and the present pine interior installed.

District 9 School.
The Bethel Church was organized in this old school in 1838. The structure was later moved across Route 12 to its present location.

Bethel's membership reached its peak in 1887 when it had 91 members. Shortly thereafter, the second and third generation Welsh began to leave the area and membership began to decline. Bethel had always been a rural parish, serving the many small farms in the area. By the turn of the century, a 40 to 50 acre farm could no longer support a family. Thus many farms were combined and consequently fewer Welsh lived in the area surrounding the church.

By 1917 membership had declined sharply to 34. As the Welsh moved from the area, Polish and other ethnic groups moved into Remsen and Steuben. These new residents had their own churches and were not inclined to join a church where they could not understand the language. What had been the church's strength, namely a commitment to the Welsh language, became its weakness. Bethel used Welsh exclusively until 1901 when English was introduced at the morning service. The evening service continued in Welsh until 1920.

Welsh churches were very closed societies and membership from outside the Welsh community was not sought. After World War I, Bethel's new members were generally relatives of members. The last person to become a member was Bernard Williams, now of New York Mills. He joined the church in 1932. His great-grandfather had built a log cabin in the vicinity and had belonged to Bethel.

Bethel combined with two Calvinistic Methodist churches, Penygraig and French Road, to share a minister for a time. Rev. Richard Owens served under this arrangement during the early 1920s. The last full-time minister for the Bethel church was Rev. Howland Bantham of the Remsen Baptist Church. During his tenure the Bethel Cemetery Association was established to care for the large cemetery. The most enduring contribution of Rev. Bantham's era was the annual Old Home Day service which began in 1926.

In 1928 regular services were discontinued and from 1929 until 1942 services were only held during the summer months. Rev. Bantham conducted these services. Membership continued to decline during this time so that by 1940 there were only ten members.

From 1943 until 1990 the Old Home Day service was the only service held at the church. The collection taken at that time was the society's only source of income. For many years Waldo Williams was instrumental in perpetuating that service.

Originally, the Old Home Day festival lasted an entire weekend and included a basket lunch on Saturday and an afternoon of preaching on Sunday. The weekend festival often fell during oppressively hot weather. The windows would be opened which allowed both cooler air and flies into the church. The children in the congregation often amused themselves during the service by watching to see if a fly would land on the preacher's nose.

Since the church was shut during the year, the building had to be opened and cleaned the week before the big gathering. This cleaning involved sweeping the church of the many flies which had entered, but not left, the church during the preceding 51 weeks.

Bethel.
This Congregational church sits at the corner of Bethel Road and Route 12.
Its Old Home Day service was held annually until 1991.

The annual August service was well attended for many years. However, in the 1980s the congregation had dwindled to about 15. In 1991 it was decided to discontinue the tradition. The last service was attended by four trustees of the church and only nine others. The three local trustees were Bernard Williams who had been secretary-treasurer for about 25 years,

Norman Williams, a former President of the Welsh National Gymanfa Ganu Association and Dr. Thomas Kent, a dentist from Whitesboro. Dr. Kent's great-grandparents, Silas and Elizabeth Kent, had been early settlers in the area and his grandfather, John S. Kent, had been a trustee of the church for many years.

As Bernard Williams, at age 69, was the youngest trustee it was agreed that a decision had to be made as to the church's future. The trustees had to choose between spending the church's treasury to raze the church structure before it fell into decay or giving the property away. The trustees decided to do the latter, and gave the church, including its furnishings and treasury, to the Remsen-Steuben Historical Society. In 1992 the church was in the process of being legally dissolved by attorney Emlyn Griffith.

Peniel

On Main Street in Remsen, set back behind the Ackley-Barry Funeral Home, is the former Peniel Congregational Church. Like Bethel Congregational Church in the northern portion of the township, Peniel was closely linked with Morris Roberts. "Old Morris," as he came to be known, was a mighty preacher whose fiery sermons made him a legend among the Welsh. He had been removed from the pulpit of Capel Cerrig in 1837 and had gone on to organize Bethel in 1838. In 1839 Peniel was organized in the village of Remsen. Many of its members came from Capel Cerrig, while others came from Steuben's Congregational Church, Capel Ucha. Rev. Roberts preached at both Bethel and Peniel until his retirement.

For the first two years the congregation met in the academy building in Remsen. Rev. Roberts raised money for the construction of a church during this time by making fundraising tours through Madison, Cattaragus, and Allegheny counties. He even traveled as far away as Ohio to solicit funds.

Between 1841 and 1842 the congregation erected a church large enough to accommodate 500 to 600 people. Set far back from the Main Street, the church was reached by a wide boardwalk shaded by towering elms. Inside, the church was austere in its simplicity, with straight-backed wooden pews and a partition separating the men from the women. Upstairs, along the sides ran a balcony under which were alcoves with wood-burning stoves. Sunday School was held in one of those alcoves.

Through Peniel's early history Morris Roberts was its driving force. He ministered for 33 years, stepping down in 1872. Rev. Roberts was a man of attractive personality, a fine preacher, a strong abolitionist, and a great fundraiser. He frequently went on mission tours throughout New York and Ohio. Six years after his retirement he passed away.

Peniel.
Peniel Church worshiped in what is now the St. Anne's Catholic Center from 1842 to 1944. A monument to Rev. Morris Roberts sits in front of the former church.

Roberts was succeeded by Rev. Robert Evans (Togwy) in 1872. At that time the church had a congregation of 80. Rev. Edward Davies was pastor for two years, from 1882 to 1884. Davies, the editor of *Y Cenhadwr,* had been a student of Morris Roberts and had traveled with him to Wales in 1866. He later wrote a biography of the famous pastor: *The Life of Morris Roberts.* Until 1889 the church shared its pastors with Bethel, located in the rural northern section of the town. After 1889 the two churches ceased to share a pastor, even though Davies continued his pastorate at Bethel.

After Rev. Davies, Rev. Morien Mon Hughes served Peniel, followed by Thomas Jenkins who was there until 1902. Jenkins later served in Madison and also at Rev. Davies' old church in Waterville. Rev. J. Vincent Jones was pastor of Peniel in the early part of this century. He went on to become pastor of Bethesda in Utica in 1917.

Every autumn a Gymanfa Mawr or Big Meeting was held in Peniel Church. The village overflowed with visitors from other Welsh areas, much like the present day Gymanfa held each fall in Remsen. Then, however, the Gymanfa would last for a number of days.

In the early part of this century Peniel's membership dwindled to a handful. Their pastor also served the few remaining members of Capel Ucha. The services were totally in Welsh, and it was the last church in Remsen-Steuben to maintain services solely in the old tongue.

In 1944 the church was sold to the local Grange. More recently it has been used by St. Anne's Roman Catholic Parish of Hinckley as a parish hall. This is ironic, as Pomroy Jones, in his *Annals of Oneida County*(1851), almost boasts that Remsen had only one Catholic resident. Today, a marker stands on Main Street in memory of both Rev. Morris Roberts and Peniel Church.

Ninety-Six (Congregational)

Ninety-Six is located in the southeastern section of the Remsen township. It is six miles from the village of Remsen and four from Prospect. The hamlet, or four corners, is so named because it was located in the 96th of 120 lots in the township. Lot 96 was subdivided causing a higher density of population in that area and thus became the hamlet of Ninety-Six.

In 1841 a Congregational church was organized at Ninety-Six at the corner of Fairchild and Swamp Roads. A two-story church was erected shortly thereafter. The church was ministered to by Rev. Morris Roberts who probably conducted services there on Sunday evenings, after preaching at Peniel and Bethel.

In the 1850s the church at Ninety-Six shared its minister with the Welsh Congregationalists in Prospect. It was never a large church and in 1872 its membership was only 16. Sometime during the 1870s the church was dissolved and the structure was torn down. Today all that remains is the foundation.

Baptist Churches

Capel Isaf

Steuben's Welsh Baptists gathered in 1803 to form their own society known as the Second Baptist Church of Steuben. The First Baptist Church was English-speaking and had been formed at Steuben Corners in 1802. The new society had twelve charter members and was led by Morgan Williams. While the theology of the church was in many ways the same as that expressed by Baptist churches today, it placed a greater emphasis on the teachings of John Calvin.

In 1806, the society built a log cabin as its first chapel. The chapel was officially known as Bethesda; however, it was more frequently referred to as Capel Isaf, or Lower Chapel. This distinguished it from Capel Ucha, the Upper Chapel, which was built on a hill to the east.

Capel Isaf sat on Starr Hill Road on land which had originally been a part of Baron Steuben's farm. The church received its property on the condition that the society maintain the Baron's grave and the five acres surrounding it as a virgin forest.

In the early years Rev. James Harris and Rev. John Stephens of Utica would travel to Steuben to preach to the Welsh Baptists. Harris was said to have been an excellent preacher, while Stephens was considered a great evangelist. It was Stephens who wrote the church's confession of faith. One attribute these early ministers surely had was dedication. They were known for walking from Utica to Rome to preach to Baptists in that city on Saturdays and then walking through the wilderness to Steuben to preach there on Sundays.

Many of the early Welsh settlers in Oneida County had not come directly from Wales but by way of Pennsylvania. These Pennsylvania Welsh called their former pastor, Rev. Richard Jones, to Steuben. In 1806 Rev. Jones came to the area from Dyffryn Mawr (Great Valley) near Philadelphia. He also ministered to the Welsh Baptists in Utica and Trenton and was known for his strong sense of discipline. The first church was built through the efforts of Rev. Jones' former parishioners. Richard Jones remained at the Steuben church until 1821.

In 1818 Rev. Thomas Morgan joined with Rev. Jones in ministering to the Baptists. In that same year a new church was built on the site of the original 1806 log church. The contract for the construction of the church required that the building be "erected on the site where the old meeting house now stands, to be 32 x 36 feet on the ground, and lighted by eight, 28 lighted windows of 8 x 10 glass, three windows on each side and two on the west end. Also, one 24 lighted window in the front of the east end, with a circle on top."

Inside, the building was to have "a gallery across the east end, elevated nine feet above the lower floor" with a "pulpit in the center of the west end of the building between the windows," and was to be finished in the same manner and form as the new church in Trenton, with a good and decent sounding-board over the same. There were to be "three pillars on each side of the interior."

Shortly after the construction of the above church, Rev. Joseph Richards began preaching and assisting Rev. Richard Jones. About this same time, Rev. Griffith Jones also came to Capel Isaf to assist Rev. Jones, but two years later he became the minister to the English-speaking Baptists in Holland Patent remaining there from 1822 to 1825. Joseph Richards became pastor to the Baptists in South Trenton in about 1820.

Next came Rev. David Griffith of Wales, preaching in both English and Welsh, but he only stayed for a brief time. He and Rev. Richard Jones left the church in about 1821. Griffith went on to help establish the First Particular Baptist Church of Steuben in 1823. Rev. Jesse Jones of Aberystwyth came to Steuben in 1823 and preached at Capel Isaf for the next seven years. Shortly after his arrival, a Christmas Eve fire destroyed the church. Services were held in the home of Morris Ellis, located across the street, until a new structure was erected on the same site in 1825.

In 1826 Richard Roberts was ordained, and he began to share the pulpit with Jesse Jones. This arrangement lasted for four years during which time the church's membership grew to 109. In 1830 Jesse Jones moved to Radnor, Ohio and the pastor of the Ohio church, Rev. Thomas Stephens, came to Steuben. The arrival of the new pastor was to have a divisive effect on the church.

In 1830 the church had two pastors and members began to debate who should be the senior pastor. The majority favored Thomas Stephens who was known as a "Super Calvinist." The minority were said to favor an Arminian theology, holding beliefs closer to those of John Wesley than John Calvin. This minority, dissatisfied with the decision to make Stephens the senior pastor, withdrew to form its own church, known as the Third Baptist Church. That Church will be discussed later.

After the schism, Capel Isaf's membership increased to 142. Rev. Stephens, who had been the impetus for the division remained as pastor only until May of 1832 when he returned to Radnor, Ohio. Over the next few years Rev. Thomas Hughes (1831), Rev. Robert W. Roberts (1832), and Rev. John Hughes (1832-1834) also preached at the church. Stephens returned briefly in about 1834, but then went back to Ohio again. Jesse Jones also returned and preached from 1835 to 1847.

In 1840 Rev. Griffith Jones of Garn, Wales came for one year, followed by Rev. David Prichard (1841-1843). At this time the church had another dispute regarding who should be the senior pastor. A majority of the membership preferred Jesse Jones to David Prichard, so Prichard and his supporters left in 1843 and worshiped in other parts of the town. Many of these persons eventually joined the Third Baptist Church. Jesse Jones died in 1847 at the age of 68. It was said that he was a quiet man, though he had been an animated preacher in his younger days.

Other pastors who followed were Rev. John D. Jones (1843-1850) and Rev. David J. Williams (1850-1853). Like many of his predecessors, David Williams caused a division in the church and later founded his own church in Prospect. Eventually, in 1870, he became a Calvinistic Methodist minister. He is buried in the Penycaerau Cemetery.

Rev. Edward Humphreys brought stability to the church and served from 1853 to 1871. After Humphreys' death the church was without a regular pastor. At that time membership had dwindled to 40. Although the Second and Third Baptist Churches were unwilling to merge, in 1875 they did decide to share the same minister. This they did until 1892.

In 1892 a meeting of Capel Isaf's officers was held at the home of John Ellis. There the officers decided to abandon their church and join with the Third Baptist Church, by then known as the Remsen Baptist Church. Soon thereafter, the old chapel was torn down.

Over the course of its existence the church had maintained the grave of Baron Steuben. That site and the fifty acres which surrounded it, including the church property, were transferred to the First Baptist Church of Remsen.

Later, in 1899, the State of New York took over the tract for preservation as an historic site. In 1932 it erected a message of appreciation to the church on a giant stone near the Baron's tomb. A framed copy of the plaque hangs in the First Baptist Church on Main Street in Remsen.

Capel Isaf Cemetery.
A marker sits at the site of the Second Baptist Church of Steuben,
also known as Bethesda and Capel Isaf.
A church stood on this site from 1806 until 1892.

As the years went by Capel Isaf's cemetery became overgrown. The graves of the church members who had long watched the Baron's grave were left unattended. Many of the old stones were knocked over, leaving numerous graves unmarked.

Ola Shufelt, whose great-grandfather is buried in the Capel Isaf Cemetery, set in motion an effort to restore and clean up the old graveyard. In 1989 the responsibility for maintenance of the cemetery passed from the First Baptist Church to the Town of Steuben. Today the site is cared for and neatly kept, a fitting memorial to those early pioneers.

Third Baptist Church

The Third Baptist Church of Steuben began as an off-shoot of the Second Baptist Church, Capel Isaf. At first, after having separated from the old church, members met in a barn owned by Robert Thomas who lived in a stone house at the foot of Ty Goch Hill, the intersection of Pritchard and

Starr Hill Roads. Later, a church was erected to the south of that house, within ear shot of the Capel Isaf. A small cemetery was established behind.

The new church was painted red, so it was commonly called Capel Goch or Red Church. Its official name however was Capel Zion. That name was retained until 1892.

The church's first pastor was Rev. Richard Roberts. He was followed by Rev. William H. Thomas. Rev. David Michael replaced Thomas and served until 1842. It was during his tenure that the structure was physically moved from Steuben to the west side of the "turnpike," north of the Cincinnati Creek in Remsen. The Third Baptist Church had not prospered in Steuben, due in part to its close proximity to Capel Isaf. When the congregation moved, they left behind a small cemetery which is no longer visible.

In the mid-nineteenth century, the center of the Welsh population was shifting from Steuben to Remsen. When the "plank road," which was later to become Route 12, was opened, it ran through Remsen, by-passing Steuben. Consequently, many of Steuben's residents moved to Remsen. New immigrants were attracted to the village as well. Thus, the Baptists were wise to relocate their church.

Even after the splinter church relocated to Remsen, the animosity between the two Welsh Baptist churches remained. Families refused to speak to each other for generations. They were said to have "faces set like a flint and hearts as the nether millstone." Each side refused to recognize the existence of the other.

Rev. James Harris followed Rev. Michael and in 1846 oversaw the building of a large new structure on Maple Street. The old Capel Goch was sold to Major Samuel Dustin who moved the building east 100 feet into what is now, and probably was then, an open field. Here he planned to remodel the church into a private residence. Sitting alone in the field the old church was described as "a cleric cravat on the neck of a lay man" with an air of solemn, ecclesiastic dignity to which it was no longer entitled.

Rev. William Jones succeeded Rev. Harris in the pulpit of the new structure. He remained until 1858 when he moved to Wisconsin. Rev. John W. Jones of Scranton, Pennsylvania was the next pastor. During his tenure, which lasted until 1863, membership increased. Rev. Stephen Howell served briefly thereafter as did Rev. Ambrose Williams who died in 1866.

Rev. Morris Williams, an able speaker in both English and Welsh, who came originally from Pwllheli in Caernarvonshire, North Wales, followed. In 1872 church membership stood at 70. Shortly thereafter, Morris Williams also began preaching at Capel Isaf. He served both churches until his death in 1882. During the next decade Rev. John Seth Jones, Rev. Henry Thomas and Rev. D. P. Griffith also served as pastors of both Capel Zion and Capel Isaf.

In the summer of 1892 Capel Zion burned. The fire may have been caused by sparks from one of the many trains that ran by the church. The actual cause was never determined.

First Baptist Church of Remsen

After the fire, the members of Capel Isaf and Capel Zion decided to mend fences and the two congregations joined to build a new church on Main Street in Remsen. It was named the First Baptist Church of Remsen. This title is misleading as the "first" Baptist church had been founded in the town of Remsen at Bardwell Mill more than 80 years previously.

First Baptist Church.
This church was erected in 1892 and was built
after the reuniting of Capel Isaf and Capel Zion.

With the new church came a new language. Zion had primarily used Welsh until 1892, though some English was occasionally used in the services. When the new building was constructed a decision had to be made as to which language would be used. The English faction of the church prevailed and English was used thereafter. The new church was dedicated by Rev. Dr. Taylor, pastor of the Park Avenue Baptist Church in Utica, on January 15, 1893.

Over the next 50 years the church continued as the only surviving Welsh Baptist church in Oneida County. Rev. A. E. Lawrence and Howland Bantham were among the ministers who served during that period.

In 1952, the church combined with Capel Cerrig (First Presbyterian Church of Remen) to form a Federated Church. Throughout the period of federation, the Baptists still had their own membership and kept their own books. By 1986 the combined congregation was less than 20, with only four Presbyterian members. As the four Presbyterian members could no longer afford to maintain their church, the federation ended. Since then the Baptists have continued to meet year round at the Main Street church.

From the time the Presbyterians removed themselves from the federation, the Baptists have struggled to survive. While the church is financially well off, the congregation usually numbers less than 20. The church plans to celebrate its centennial in 1993 with hopes for revitalization in its second century.

Bardwell Mill

The hamlet of Bardwell Mill is located in the northern section of the town of Remsen. There, in 1809, Remsen's first religious society was formed. The first settlers in that part of town were English, not Welsh, and therefore the first services in Bardwell Mill were in English.

This small group of Baptists began to meet in the north schoolhouse in 1809. The members came from Alder Creek and the northern part of the Remsen township. Membership was small and was held together by Deacon Daniel Dayton who led the church for many years.

Some of the ministers serving this group were Revs. William A. Wells, Philetus Pirsons, and Thomas Z. R. Jones, son of Rev. Richard Jones. These pastors also served in Trenton Falls and Prospect.

Finally, in 1829 a small church was built in the hamlet by these English-speaking Baptists. Four years earlier, in 1825, Rev. David Morris had organized a Welsh Baptist Society at Bardwell Mill with the aid of Richard Roberts and Thomas Stephens, who were then the ministers at Capel Isaf.

At some point in time thereafter it appears the Welsh took over the English church and became the sole religious society in the hamlet. By 1830 the church was reported to have 150 members. Rev. Owen F. Perry, a rich farmer in the area, was the pastor for many years. Eventually the Welsh congregation had to share a minister with the Remsen Baptist Church. Perhaps it was this yoked arrangement that helped the Bardwell Mill Church survive into the twentieth century. In later years the church was well known for its annual ice cream social.

Bardwell Baptist Church.
A small marker stands at the site of Bardwell Baptist Church which was in existance from 1809 to 1927.

In 1927 the church closed for lack of membership. All that remains is a marker located on a dead-end driveway in the middle of the hamlet. The marker simply says "In Memory of Bardwell Church."

Capel Bont

There is not much to say about Capel Bont. Just as there is a Capel "Nant" or church of the "brook," there has to be a Capel "Bont" or church of the "bridge." On the corner of Jones Road and Welsh District Road, Capel Bont's small cemetery remains. Many of the stones are broken while others have been tipped over.

Capel Bont Cemetery.
A sign has recently been erected to mark the site of the
Baptist church which stood circa 1830 to 1860.

Capel Bont was a Baptist church organized around 1830, or maybe earlier. The church lasted until the 1850s and may have been an outgrowth of one of the many splinters from Capel Isaf which occurred around 1830.

In the early 1840s, Capel Zion moved to Remsen and then in 1851, another Baptist church was formed in Prospect. With two Baptist churches in the region the need for a third was greatly diminished. Therefore, sometime between 1854 and 1870 Capel Bont was dissolved. Today, the local historical society has erected a sign in its honor.

Calvinistic Methodist Churches

Penycaerau

The Welsh churches of Remsen and Steuben were all born out of Capel Ucha, the mother church. So it was for Penycaerau, which itself became the mother of the Calvinistic Methodist churches in Central New York.

The name "Calvinistic Methodist" has caused great confusion for those not acquainted with the denomination. The Calvinistic Methodist Church is not to be confused with what is presently known as the United Methodist Church or its predecessor the Methodist Episcopal Church. It should also not be confused with the Presbyterian Church with which it united in 1920, although many of its churches adopted the name "Welsh Presbyterian" after the turn of the century. The confusion with the name has led to errors in many local history books and in improper identification of churches on nineteenth-century atlases.

The Calvinistic Methodist movement began in Wales and had its roots in the great revival of the early eighteenth century which swept over much of Great Britain. In 1735 George Whitefield joined with a small prayer group which had a three-fold practice of study, devotion, and visitation. Because of their consistent and orderly conduct, those in the group were called Methodists. In 1741 the English Methodists divided into two schools of thought: one led by John Wesley and the other by Whitefield. Whitefield and Wesley split over the former's strict adherence to John Calvin's teachings.

George Whitefield was English, but Calvinistic Methodism was born in Wales. One of Whitefield's students was Howell Harris of Trefecca, South Wales. When Harris returned to Wales from Oxford, he spread the word of George Whitefield and even invited Whitefield to speak in Wales. Whitefield accepted Harris' invitation and shortly was drawing enthusiastic crowds. His message fell on receptive ears and soon thereafter the Calvinistic Methodist Church was born. In 1742 George Whitefield presided over the first conference of what later became the Calvinistic Methodists at Watford, Glamorganshire, South Wales.

The birth of Calvinistic Methodism in Central New York can be directly traced to one man, James Owen, who often went by his Welsh name, Owen

Ap Iago. Mr. Owen immigrated from Aberdaron on the Lleyn Peninsula as did many of the other early settlers in Remsen. He arrived during the great wave of immigration in 1818. In Wales he had been deeply involved with the Calvinistic Methodists since his youth. He carried the denomination's teachings and practices to the New World with him.

The Calvinistic Methodists were very strict and initially set themselves apart from other Welsh men and women by their dress and appearance. They attempted to rid themselves of all worldly pleasures and were fervent observers of the Sabbath. Even the reading of a newspaper on Sunday was considered sacrilegious. In the early days of the denomination men refused to part their hair, as they considered doing so vanity. In some parts of Wales a wooden bowl was used to "fashion" the hair and hence the members were called "round heads." Of the four primary non-conformist denominations the Calvinistic Methodists were the most recently formed and, as a consequence, looked upon as upstarts by the older groups.

Upon his arrival in Central New York, James Owen purchased a farm just north of Prospect on the Old Stage Road. His large stone house still stands and is well maintained. Above the front door is an inscription which reads:

Adeiladwyd Hwn
i James Owen
1822
'Os disgwyliaf, y bedd sydd dy i mi' Job 17:13
Daethom o Gymru i'r wlad hen yn 1818

Translation:
This house was erected for James Owen, 1822. "If I wait, the grave is mine home," Job 17:13. I came from Wales to this country in 1818.

Shortly after coming to the area Mr. Owen became a deacon of Capel Ucha and was soon made secretary of same. Despite his position, his membership at Capel Ucha was of short duration.

In 1819 Mr. Owen attempted to introduce a Sunday School to the Congregational church. The other officers of the church thought it was inappropriate for children to study on Sunday and so opposed the idea. Mr. Owen persisted in his attempts to organize the school until he discovered a note posted to the church's door with a strict warning prohibiting Sunday School in that structure. Unfazed, Mr. Owen continued the school in his home during winter months and in his barn during the summer.

In 1824 the first Calvinistic Methodist church in America was formed with James Owen, Lewis Lewis and Hugh H. Owen as its first elders.

Worship services and Sunday School were held at the Owen home until a church could be constructed.

In the same year the first church structure was completed on the corner of James Road and Jones Road in the southern portion of the Remsen township. The new chapel was named Penycaerau after the chapel Owen had joined in Aberdaron at the age of nine.

Home of James Owen.
This house was built by James Owen in 1822 and was the meeting place for Calvinistic Methodists from 1822 to 1824.

The first sermon given in the chapel was by Rev. William G. Pierce, then the pastor of Capel Ucha. He chose as his topic Matthew 16:18, "Upon this rock I will build my church and the gates of hell shall not prevail against it."

In 1826 Mr. Owen contacted church officials in Wales and on November 24, 1826 Penycaerau was officially accepted into the Calvinistic Methodist Church of Wales. It thus became the first church of its denomination in this country to be so accepted.

Penycaerau had difficulty finding a minister as it was the first and only church of its denomination in the country. It therefore looked to its own congregation to obtain a pastor. A young man, Benjamin Davies, immigrated to Oneida County at the age of 20 in 1822 and joined Capel Ucha. When the other Calvinistic Methodists left that chapel he left with them.

Soon Davies decided he wanted to become the new church's minister. Since there were no other Calvinistic Methodist ministers in the United States, the church needed to make special arrangements and obtain permission to have Mr. Davies ordained. This occurred in 1828.

Rev. Davies was in great demand as he was the area's only ordained Calvinistic Methodist minister. He helped organize the churches of Penygraig, Nant, and French Road and was the first pastor of each. On those weekends when Rev. Davies was not preaching in the Remsen-Steuben circuit he would walk 20 miles to Utica, preach twice on Sunday, and return home by foot on Monday. For this grueling schedule he was paid one dollar.

In 1830, William T. Williams became the second ordained minister of the denomination in this country and began assisting Rev. Davies. In 1831, exhausted from his duties, Rev. Davies went to Wales to recruit others to come to preach in America. It was on this trip that he met Rev. Morris Roberts who shortly thereafter came to Remsen. Rev. Roberts was to become one of the most influential and highly regarded Welsh preachers in America.

In 1833 Morris Roberts began preaching in Remsen. He was compensated only slightly more than Rev. Davies had been. While he received two dollars for preaching in Utica, the other churches were less generous. Penycaerau and Remsen paid one dollar, Penygraig and Nant, 50 cents and French Road, a quarter. Morris Roberts served this circuit of churches until 1837.

In 1836 Rev. Davies passed away at the age of 34 after ten strenuous years as a minister. Fifty years later he was remembered by the New York Gymanfa of the Calvinistic Methodist Church when they erected a monument in his honor in the Penycaerau Cemetery.

With an increase in Welsh immigration to Remsen, the Penycaerau congregation outgrew its chapel. The membership, therefore, purchased an adjoining parcel and erected a new church slightly south of the original building. The old church was moved to the B. F. James farm on James Road in Trenton where it was used as a barn. It could still be seen there in the 1920s, but it is now gone.

The first person buried in the Penycaerau Cemetery was Mary Roberts, who died in 1826. As the church yard was small, people often cut across her grave to reach the horse sheds in the rear. The family of the deceased was outraged by this practice and put an iron fence around her grave. When someone removed the fence in the middle of the night, the family removed Mary Roberts' body and her headstone to the Fairchild Cemetery on Fairchild Road. The stone which marks her grave still proudly proclaims that she was the first person buried in Penycaerau Cemetery, but does not mention that she was also the first to leave.

Also buried in the Penycaerau Cemetery are a number of the church's ministers: David Stephens (d. 1835), Benjamin Davies (d. 1836), John Davies (d. 1842), David E. Davies (d. 1843), Evan Morris (d. 1876), and David J. Williams (d. 1882).

Penycaerau Cemetery.
The first burial in the cemetery was in 1826. A monument to the first Calvinistic minister ordained in America stands to the left of center.

The second church at the site was constructed in 1852. It was notable in that it had a basement with four rooms. During the 1870s their minister, Evan Morris, lived in those quarters. In later years the basement was occupied by Catherine Humphrey and her son. Prayer meetings were often held in her apartment.

The building itself was both small and simple. Nevertheless, T. Solomon Griffiths of Moriah in Utica observed "(t)he Jews could not have had more respect for the temple in Jerusalem than I had at the time for the old temple at Penycaerau."

On July 30, 1853, one year after the new church was constructed, James Owen passed away at the age of 72. He had been an elder at various churches both in America and Wales for 54 years. During the quarter century since he had formed the first Calvinistic Methodist church in America, more than 50 other churches of that denomination had been established. While at Penycaerau, he had made it his business to keep copious records of the church's activities and kept a summary of every sermon preached. If a member were absent he would make a record of it together with the excuse which the member was required to give.

Owen outlived two wives, each of whom gave him many children. Alexander Pirnie, Republican Congressman from the 32nd Congressional District from 1958 to 1972, was a descendant of Owen. It is interesting to note that Mr. Pirnie practiced law with descendants of Rev. William G. Pierce of Capel Ucha, namely Arthur and Philip Evans.

The death of James Owen was profoundly felt by the church. He is buried in the Penycaerau cemetery and a stained-glass window in honor of one of his daughters can still be seen at Moriah-Olivet Church in Utica.

At the time of its organization, Penycaerau's strength lay in its central location, being equidistant from Remsen and Prospect. This attribute, however, became a detriment and a reason for the church's eventual demise as new churches drew from its membership. No sooner had the church been organized in 1826 than members began leaving to form other churches at Penygraig, Nant, and French Road.

In 1831, Penycaerau's members from the village of Remsen withdrew to form Capel Cerrig. Another church was formed at Ninety-Six in 1841, where the Calvinistic Methodists worshiped in a schoolhouse, and in 1847 a church was established two and a half miles away at Enlli.

In 1850 the membership of Penycaerau was 45 with many of its members coming from Prospect, one mile to the south. In 1857, shortly after the new church was erected, the members from Prospect also left, leaving only a small number of local residents to continue the church. After Rev. Evan Morris' death in 1876 the church was ministered to by supply pastors. In the 1890s Penycaerau was joined in a circuit with Enlli and Prospect and were ministered to by Rev. E. C. Evans and Dr. Evan G. Williams.

In 1908 or 1909 the church was abandoned by the few remaining members who transferred their membership to the Prospect church. Four years later some area Welsh leaders proposed to repair the church because of its historical significance. The structure was thus rehabilitated and its churchyard cleaned up. New windows were installed and other repairs were made. Committees were appointed to oversee the repair of the church.

In 1914 a decision was made to use the church for funerals and for an annual service. Upon completion of extensive repairs to the building, a large celebration was arranged. On the morning of the appointed day Dr. E. G. Williams of Remsen conducted a service in English. A mid-day dinner was held on the lawn of the residence of W. N. Jones, whose farm was near the church. Dr. R. T. Roberts of Rome conducted a devotional service in the chapel that afternoon. There were twice as many in attendance as could gain admittance. In the evening David Ames, a descendant of James Roberts who was active in the founding of the church, was called upon to address the congregation. Unfortunately, the 1914 "annual" service was the last such service held.

Penycaerau Monument.
This monument was erected by the Oneida (Welsh) Presbytery in honor of the first Calvinistic Methodist church in America. Two structures stood on this site between 1824 and 1924.

Over the next few years the church again fell into disrepair and became the target of vandals. On September 13, 1924, one hundred years after the church's formation, the structure was sold and moved from the site. Dr. James Francis, a dentist in Clinton, indicated that his father purchased the old church and moved the structure to his residence in Remsen where it was converted into a garage. Dr. Francis related that throughout his childhood his father always spoke of parking his car in Penycaerau.

On October 11, 1924 a monument was erected in honor of the church with a likeness of the church on a bronze plaque set on a stone. In 1930 the Oneida Presbytery passed a resolution that an annual pilgrimage should be made to the Penycaerau site on the second Sunday in July, and that the sermon be preached in English in the afternoon and in Welsh in the evening.

These pilgrimages were made over the next decade or more. Mrs. Margaret Jones remembers her father using a scythe to cut the tall grass that grew in the cemetery and in the area where the picnic was to be held. A hand- and foot-pumped organ was brought from Capel Cerrig in Remsen and Margaret Griffith, then the organist at Moriah in Utica, accompanied the hymns.

The afternoon session at the Penycaerau cemetery was followed by a picnic, and later, an evening of singing at Capel Cerrig. Often there would be standing room only and the congregation would overflow the church.

Today, only the cemetery's headstones bear witness to those early Calvinistic Methodists. In 1984, in connection with the coming of the Welsh National Gymanfa Ganu to Utica, Margaret Jones and her sister Catherine Jones Roberts began planting daffodils, the national flower of Wales, on the graves. Soon, all of the graves had daffodils. Many of those daffodil bulbs still bloom every year to honor the early Welsh settlers.

The memorial to Penycaerau ends with a reference to Psalm 48:12, 13, and 14:

> Go through Zion, walk around her, counting her towers, admiring her walls, reviewing her palaces, then tell the next generation that God is here, Our God and leader for ever and ever.

Penygraig

In the eighteenth century the Welsh generally walked to church both for religious reasons and because of poor road conditions. It was therefore difficult for many Welsh to attend services at the one Calvinistic Methodist church in the area. Some of Penycaerau's members, such as Robert G. Jones, walked five miles to attend services. A decision to build a new church was made at a special meeting of the Remsen Vestry on December 2, 1827. On December 17, 1827 a meeting was held at Ty Howel, the home of Henry Pritchard on Old State Route 12, for the purpose of organizing a church in that section of the township. The church was named Penygraig which means "top of the rock."

There were 14 charter members including deacons John Davis, W. S. Prichard, and Edward Jarmon. Services were held in the neighborhood until a church could be built. A parcel of land was purchased for $14.00 and in the summer of 1828 a frame church was constructed.

In the early years the church was served by the circuit preachers, including Benjamin Davies. William Edwards was a candidate for ordination at the church in 1829, but did not serve as its pastor.

In 1845 a new church was built to replace the smaller structure. At that time David R. Williams was the pastor. He preached in Oneida County from 1843 to 1848, having come from Carbondale, Pennsylvania. Later he moved west to Columbus, Wisconsin. Also in 1845 William Jones from Snowden in North Wales was ordained in the church. One year later he moved to Wisconsin. In 1855 John Davies was called to the church from Llanfachreth, Merionethshire, North Wales.

In 1859 a parcel of land opposite the church on the State Road was purchased from Robert G. Jones and a manse was constructed for the church's minister. Soon thereafter Rev. Ebenezer Salisbury was called as a pastor and he served four years.

After the turn of the century, Penygraig combined with the Bethel Congregational Church to share a supply minister. If the preacher supplying was Congregationalist he would give two sermons at Bethel and one at Penygraig. The situation would be reversed if the minister were Calvinistic Methodist. Supplies during this time included Rev. John Isaac Hughes, Rev. Lewis Williams, and Rev. Richard J. Williams. For a brief period Rev. David C. Davies ministered to the Penygraig, Bethel and French Road churches.

In 1920 the church was yoked with the French Road Church with Rev. Richard J. Owen as pastor. During his pastorate Rev. Owens' son was electrocuted. This tragedy is still remembered by former parishioners. He was followed by John R. Evans, who went on to preach in New Hartford and Ilion.

Penygraig was well known for its church suppers. An annual ice cream social was also very popular. Large freezers would be brought to the church and ice cream would be made either at the church or at a house down the road. This homemade ice cream would attract people throughout the area. The festival was held on the lawn or, if there was inclement weather, in the church.

In later years Jennie Jones was the head ice cream maker. She was also in charge of the Sunday School. As there was no parish hall or class rooms, Sunday School was generally held in the sanctuary before the service.

In the church's one large room there were two stoves to provide heat in the winter and an organ which was played by Evelyn Tibbits for many years. There was no choir because the congregation delighted in its own singing.

The last regular minister of the church was R. Wynne Bellis. He served the church from 1927 to 1935. During the same period he also served Remsen, Nant, and Enlli in the Remsen Presbyterian Parish. Although he was fluent in Welsh, he conducted only parts of the service in the old tongue. Sometimes, because the service was conducted partially in Welsh, parents allowed their English-speaking children to play outside while they attended the service. This was a treat for the children, especially when they could pick wild strawberries growing in the cemetery. One of those children told me years later that those were the best strawberries she ever ate and this book would not be complete without their being mentioned.

Three of the last members to join the church were Robert Roberts, Gilbert Thomas, and his sister, Leola Thomas. These final members, particularly Gilbert Thomas, watched over the church and later the church's cemetery for many years. Thomas' family had first come to the area in 1817 and his grandfather and father had been leaders of the church. In fact, his grandfather had helped in building the church structure.

Facing a declining membership, the church disbanded in 1935 and many of its former members went to worship at Stone Church in Remsen. Although Penygraig was closed, the remaining members did not want to part with the structure. In 1949 a cemetery association was created to care for the cemetery and look after the building. Over the years the cemetery association members have personally mowed the grounds and righted fallen stones.

In 1950 the parsonage was sold to Gardner and Myfanwy Pugh. Later, in 1957, the cemetery association needed money for its operations and therefore resolved to sell the church. Everyone felt sad about the decision, but realized that it was impossible for the association to maintain the structure in a proper state. Sealed bids were solicited, and when they were opened, a neighboring farmer, Alfred Williams, had purchased the 112-year-old structure for $90. He dismantled the church and used the lumber for a building on his farm.

Penygraig Monument.
This monument was erected in honor of the Penygraig church. Two structures stood on the site from 1828 to 1844 and 1845 to 1957. Today a cemetery association maintains the property.

A memorial stone was erected on the hill in front of the cemetery in honor of the church. Gilbert Thomas and his wife Nadine planted two pine trees on either side of the marker. The trees have now grown so tall that the stone is almost obscured.

Upon Mr. Thomas' recent passing, his wife assumed the position of secretary-treasurer of the cemetery association. She has mowed the grounds in the past, but more recently has hired a neighborhood boy to maintain the grounds where the old church once stood.

Nant-Cobin

While Penycaerau is regarded as the first Calvinistic Methodist church in America, an argument can be made that the Nant-Cobin chapel is deserving of that honor. Nant can trace its roots to 1802, when the "First Methodist Society of Steuben" was formed. In 1828, four years after the first group of Methodists removed themselves from Capel Ucha to form Penycaerau, the remainder of the Methodists, including the church's pastor, formed or relocated the "First Calvinistic Methodist Society of Steuben" to the Cobin area of the township. Soon thereafter, in April 1829, Capel Ucha officially changed its corporate name to reflect the fact that the Methodists had gone elsewhere. The "new" society at Nant could legitimately claim to be a direct continuation of that first society and thus actually 22 years older than Penycaerau. Penycaerau was, however, the first church actually accepted into the Calvinistic Methodist Church of Wales, and thus has the honor of being "first."

The new church was located in the southern portion of the township. Traveling down Sixty Road from Sixty Corners and heading towards Holland Patent, one has a gorgeous view of Utica and the Mohawk Valley. At the bottom of that hill, just beyond Fuller Road, on the east side of Ellis Road, stood the chapel known either as Cobin or Nant.

Cobin Cemetery.
This is the site of the First Calvinistic Methodist Church of Steuben. Rev. William G. Pierce, its first pastor, is buried here.

It is unclear why the church is referred to by both the names Cobin and Nant. Cobin was the name of a farm which is located in the vicinity of where the chapel stood. Capel-y-Nant means "church by the brook," and a small stream does run nearby. Whatever the reason, the church was known by both names.

The records of the early church appear to have been lost over time, so not much is known about the first thirty years of the church's history. In 1828 a church was erected and the congregation called Rev. William G. Pierce of Capel Ucha to be its first pastor. When he died in 1847 he was buried in the Cobin cemetery.

In 1856, the church reorganized and the old church was moved across the road. It was converted into a house which was later owned by Humphrey Ellis, one of the last trustees of the church. It was recently taken down to make way for power lines.

The new society was organized at a meeting held on January 7, 1856, at which time seven trustees were elected. The first elders were Evan Jones and T. Richards. Other early elders were Robert Owens, and the brothers Hugh and Richard Hughes. In 1860, at the age of 30, Richard Davies was made an elder. He served for 62 years until 1912. Thus, the history of Nant is closely linked to that one man.

A new church was constructed in 1856 at the cost of $1,200. It was a two-story structure with three windows across the front on top and two below flanking the single entrance. Inside there was a balcony for additional seating.

Rev. Edward Rees who spent much of his life ministering to the various churches in Lewis County also worked closely with Nant for many years. Rees was known to be quite a character with a keen sense of humor and a powerful presence in the pulpit. In 1872, while the church was under his care, there were 46 members. He died in 1876.

After Rev. Rees' passing, Nant shared its pastor with Capel Cerrig in Remsen. By the turn of the century these were the only two Welsh churches in the Remsen-Steuben area which could support a full-time minister. Over the following years the church was served by Revs. George Lamb, David M. Jones, E. C. Evans, Morris S. Jones, and Hugh Rowlands. When Rev. D. C. Davies was ordained, an installation service was held in the morning in Remsen and in the afternoon at Nant. Later, under Rev. Bellis, Nant was associated with Capel Cerrig, Penygraig, and Enlli in the Remsen Presbyterian Parish.

By 1903 Nant began using English in its services. Its weekly services were held on Sunday afternoons because the pastor had to preach in Remsen on Sunday mornings. In the church's last years, services were only held during the summer months.

The last congregational meeting was held in April of 1937 at which time there were 38 members. The last two elders were Nelson Meade and Humphrey Ellis. Mr. Ellis, for whose family Ellis Road is named, led the singing at regular services while his wife played the organ.

In 1944 the church was dissolved by the Utica Presbytery. Soon thereafter, the Presbytery decided that the building should be sold as quickly as possible and a price of $200 was placed on the structure. Ethel A. (Jones) Evans who lived approximately one mile west of the church on Fuller Road had attended the church as a girl. She was very distressed to hear that the church was going to be sold. She therefore insisted that her husband, Sylvanus, purchase the structure and bring it to their farm. This he did with the help of a contractor from Boonville.

Once on the Evans' farm, the building was converted into a storage barn. The building remained in use in that capacity until about 1975. By that time Spencer Evans had inherited the farm. As the Highway Superintendent of the Town of Steuben for many years, Spencer Evans was not farming the land any more and did not need a barn. However, his wife needed an addition to their home for her beauty parlor. Mr. Evans took down the old building and used the lumber to construct the addition. Most of the outer shingles of the former church and much of its floor had rotted away. The frame, however, was still in good condition. Many of the huge beams were still sturdy and therefore were put to a new use.

The cemetery on Ellis Road, containing the remains of Rev. Pierce together with many of the other faithful members of the church, is still maintained. Rev. Pierce's descendants continue to be prominent citizens of Oneida County. Two, Arthur and Philip Evans, are senior partners in one of Utica's premier law firms: Evans, Bankert, Cohen, Lutz and Panzone.

French Road-Hebron

French Road, located in the northern portion of the town of Steuben, gets its name from the French royalists who fled to America during the French Revolution. Apparently these expatriates constructed the road as they headed toward a settlement further north. This occurred during the brief time that Baron de Steuben lived in the township. Thirty years after the French passed through the area, Welsh settlers established a Calvinistic Methodist society on French Road. The society was formed contemporaneously with Penygraig and Nant.

Although the church was formed in 1828, the members were not able to erect their chapel until 1835. At that time William P. Williams, Evan Perry and David George were the trustees. The church incorporated as the Welsh Whitefield Calvinistic Methodist Church in Steuben on June 18, 1857. This church was more commonly known as the French Road Church or Hebron Church. Hebron was the site where Abraham erected an altar to God

(Genesis 13:68). At the time of its incorporation its trustees were John O. Roberts, Evan Perry, and Robert G. Meredith.

The church was always small and in 1872 had only 23 members. Because of its size the church was never able to support its own pastor. Since the 1820s and 1830s when Benjamin Davies first began preaching on the circuit of the Remsen-Steuben churches, the French Road Church always shared its pastor with at least one other church.

French Road Church.
This church, also known as Hebron, was erected in 1835.
An annual Old Home Day service is held in July.

In the early part of the twentieth century, regular services were discontinued and the society only met during the summer. It was yoked with Penygraig and Bethel churches in 1913 under Rev. David C. Davies. At that time winter services may have resumed. Later, French Road shared its pastors only with Penygraig. Rev. Richard J. Owen served both churches beginning in 1920. Rev. John R. Evans followed in 1922. Finally, in 1928 the church dissolved.

When the church closed its doors the structure faced the same fate as many of the other Welsh chapels. The structure appeared destined to fall into disrepair to the point that the building would have to be torn down and its lumber sold. Fortunately, shortly after closing, an event occurred which saved the tiny chapel.

On May 1, 1928 Augustus Loring Richards wrote the following to Robert C. Meredith:

> Mrs. Richards and I were up at Steuben a couple of weeks ago over the weekend. There was so much snow left and the roads so bad that we had to walk nearly everywhere we went. During our walk back from camp we noticed the Old French Road Church was closed up. I am wondering whether this church is going the same way as the Old Sixty and Pen Mount Churches went. Personally, I should be very sorry to see it lapse into decay. Many members of my family and many of my good friends have attended there. I am wondering whether, if they are not going to use it anymore, it would be possible for me to buy it at a small figure. I would not want to move it away or to injure it in any way, and while I would not be willing to agree to keep it in repair, I should probably be willing to spend some money in protecting it from the elements.

Augustus L. Richards, a graduate of Harvard Law School, was associated with Hughes, Rounds & Schurman in New York City, then headed by the prominent Welsh-American, Charles Evans Hughes. He later returned to Steuben to retire in 1941.

In 1929, Mr. Richard's request was granted and the church was transferred to him by the Oneida Presbytery. He remodeled the church at his own expense and then made it available to the Presbyterian Church for religious purposes.

During the 1940s a neighbor, Edward Creedel, attempted to purchase the church, but Mr. Richards would not convey the property unless it was agreed that it would only be used for religious purposes. Therefore, Mr. Richards continued to own the property until his death on January 8, 1951, when it passed to his wife. Upon her death in 1964, the property was to pass to a son. However, the son did not want the responsibility of owning the church. Alex Senchyna, a local resident, persuaded the executor of the estate to transfer the property to the newly organized French Road Cemetery Association for $50.00.

Since the Cemetery Association's purchase of the property, an annual Old Home Day service has been held on the third Sunday of July. Occasionally the old chapel is the site of a wedding or funeral as well. In recent years Rev. Paul Creedel, vice-president of the Cemetery Association and pastor at the Ava United Methodist Church, has led the services. His father, Edward, was one of the original Cemetery Association trustees.

The annual service often attracts 100 people and is a celebration of the community and its heritage. While the St. David's Choir has participated in the service, the church is no longer exclusively Welsh. In fact, many of those who attend are of Polish or Ukrainian heritage.

Burials still continue in the cemetery at the rate of two or three each year. The grounds are maintained by the Association and, over the years, children of the Association's trustees have been hired to mow the grass.

In 1988 the Association undertook its most ambitious project since the purchase of the church. A large rock beneath one corner of the church would move with each frost and thaw. This was causing structural damage to the building. The church was also being damaged by the snow pushed against it by the town's snow plows. A national campaign was undertaken to raise funds to move the church. The fund drive was successful and the church was moved approximately twenty feet back from the road.

One final point of interest regarding the church. Located on the wall directly behind the communion table is a mural. For years this art work was obscured from view because it had been covered up with interior wall paint. Once discovered, however, the Association hired a local artist to bring the hidden picture to light. The meaning of the picture still remains a mystery, but it has been theorized that the door which figures prominently in the mural depicts the door to Heaven.

Capel Cerrig

No church structure is more associated with the Welsh in Central New York than Capel Cerrig (Stone Church) on Prospect Street in Remsen. Because of its size and location it was the focal point of Welsh Calvinistic Methodism in what would become known as the Remsen Gymanfa.

In 1830 the Remsen members of Penycaerau left the mother church and formed their own society. On January 1, 1831 Hugh H. Owen, Edward Jones, and William Pritchard, as trustees of the First Welsh Whitefield Methodist Society of Remsen purchased a one acre parcel on Prospect Street from Moses and Dinah Jones. That same year a stone church was erected as the first church built in the village of Remsen. The church's masonry was laid by Rev. William T. Williams (Bryn Coed) while the interior woodwork was constructed by brothers, Hugh, John, and Robert Hughes. Hugh Hughes became an elder and served the church for the next 50 years.

Capel Cerrig.
Today the Stone Church is the home of the Remsen-Steuben Historical Society and the site of Remsen's annual Gymanfa Ganu.

The outside of the building is just as it was in 1831 with the exception of a new Vermont slate roof added in 1888.

On the front of the church is the inscription:

Adeiladwyd y Ty Hwn
gan y Trefnyddion (Whitefield)
Calfinaidd Cymreig
i addoli'r Arglwydd yn y flwyddyn
1831

Translation:
This house was built by the Welsh Calvinistic (Whitefield)
Methodists to worship the Lord in the year 1831.

Because of the frequent confusion of the name "Calvinistic Methodist" with "Methodist Episcopal," the society specifically used the name "Whitefield," after George Whitefield, the founder of the denomination.

William T. Williams was instrumental in the building of Capel Cerrig and also served as the first pastor there. He did this in addition to his main pastorate at Penycaerau. Williams had come to Oneida County directly from Wales in 1829 and became the second person ordained in the Calvinistic Methodist Church in America in June of 1830. It was said that he was short on talent but "did his best." He later moved to Wisconsin where he died in 1853. Rev. Benjamin Davies, the first Calvinistic Methodist minister ordained in America, also supplied the pulpit of the church, but was never its principal pastor.

The first permanent pastor of the church was Rev. David Stephens. In an effort to raise money to pay for the church and to further the cause of the denomination, he would often take trips to other Welsh settlements. After one such trip to Ohio he returned to find the congregation clamoring for the newly-arrived Rev. Morris Roberts to replace him. Rev. Roberts was known for his forceful preaching style and was full of fire and enthusiasm which Stephens could not match. In 1833, after much debate, the congregation dismissed Stephens and called Roberts to succeed him. This was a devastating blow to Rev. Stephens from which he never recovered. He reportedly died shortly thereafter of "wounds received in the house of his friends."

While Rev. Roberts initially was very popular with the congregation, he was considered by some to be too liberal in his theology. When he preached a sermon on the subject of " 'Gallu dyn' 'the power of man' " which the more conservative members of the church considered heretical, he was removed from the pulpit. Thus, within the space of only six years, the church faced its second major crisis. As Millard Roberts observed in his *History of Remsen*, "the stone this church selected for its up-building when it rejected David Stephens proved the rock upon which it split."

When Morris Roberts left the church in 1837 a good portion of the congregation left as well. On May 22, 1839 Peniel Congregational Church was organized in Remsen with Rev. Roberts in its pulpit and many former members of Capel Cerrig in its pews. As pastor of the Peniel, Bethel, and Ninety-Six churches, Rev. Roberts was to continue to play an important role in the religious life of the village for decades to come.

Over the next decade the church was served by supply preachers. Rev. Edward Rees from Lewis County came regularly and Rev. Thomas T. Evans of Floyd also was a frequent visitor.

In 1850 Rev. David Williams came from Wales and served the church for three years before moving to Pittsburgh. He was followed by Rev. Thomas Williams who served for a number of years. At that time Welsh immigration was at its peak. By 1850 three-quarters of the population of Remsen and Steuben was Welsh.

The church was supplied by a number of pastors until 1872 when Rev. David M. Jones began his three-year tenure. Rev. Jones had been ordained in Minnesota in 1871. While in Oneida County he also served the Camroden Calvinistic Methodist Church. In 1883 he moved to Wisconsin with his wife, who had been a member of Capel Cerrig's congregation. They were married during his tenure in Remsen. Capel Cerrig's pulpit was built by Rev. Jones and serves as a tangible reminder of his brief pastorate in Remsen.

Rev. Edward C. Evans arrived from Shenandoah, Pennsylvania in 1878 and served until 1884 when he left for Cincinnati, Ohio. While in Remsen he married one of the church's members, Miss Lizzie Richards. It was probably this familial tie which caused him to return to Remsen one year later as editor of the English-language monthly *The Cambrian*.

Rev. Edward Thomas followed Evans, coming to Remsen from Wales. He only stayed for eight months and then returned to his homeland. Rev. George Lamb, who became pastor in 1886, had come to New York from Wales in 1872. He, like his predecessors, married a member of the parish before moving on to Wisconsin in 1889.

For the next 20 years Revs. Edward C. Evans and E. G. Williams served the church and each preached once per month. Evans took the first Sunday and Williams the last. Supplies would take the other two Sundays.

In the early part of this century Rev. William J. Owens came from Wales and supplied for a few months and was followed, in 1912, by Rev. R. J. Jones who also came from Wales. He preached to large crowds for six months before returning to Wales. Rev. Jones' sermons were couched in the scholarly Welsh of the great Welsh preacher, Christmas Evans. It is said that he refused to acknowledge how limited the knowledge of Welsh was among his congregation.

It was at about this time that English began to make its way into this church. This caused some members to leave. While the morning service remained exclusively in Welsh, the evening service every other Sunday was in English.

Rev. Morris S. Jones of Alliance, Ohio followed Rev. Jones and served as pastor during the First World War. In 1919 he left to assume the pastorate at Hebron Church in Chicago. During his stay in Remsen the church purchased its manse.

Capel Cerrig was the largest of the Calvinistic Methodist chapels in the Remsen-Steuben area and therefore became the center for many of the other Calvinistic Methodist chapels in the area. Thus, the church was better able to sustain itself than the chapels in the surrounding rural areas. By World War I the majority of the congregation did not use Welsh in their homes and therefore did not pass the language on to their children. As a consequence many of the children joined the Methodist Episcopal Church on Main Street in Remsen.

In 1920 the national Calvinistic Methodist Church and the Presbyterian Church in America merged. At the time of merger, the denomination which had established its first American church in Remsen less than 100 years before had 142 churches with 14,000 members. When the merger occurred, Capel Cerrig assumed the name First Presbyterian Church of Remsen. The Oneida (Welsh) Presbytery continued until 1936, serving the former Calvinistic Methodist churches in the area.

Rev. Hugh Rowlands of Stratonville, Pennsylvania served as pastor for one year and was succeeded in 1921 by Rev. D. C. Davies. Davies came by transfer from the Wesleyan Church in Wales and was ordained by the Oneida (Welsh) Presbytery in Remsen. He had come to America in about 1913. Prior to his ordination he had supplied the Penygraig, French Road, and Bethel churches. After leaving Remsen he went on to preach in Poultney, Vermont and Long Creek, Idaho.

In 1927 R. Wynne Bellis, the last clerk of the Oneida (Welsh) Presbytery and the Gymanfa of New York and Vermont, began his long tenure at Capel Cerrig. He had served in Pennsylvania and South Dakota before coming to New York.

Rev. Bellis was not only Capel Cerrig's pastor but also served the rural parishes of the area. By the 1920s Capel Cerrig had become affiliated with a group of churches known as the Remsen Presbyterian Parish which also included Nant, Penygraig, and Enlli. This association continued into the 1930s.

Rev. Bellis was the last minister to preach in Welsh and continued to hold some services in the old tongue until he left in 1941. In 1931, when the church celebrated its centennial, the entire service was in English. It should be noted that at the time of the centennial celebration Elder George Whitefield Jones had served as an elder for 42 years. He was to remain as an elder until his death at age 105.

On September 12 and 13, 1936, the last meeting of the Oneida (Welsh) Presbytery was held at Capel Cerrig, and was presided over by Rev. Walter H. Jones of Rome, the moderator of that Presbytery. It was fitting that the last meeting was held in Remsen as it had been the site of many important meetings during the early years of the Calvinistic Methodist churches in the area. At the time the Oneida (Welsh) Presbytery was disbanded there were seven churches remaining: Capel Cerrig, Moriah (Utica), Camroden, Nant, Penygraig, Enlli, Bethel (Rome) and Zion (New Hartford).

In the 1940s Capel Cerrig was yoked with the Holland Patent Presbyterian Church in what was known as the Holland Patent Larger Parish. Revs. Cedric Haggard and Ernest Grant supplied briefly until Rev. Frank W. Twitchell was installed in 1942. Other ministers who followed were Revs.

George Murdock, Wilford Hasbrouck, Bertram Humphries, and James W. Kemmerer.

In 1952 Capel Cerrig and the Remsen Baptist Church joined together to form a federated church. The two churches held services together until 1989. During those years the two churches kept separate books, records, and members. Summer services were held in the old Stone Church while in the winter months the congregation gathered at the Baptist Church on Main Street.

During the federation, Alan B. Peabody, Executive Director of the Council of Churches of the Mohawk Valley Area, showed a great deal of interest in the church, worked hard to sustain it, and even served as pastor for a number of years. He was followed in the pulpit by two lay preachers Charles Mahaffy and Curry M. Bartlett Jr. It was during Mr. Bartlett's tenure that the church celebrated its 150th anniversary.

I had the opportunity of attending one service at the church prior to it being closed. My father, Dr. Jay G. Williams, was supplying and therefore we rode up from Clinton together so I could hear him preach. We arrived early and waited in the car until someone came to open the church. The congregation was small with only 13 Baptist members and four Presbyterians. I believe they had perfect attendance that morning. The membership was old and greying and, as I recall, the hymns were accompanied on the piano, not the organ. Despite the small congregation an usher stood at the door greeting the morning's worshipers. I will never forget Leonard Wynne's smiling welcome as he passed out the morning bulletins.

A brief word should be said about the structure itself. Like so many of the Welsh chapels, the building reflected the theology and spirit of the church. Rule Number Six of the Calvinistic Methodist's confession of faith ordered church members to "part with the vanity of the world and its corrupt practices: such as vain society, feasts of patron saints, dances, play acting, revelry, carousal, drinking and the like." The stripping away of pretensions was meant to allow the inner light to shine through.

In keeping with that spirit the exterior of Capel Cerrig is very stark. The sides are simple; it has two stories with four windows on each level. At present the windows have been returned to their original clear pane style. Behind the church once stood horse barns. Today, an unpaved parking lot is on the side.

The interior of the church has been remodeled on four occasions: in 1872, 1888, 1923, and 1991. In the course of the most recent remodeling an attempt is being made to return the interior to its original state. The old varnished pews in the balcony are thought to be original. Be wary of those pews on a warm summer day. I recall once walking away with a seat full of varnish. The balcony at one time extended on all three walls of the church, but in 1921 the back portion of the balcony was enclosed. In that same year new pews were installed on the first level.

At one time on the main floor there were wood stoves on each side of the sanctuary. In the front stood the communion table and behind it three tall straight-back chairs. Originally a wooden archway graced the front wood-paneled wall. Later the archway was removed and the wall was covered by plaster. A three-dimensional picture of gothic arches was painted behind the pulpit, in a style similar to that found at the Richville and French Road churches.

In 1943 the downstairs was painted and the picture was covered over. A cross was purchased and hung behind the communion table where it remained until the church closed. During the most recent renovations, the paint was removed to reveal the original wood paneling and a bare archway with space where the wooden arch once was. At a presentation of "A Child's Christmas in Wales" evergreen branches were placed in the bare area to form a green arch. In 1992 a new arch was installed.

In the final years of its existence Capel Cerrig was served by Rev. John Harris, a Utica pastor. He was involved with the Utica Rescue Mission and frequently brought persons from the shelter to services. This allowed them to have a warm church environment and gave the church more people in the pews.

The last minister was Rev. Susan Loper, the church's first woman pastor. She was there when the church closed forever in 1986. In that year both the Baptist Church and Capel Cerrig were in need of repair. Therefore, the churches had to decide which of the two buildings to maintain. The Baptists were prepared to repair their church but not Stone Church. The four Presbyterians realized that the burden of maintaining the 155-year-old structure would fall on them and determined that they could not maintain the building on their own.

The last four members of Capel Cerrig were Hugh Black, Hazel Black, Jennie Jones and Dorothy Wynne. Mrs. Wynne had been the last person to join, having become a member in about 1981. Upon the church's dissolution its property was turned over to the Utica Presbytery.

Every year since 1961, the Remsen Fortnightly Club has sponsored a Gymanfa Ganu at Capel Cerrig. A regular feature at that event each year has been Evan Gwyndaf Roberts at the organ. Since its inception he has accompanied conductors from the United States, Canada and Wales at Remsen's hymn festival.

In 1981 the village began its annual Festival of the Arts, billed as a celebration of rural Welsh traditions. The crafts fair attracts tens of thousands of people and culminates with the Fortnightly Club's Gymanfa on Sunday: the afternoon session is at Capel Cerrig and the evening session, at the United Methodist Church on Main Street.

When Capel Cerrig closed, the Remsen-Steuben Historical Society offered to pay the Presbytery for its expenses involving the upkeep of the building. The Presbytery, however, felt that it had to attempt to obtain the highest possible price from the sale of the church. There was talk of selling the building to a commercial enterprise, of converting the church into apartments or of even tearing it down.

The Presbytery appraised the old church at $15,000 and demanded that amount from the Historical Society. In order to raise the necessary funds a national campaign was undertaken. Advertisements were placed in local and Welsh newspapers soliciting contributions.

As the time for the annual Gymanfa approached, Dorothy and Leonard Wynne went to the old Stone Church to clean in preparation for the event only to find that the locks on the doors had been changed. The keys would be given out by the Presbytery only if certain forms were signed and assurances given. Further, the Presbytery, feeling "pressure" from the Historical Society, refused to compromise or allow the use of the building until a sale was finalized. The reason given for not allowing the event to proceed was "(w)hen they start singing and get those rhythms going it could be enough to make the place collapse and we're concerned about the health and safety of people." The force and power of Welsh hymn singing is obviously widely known.

Since the Stone Church could not be used, both sessions of the Gymanfa were held in Remsen's United Methodist Church. The opening hymn, "Oh Jesus, Thou art standing outside the fast-closed door" was a subtle statement of protest to the Presbytery's position.

Eventually the Remsen-Steuben Historical Society did raise the necessary funds and the building was purchased. Thereafter, an extensive renovation was undertaken. The building has been the site of many events including a Christmas party and St. David's Day festivities.

In 1991 I had the great pleasure of being asked by Dorothy Wynne to conduct the annual Gymanfa Ganu. What a feeling of excitement it was to climb the steps to the front of the church and stand behind the pulpit crafted by Rev. David M. Jones where so many great Welsh preachers have stood. Rev. Paul Creedel, an officer of the French Road Cemetery Association, gave the invocation and Mair Lloyd, widow of former Moriah pastor R. Glynne Lloyd, gave the readings in Welsh. It was a moment I will never forget.

Today, as the home of the Remsen-Steuben Historical Society, renovations are ongoing. During some recent work, old plaster was stripped away, revealing a poster signed by members of a Sunday School class from the nineteenth century. The poster contained a message to future generations. It said, "Remember Lot's wife." That is to say, "Don't look back."

Enlli

Three miles from Remsen, on the road leading to Ninety-Six, there sits a small white chapel on the side of the road which is often mistaken for an old schoolhouse. It is located immediately adjacent to the White Birch Inn, the premier restaurant in the Remsen area.

Enlli.
This church is located on Fairchild Road in Remsen. It was active from 1848 to 1965. The structure is unusual in that it is wider than it is long.

This small church was organized in 1848 and was named for Ynys Enlli (Bardsey Island), an island located off the coast of North Wales near Aberdaron. Henry D. Williams, a distant relative of mine, is a local historian in Aberdaron and is an expert on the history of the island. On our trips to

Wales, he offered to take my brother, my father and me across the fierce seas to visit the island, but the strong possibility that a storm could strand us on the island always kept us from visiting it. The island has about 250 tillable acres and in 1886 was inhabited by 72 people, 36 men and 36 women. Today it is an uninhabited bird sanctuary.

In 512 A.D. a monastery of the Celtic Church was established on the island and it existed for many years. The locals will tell you St. David himself ran the monastery for three years. In the Middle Ages a pilgrimage to Enlli was equal in importance to a pilgrimage to Rome. Because of its religious signifigance, many believers chose to make Enlli their final resting place. At least 20,000 saints of the Celtic Church are said to be buried on Bardsey Island.

Enlli at one time considered itself a separate nation and in the nineteenth century a John Williams was crowned "King of Bardsey." The story is told that the "King" appeared at the National Eisteddfod in Pwllheli on the day set aside for welcoming Welsh exiles. He presented himself as an "exile" from the nation of Enlli.

In the early nineteenth century many of the settlers in the Remsen area were from the Aberdaron-Ynys Enlli region in North Wales. In the small cemetery across the road from the Enlli Chapel is a headstone which reads, "John W. Prichard: A native of Enlli, North Wales – immigrated to America in 1826, died February 5, 1861." Mr. Prichard may have been instrumental in forming the church. It is also possible that he was a relative of Love Prichard who was at one time "King" of Enlli.

John R. Jones, another native of the tiny island is credited with founding the church. He, his wife, and five children were the first settlers in that area of the township, so he named the church after his old homeland. The first elders of the church were Jenkyn Jones and James Williams.

Soon after the church was organized, timbers were cut from the virgin forest and brought to the site for the construction of the chapel. After the front of the church had been erected it was decided that the building, as designed, would be too large. The timbers for the sides were re-cut. Thus, the building is not as long as it is wide.

The church is small with two stoves on either side of the sanctuary. The older men and women would sit on benches which surrounded the stoves, with men around one stove and women around the other. The building has two entrances, one for men and one for women. The sexes sat separately until the 1940s. While this division may originally have been for "moral" reasons, it also conveniently divided the church into vocal parts for singing in four-part harmony.

In 1860 the church was officially incorporated, but little is known about its activities at that time. In fact, no church records exist from 1848 to 1887.

In the 1890s Enlli was part of a circuit of churches, including Penycaerau and Prospect, that shared pastors. Those who served in that decade were Rev. E. C. Evans and Dr. E. G. Williams. Services were held only during the months "when the cows were in the field" (May through November) and were generally held in the afternoon because the minister preached elsewhere in the morning.

Church minutes were kept in Welsh until 1914. All services were in Welsh until that time as well. The last person to preach in Welsh was Dr. E. G. Williams, a pharmacist from Remsen who wore chin whiskers down to his belt. He had given up medical practice to become a minister.

By the 1920s the churches at Prospect and Penycaerau had closed. Therefore, Enlli joined a rotation with Capel Cerrig, Nant and Penygraig. During the twenties, the church enjoyed a rebirth. In 1927, three years before his death, my great-grandfather, John S. Williams, founded a Sunday School at the chapel. "Sunday School" is a misnomer as these Bible study meetings were generally held on Wednesday evenings. Oliver Jones, the last trustee of the church, was in John S. Williams' class.

During the years which followed, Enlli was often supplied by Methodist ministers from the Remsen United Methodist Church. For a time the Presbyterian minister from Holland Patent had the services. Rev. Richard J. Owen also served the church as part of a circuit.

In 1941 electricity was installed at the same time electricty was brought to the neighborhood by President Roosevelt's Rural Electrification program. Wires were run directly from the ceiling into the converted kerosene lamps behind the communion table. The stoves were retained and they remain today. An arch behind the pulpit with the inscription, "If God be for us, who can be against us" written in gold, was covered over by wallpaper.

In the 1940s the church had a membership of 24. Rev. Ernest Grant was engaged to conduct summer services. The congregation held regular services until 1965, but after that date, regular services were abandoned even though the church continued to exist. The last service was held on August 20, 1971 when Rev. Morton Magee of the Remsen and Prospect United Methodist Churches preached to 61 people. The church was to stand unused for the next twenty years.

In the late 1980s the Utica Presbytery tried to sell the church. However, they were advised that the land on which the church stood was not owned by the Presbytery but by an adjacent landowner. Therefore, the building was saved.

In 1991 the church was conveyed to the Remsen-Steuben Historical Society. In celebration of this conveyance, an old-fashioned ice cream social was held in the chapel and under a tent. People came from as far away as Long Island. Some were former members or relatives of former members. Some just came to walk through the church and savor that atmosphere and the refreshments. Henry D. Williams' book on Ynys Enlli was on sale, the ice cream was delicious, and the mood was jovial as the past was celebrated.

The last elder of the church, Oliver Jones, and his wife, Leona, recently celebrated their 50th wedding anniversary and invited the entire town of Remsen to share in the festivities. They asked that those attending contribute to the church in lieu of a present. This raised $4,500 for church improvements. New windows, a new roof, and a new chimney were installed. The building is to be repainted in the near future.

On May 9, 1992, the first sermon in twenty years was preached in the church by my father, Dr. Jay G. Williams. The sun shown brilliantly into the sanctuary and red geraniums stood on each window sill. The beauty of the day made the peeling plaster almost unnoticeable. A hand- and foot-pumped organ was brought from Capel Cerrig and played by my mother, Hermine Williams. Rev. James Dick, a retired Baptist minister, who had preached at the church once in the 1960s, assisted in the service. I had the good fortune of leading the hymns. I made sure that a number of verses were sung in Welsh so that I could write that in 1992 the Welsh language still filled the church. After such a wonderful reopening one can only hope the service will become an annual event. Maybe the church will once again be open for weddings and other services.

Ninety-Six (Calvinistic Methodists)

The Welsh Calvinistic Methodists began to worship in a schoolhouse at Ninety-Six in about 1840. The hamlet of Ninety-Six is so small it is hard to imagine the area could support even one church, yet four were located there at one time. Of those four, three were Welsh: the Wesleyans, the Congregationalists and the Calvinistic Methodists. The fourth was a society of Campbellites who worshiped at the Ninety-Six schoolhouse for a time.

Of the three Welsh churches, the Calvinistic Methodist one was the smallest. It never had its own building, always worshiping in the hamlet's schoolhouse. The church remained until the 1850s when it ceased to hold services.

Wesleyan Methodist Churches

Sixty Corners

Sixty Corners is located at the intersection of Starr Hill Road and Sixty Road, just west of the Steuben Memorial. The name "Sixty" comes from the 60 acres the Baron cleared for his farm.

Sixty Corners.
A Wesleyan Methodist church stood at Sixty Corners for many years.
The cemetery is located at the intersection of
Starr Hill and Sixty Roads in the town of Steuben.

The church at Sixty Corners was one of the few Wesleyan Methodist churches in the area and the only one in the town of Steuben. It was made famous in Howard Thomas' 1966 novel *The Road to Sixty* and was the church attended by the protagonist, Gwen. The Sixty Wesleyan Church was located in a region dominated by Calvinists. This conflict in theology is the central theme of Thomas' story. As one character notes, "There are lots of good masons in Remsen and Prospect, and every last one of them a Calvinistic Methodist or hard shelled Baptist or a Congregationalist. They would rather burn in hell than touch a hand to a Wesleyan Methodist Chapel."

The "First Society of the Welsh Methodist Episcopal Church at Steuben" was established in 1830. The name "Methodist Episcopal" was used interchangeably with "Wesleyan Methodist" by the Welsh, though today the Wesleyan and United Methodist churches are very different.

In 1833 the congregation purchased land from Thomas Jones on the southwest corner of Sixty Corners for the site of their church. In the 1830s Rev. John Jones was a frequent preacher. Later, Revs. John R. Williams, Thomas Thomas, and others served Sixty in a circuit with the Wesleyan churches of South Trenton and Ninety-Six. The church continued until the 1870s.

Today the cemetery remains enclosed in a wire fence installed by John Davis and his brother. An outline of the church's foundation can still be seen directly in front of the entrance to the cemetery. The old Welsh graves are well maintained and stand side by side with more recent headstones bearing Polish inscriptions.

Ninety-Six (Wesleyan)

The Welsh Wesleyans erected a church at Ninety-Six in the early 1850s. This congregation shared its pastor with the church at Sixty Corners in Steuben. The society was never very strong and dissolved in about 1890. The church remained shut for about 15 years, until after the turn of the century. At that time the funeral of a rich lady from the area was conducted at the old church. The people present at the service resolved to keep the church open. Subsequently, for a number of years services were held there on Sunday afternoons by the pastor of the Methodist Church in Remsen. These services continued until 1915 when the church was torn down.

Chapter II

Neighboring Towns

AS REMSEN AND STEUBEN GREW, the Welsh began to move into the adjoining towns of Trenton, Marcy, Deerfield and Newport. Unlike Remsen, these towns were not primarily Welsh, though they did have large Welsh populations. The Welsh churches in these towns grew out of the older churches in Remsen and Steuben. Today not one of the Welsh churches in these towns continues, the last one having closed in the 1950s.

Trenton

The town of Trenton is located directly south of Remsen and Steuben. It has three villages and one major hamlet, namely Prospect, Holland Patent, Barneveld, and South Trenton.

Prospect

Prospect, being the closest of Trenton's three villages to Remsen, had a large number of Welsh residents in the early nineteenth century. James Owen, the founder of Penycaerau, for example, lived just north of the village. Because of its proximity to Remsen, the village's Welsh residents were members of the older, more established churches in Remsen and Steuben and did not begin to establish their own churches in the village until the 1850s.

Prospect's greatest contribution to the Welsh community came long after its chapels had closed. In the 1950s, 1960s and 1970s, Howard Thomas of Prospect was the founder and proprietor of a small local press, Prospect Books. Aside from writing and publishing numerous local history books he also authored two novels about Welsh life in Oneida County during the nineteenth century. *The Singing Hills* and *The Road to Sixty* are both classics and should be read by anyone interested in the Welsh of Central New York. In recognition of his work the Prospect Library established the Howard Thomas Room which houses its local history collection.

Baptist Church

The first Welsh church in Prospect was formed by the Baptists in 1854 under the direction of Rev. David J. Williams. He had been the pastor at Capel Isaf since 1850, but when a theological dispute arose within that church, Rev. Williams and his supporters removed themselves and establish their own church in Prospect. Prior to this time Welsh Baptists in Prospect had attended Capel Bont.

The Prospect Welsh Baptist Church was built by and for Rev. Williams. The small church was located on State Street, just to the south of Prospect's present cemetery. The Welsh Congregationalists worshiped in the structure as well as the Free Baptists, who began meeting there in 1857 and remained for several years thereafter. The cemetery was known as the Baptist cemetery long after the church closed.

In 1870 Rev. David Williams left the Baptist church and became a Calvinistic Methodist minister. He continued to preach in the Remsen and Prospect area until his death in 1882.

In 1872 the Baptist church in Prospect closed its doors and its members joined with Zion Baptist Church in Remsen. The structure stood for a number of years after it ceased being used as a church. Its final use was as John Jones' tire shop. It has since been torn down.

Moriah

Prior to 1853, the Welsh Congregationalists in Prospect attended Capel Ucha. In that year they began holding meetings in the village with a view towards forming their own church. In 1856 the society began to hold worship services in the local school and in the Welsh Baptist Church.

In 1857 the congregation constructed a church on what was then Hinckley Street and named the chapel Moriah. Moriah is the land to which God instructs Abraham to take his son Isaac and offer him as a sacrifice. It is also the name of one of the Welsh churches in Utica.

Moriah.
This home was Prospect's Congregational church from 1857 to 1947. Since that time it has been used as a private residence.

The church's first pastor, Rev. Hugh R. Williams, solicited funds for the construction of the chapel from throughout New York and Pennsylvania. When the church was unable to pay all its construction expenses, Rev. Morris Roberts, of Remsen's Peniel Church, loaned the society money to cover its debt. Hugh R. Williams remained for two years. He was followed by Rev. Robert Evans, who went on to become the pastor of both Peniel and Bethel in Remsen.

Over the years Moriah generally relied on supply pastors and often shared its minister with the Congregational Church at Ninety-Six. It also frequently yoked with the Calvinistic Methodists in the village for joint services. In the 1870s it had a membership of about 30.

In 1896 Moriah merged with the English-speaking Congregational Church. One year later the church was extensively remodeled to accommodate the merged congregation. At that time Rev. T. I. Jones was the acting pastor. On September 26, 1907, the church celebrated its 50th anniversary. Most of the choir members listed for that Sunday had Welsh surnames, so it is clear that the church did not forget its Welsh roots. Rev. George O. Phelps was the pastor at the time of the celebration.

In 1938 the Congregational Church joined with the Free Will Baptist Church and formed the Federated Churches of Prospect. Millard Roberts was the first pastor of the new society. The association continued for nearly a decade with the congregations alternating between the two structures. In 1947 the Baptists left the federation and the Congregational Church was dissolved.

The church was converted into a private residence and has been owned by the Helmer family for many years. The building, located at 604 Summit Street, does not look like a church at first glance. The steeple and bell tower have been removed, and the large stained-glass window in the front has been replaced by smaller windows. Yet, if one looks carefully, one can still see structural evidence of the church beneath the surface.

Calvinistic Methodist Church

Calvinistic Methodist Church.
Prospect's Calvinistic Methodist Church was located at 216 Church Street from 1860 to 1913. Today it is a private residence.

The Calvinistic Methodist Church in Prospect was organized in 1857. Its membership came by transfer from Penycaerau, located one mile north of the village. As a consequence it had a strong relationship with Penycaerau throughout its existence.

The society was officially known as the Second Calvinistic Methodist Society of Trenton, the First Calvinistic Methodist Society of Trenton having been established in Holland Patent. Its church was erected at 216 Church Street in 1860. Generally it was served by the same minister who served Penycaerau and Enlli. Membership was always small, having only 30 members in 1872. Rev. Ebenezer T. Jones served as pastor for a time. In the 1890s Rev E. C. Evans and Dr. E. G. Williams preached there.

When Penycaerau closed its doors in 1908 its members and assets were transferred to the Prospect church, which itself had only 11 members. By 1913, the Prospect church's doors were also closed.

Like Prospect's Welsh Congregational Church, the Calvinistic Methodist chapel was converted into a private residence. It has been the home of the Rickards for many years.

Holland Patent

The village of Holland Patent sits in the western portion of the town of Trenton. The Welsh started to settle in the village in 1836, and in 1838 the Baptists, Congregationalists and Calvinistic Methodists began worshiping in private residences. Eventually, in about 1843, the three groups rented the local school for Sunday worship. One group would hold services in the morning, one in the afternoon and the third in the evening. The children met in a unified Sunday School.

Baptist Church

The Welsh Baptist Church was organized in the early 1840s. It was a small society which never had its own church building. The society may have lasted until the early 1870s. It is interesting to note that some of the ministers at the English-speaking Baptist Church were Welsh and may have served the Welsh Baptists in Holland Patent before the formation of the Welsh Baptist Church. These included Revs. Griffith Jones (1822-1825), Robert L. Williams (1827-1834), Thomas Roberts (1837-1841) and Thomas Jones (1849).

Zion

Holland Patent's Calvinistic Methodist Church was organized in 1840 by the Merediths, a prominent Holland Patent family. Prior to this time the Methodists had worshiped with the Welsh of other denominations. The first meeting of the society was held at the home of Hugh Edwards. His home, along with those of William Roberts and William Williams, was used for holding services during the church's early years.

The first pastor, Rev. Robert Meredith, had emigrated from Ffestiniog in 1831 and came to Holland Patent in 1840. He was responsible for the church's organization. Sadly, Rev. Meredith died unexpectedly in 1841.

After Rev. Meredith the church was served by circuit preachers such as the Revs. T. J. Evans, Isaac Davies, Thomas R. Jones and Richard W. Jones. Evans came to this country in 1840. He later moved to Brooklyn where he joined the Presbyterian church. Davies also came in 1840 from Denbighshire, North Wales. In 1842 he returned to Wales. Thomas Jones preached in Camroden, a few miles to the west, in the town of Floyd. He was officially ordained in Rome in 1857.

On September 3 and 4, 1844 Holland Patent's Calvinistic Methodists dedicated their chapel and named it Zion. It was a wood frame structure measuring 42 x 26 feet and was erected under the supervision of Hugh Edwards and Robert R. Meredith. Zion was located on the north side of Park Place in Holland Patent behind the Union School. In 1857 it was enlarged to accommodate a growing membership.

Rev. David O. Jones was the first pastor in the new church and served for a few years. Rev. Thomas J. Williams came to the village in 1847 and Rev. Hugh Roberts was a frequent preacher after 1849. In 1851 Rev. David Williams began preaching in Holland Patent. He later returned to Wales. Rev. Thomas R. Roberts, who served at the Zion Church on Welsh Hill in Turin, also ministered in Holland Patent for a time.

In 1858, Rev. William Rowlands, one of the most prominent Calvinistic Methodist ministers in America, began to preach in Holland Patent, dividing his time with the Marcy church. He remained until 1861 when he became pastor to the Methodists in Utica.

Throughout its existence, members of the Meredith family led the church and served as its elders. M. J. Meredith, son of Rev. Robert Meredith, was an elder from 1849 until his death in 1898. He also served as chorister from 1853 until his death. Robert R. Meredith served as treasurer for 40 years. He was succeeded by his son, Robert J. Meredith, in 1892.

In 1865 Rev. Robert F. Jones became pastor and remained for two years. In 1870 Rev. Thomas T. Evans came to the village from Camroden.

He continued to preach for as long as his health permitted. He died in 1898 at the age of 91. Rev. Griffith Griffith of Rome, New York also served as pastor, remaining until 1896 when he moved to Columbus, Wisconsin. Later, in 1921, he moved to Milwaukee, Wisconsin where he died in 1928. He was followed in the Milwaukee pulpit by another transplanted Roman, Jay G. Williams, who four years later died while that church's pastor.

Rev. Henry R. Williams was at the church for three years following Rev. Griffith Griffith. In 1901 Rev. John Isaac Hughes became the last pastor to serve the church.

The small church contributed more than its share of leaders to the regional Welsh organizations including the Welsh Bible Society. Nevertheless, membership dwindled and in 1905 the church dissolved. Its few remaining members joined Holland Patent's Welsh Congregational Church. The structure stood vacant for a time and then was taken down.

Congregational Church

Holland Patent's Welsh Congregational Church was formed in 1843 as an outgrowth of Capel Ucha. For the first year of its existence its members met in a schoolhouse under the guidance of Rev. William D. Williams. He conducted the church's services from 1843 to 1857. Later the congregation rented another denomination's chapel to hold services. In 1855 the church had 15 members with a congregation of 50.

In 1858 the society purchased a structure located on the village green. The building had been constructed in about 1851 and may have been used both as blacksmith and cabinetmaker shops prior to its conversion into a church. It had been owned by a John Ewing who had purchased the land from Pasqual DiAngelis in 1846.

The stone structure had a large portico which may have been a later addition. Stained-glass windows were installed on the sides and plain glass graced the front. The inside of the church contained old fashioned and uncomfortable low back pews. The sanctuary seated about 200. The pulpit was centered at one end of the church and in front of the pulpit was a hand-pumped organ.

In the 1860s, the Revs. John R. Griffith of Camroden, James Davies, and John Cadwalader served as pastors. In 1865 the church had 18 members with a congregation of 25.

Rev. James Griffith served both the Holland Patent and Trenton (Barneveld) churches in the 1870s. From 1888 until 1891 Rev. Richard Hughes served as pastor. For many years Hughes was the secretary of the

Welsh Association of New York State. He was followed by Edward Davies who also served both the Holland Patent and Trenton churches.

From 1901 to 1929 Rev. Richard Hughes returned as pastor. Rev. Henry Hughes also served the church. R. T. Williams of Bethesda in Utica conducted services from 1940 to 1951 and Dr. Glynne Lloyd of Moriah supplied the pulpit from 1948 to 1956. From 1948 to 1951 these two pastors alternated conducting the afternoon services.

Congregational Church.
Holland Patent's Welsh Congregational Church was located on the village green. Services were conducted here until 1956. It has been the Kelly residence since 1970.

The church continued into the 1950s with an average attendance of only 15 to 20. Throughout this period the church continued the use of Welsh in its services. One of the church's objectives was the preservation of "yr hen iath" (the old language). However, since the members' children did not learn the language, the congregation dwindled until in 1956 the church was closed.

For many years the church stood vacant. It was first owned by Albert Bagg and then by Ed Christiana. The stained-glass windows, which had been installed at the turn of the century, became the target of vandals. All but one of the windows were destroyed. The remaining window was removed by Christiana.

In 1970 the church was converted into a private residence. Since that time it has been the home of Christopher and Virginia Kelly.

Barneveld

Barneveld is the town seat for the Town of Trenton. It was originally known as Olden Barneveld and then for many years simply as Trenton. The name has now been returned to Barneveld.

The first Welsh family to come to the Barneveld area was John Jones "the farm" who moved to the Mappa farm in 1801. However, it was not until 1856 that Rev. William D. Williams helped organize the Congregational Church in Barneveld. There had been a small Calvinistic Methodist society in the village during the 1840s, but it never had a structure.

The church was erected on Mappa Avenue in 1858. Following Rev. Williams in the pulpit were Revs. James Davies, Robert Evans, and John Cadwalader. Rev. James Griffith, after leaving the pulpit of the Second Welsh Congregational Church in Utica, also served the parish for a number of years in the 1870s. However, after his departure services were not held regularly and the church did not engage a regular pastor. Later, when the congregation was able to retain a minister, his primary responsibility was always to the Congregational Church in Holland Patent.

From 1888 to 1891 Rev. Richard Hughes served both parishes. He had come to the area from Wilkes-Barre, Pennsylvania. In 1891 he left to become pastor of the Nelson church.

Rev. Edward Davies followed in 1891 and he was also responsible for Capel Ucha, Bethel Church in Remsen and the Welsh Congregational Church in Holland Patent. He probably was the church's last regular pastor.

Near the turn of the century the church was sold to a group of Episcopalians who named their parish St. Andrew's. The remaining members joined the Welsh church at Holland Patent. After the property was transferred the church was remodeled both internally and externally. The original windows, rectangular with small panes of clear glass, were replaced by arched windows. The pews used by the Welsh had been hard spindle-back benches, hinged so they could be folded over. These pews were given to the Methodist church in the village. The Methodists found the pews too hard and resold them to an antique dealer. Today further renovations are planned for the sanctuary to make the church larger and handicapped accessible.

*Trenton Congregational Church.
St. David's Episcopal Church on Mappa Avenue in Barneveld was a Welsh Congregational Church from 1858 until the turn of the century.*

Before St. Paul's Episcopal Church in Holland Patent closed, it merged with St. Andrew's. The joint parish adopted the name St. David's in about 1986 in honor of the patron saint of Wales. In 1991 the parish had to decide which structure to retain as it could no longer support the two buildings. The Barneveld church was selected and thus the old Welsh Congregational Church remains a place of worship today as St. David's Episcopal Church. The structure's Welsh spirit has had a great influence on the members of the church, as evidenced by the fact that at Remsen's annual Festival of the Arts, the St. David's Church booth always serves the best Welsh cakes.

South Trenton

South Trenton was first settled in 1792 and three years later was the second stop for the first group of Welsh settlers on their journey north to the town of Steuben. The first settlers in South Trenton were Col. Thomas Hicks, John Garrett and his two sons Cheney and Peter. They came to the area as carpenters to construct Mappa Hall in Barneveld. Direct descendants of the Garretts live in the hamlet today. Soon after these settlers arrived, Edward Hughes and Hugh Thomas came to the area from Wales.

Mr. Thomas arrived in 1797 and Mr. Hughes in 1806. Thus, of the first handful of settlers in South Trenton, two were Welsh.

Edward Hughes was born in Denbighshire in North Wales. He purchased 50 acres located a quarter of a mile south of the hamlet from the Holland Land Company for $8 an acre. He erected a log cabin on his farm shortly after his arrival. When soldiers returning from the War of 1812 were passing through the area and "annoying the inhabitants," Mr. Hughes allowed the soldiers to stay in his barn. Thus his family was spared being molested.

At one time South Trenton was a thriving community and the center of activity in the southeastern portion of Trenton township. It grew in importance because of its location. The highway north passed through it and it had a good water supply from the Nine Mile Creek. It had two Welsh chapels, one Wesleyan and one Baptist. It also maintained a number of Welsh social societies. One of these organizations predicated admission on the applicant being an author of at least "tolerably good" poetry. The hamlet also had its own chapter of the Sons of Temperance. In 1850, when the Welsh population was at its height, South Trenton's Welsh population was 200.

Over time, the steep Deerfield Hill caused travelers to find easier routes north. Eventually South Trenton's businesses relocated in Holland Patent and other communities. Today Route 12 by-passes the hamlet which is a quiet residential community.

Baptist Church

The first church organized in the hamlet was Baptist. There also may have been a Calvinistic Methodist society as Rev. Morris Williams was ordained as a Calvinistic Methodist in South Trenton in 1841. Rev. Richard Isaac, another Methodist minister, preached there in 1842.

When the Baptist Church on old Route 12 began is not clear. The first burial in the church's cemetery was on January 13, 1828 when Edward Hughes was laid to rest. It is quite possible that Mr. Hughes donated the land on which the church and cemetery later stood.

There were over 30 burials in the cemetery between 1828 and 1850. It is likely that a church was erected prior to 1828. Rev. Richard Jones preached to the Baptists in South Trenton during his tenure at Capel Isaf (1806-1821). The church's first full-time minister was Elder Joseph Richards. He had originally been pastor of Capel Isaf and later served as minister to the English-speaking Baptists in Holland Patent. He may have begun preaching in South Trenton in 1820. Rev. Richards died at the age of 80 in 1842 and is buried in the church's cemetery.

South Trenton Baptist Cemetery.
This cemetery is located on old Route 12 in South Trenton.
A Baptist church was located at this site for many years.

Rev. John Hughes followed Richards in the pulpit. He came to South Trenton in 1834. Like Richards he had been pastor at Capel Isaf before coming to South Trenton. Another pastor of the church was Rev. John Stephens. Stephens had been instrumental in organizing churches in Utica and Steuben. He also founded the Welsh Baptist Church in New York City where he was minister from 1806 until 1810. Rev. Stephens died in 1846 at the age of 84 and is buried in South Trenton. Also buried in South Trenton is the wife of Rev. Robert Williams who died in 1861. Rev. Williams may have been the church's pastor at that time.

In 1850 the church had 40 members. During the 1850s Rev. Robert Littler served as pastor. Rev. Littler came to South Trenton directly from Denbighshire in Wales. He also served the English-speaking churches in Prospect, Trenton Falls and elsewhere. In about 1861 he left to work as a cheese buyer in New York City. Shortly thereafter he enlisted as a chaplin for the Union army. He died of a fever in a medical hospital in Baltimore, Maryland in 1863. Littler may have been the church's last regular pastor. Littler's great-granddaughter, Gertrude Reynolds, was for a long time a resident of South Trenton and now lives in Florida.

After Rev. Littler the pastors from the Welsh Baptist churches in Remsen and Steuben supplied the chapel. Like many of the other Welsh Baptist churches, membership in the South Trenton church declined during the second half of the nineteenth century as the new immigrants were generally of other denominations. In the late 1870s the church was abandoned. Today only a small cemetery remains.

The cemetery fell into disrepair and lay abandoned for many years. In the 1960s, the Yorkers, a Holland Patent High School history club, helped restore the area. It again fell into disrepair until recently when a local man, Ken Marshall, began mowing and caring for the cemetery. Though not of Welsh descent, Mr. Marshall has taken it upon himself to keep the plot clear of the fast-growing plants and weeds.

Wesleyan Church

The Wesleyan Methodists' church in South Trenton, like the Baptists', was small. It was located on Coombs Road, just south of the Baptist church. One of the founders of the church was Jacob D. Jones who came to the area in 1818. When he first arrived he had to travel 12 miles to attend services. He therefore resolved to found a church of his denomination in South Trenton and began holding prayer meetings in his house. He was a fervent abolitionist and therefore a Free Soiler and later a staunch Republican.

On September 17, 1840 the Wesleyans purchased a parcel on which to erect a church. At that time the trustees of the church were Jacob Jones, Francis Francis and John Evans. A church was erected soon after which stood until the 1890s.

Throughout the church's history it shared its minister with the Wesleyan churches at Sixty and Ninety-Six. Its ministers included Revs. John R. Williams and Thomas Thomas.

In the latter part of the nineteenth century the church closed its doors. It was later used by a group of English-speaking Methodists. They used the structure for a time and then it was torn down.

The church had a small cemetery located behind it. Today, the cemetery is not visible from the road. The few remaining stones sit behind the home of Mr. & Mrs. John L. Sullivan. Arching trees shade the bed of myrtle which covers the graves. The area is very nicely maintained. The property was never transferred from the church and is cleaned once every year by a local Boy Scout troop.

*South Trenton Wesleyan Cemetery.
The headstones of John and Elizabeth Evans are the best preserved
of those located in the Wesleyan cemetery, located behind
the Sullivan's home on Coombs Road.*

Deerfield and Marcy

Between the town of Trenton and the city of Utica are the towns of Deerfield and Marcy. Deerfield included the town of Marcy until the latter's creation in 1832. The first Welsh settler in what is today the town of Deerfield was Ellis Roberts who settled on Smith Hill in 1818. Other settlers joined him soon after; yet no permanent Welsh settlement was established in Deerfield at that time. In the portion of Deerfield which is now in the town of Marcy, however, a settlement was developing.

Salem

In 1815 Cadwalader Richards donated a parcel of land from his farm so that a church and cemetery could be established. This plot was located on what is now Church Road, just west of old Route 12. It is located five miles from downtown Utica and two and a half from the city's corporate limits. Burials began in the cemetery in 1819 when Griffith Jones was interred there. A church, however, was not erected for some time.

In 1823 Rev. Robert Everett came to the Congregational Church in Utica. Shortly thereafter he began preaching in Deerfield and established a church. For seven years the members met in homes and schools. Then, on October 18, 1830, Rev. Everett led an organizational meeting at the District 26 schoolhouse. At that time the church was officially incorporated and the first deacons, Ellis Roberts and John Lewis, were elected.

The society was known as the "First Welsh Congregational Society of Deerfield." It retained this name even after the area where the church stood became part of the town of Marcy in 1832.

In 1831 the small congregation erected a frame church and called Rev. David Hughes of Mallory Road as its first minister. It is interesting to note that David Hughes was a Wesleyan. The church was erected on the south side of the road, directly opposite from where the present church stands.

In 1833 Rev. William D. Williams, the son-in-law of Cadwalader Richards, was ordained in the church. He had come to America only the year before. He ministered there for one year before going to Capel Ucha in Steuben and later to Ebensburg, Pennsylvania.

For the next seven years the church was supplied by ministers from Utica's Welsh Congregational Church. In 1840 "Salem" was adopted by the church as its name. From 1841 to 1848 Rev. Samuel A. Williams, formerly of Llanidloes, Wales, served as pastor. He later moved to Bradford, Pennsylvania. In 1848 Rev. William D. Williams returned to the area and began a 40-year tenure at the church. In late 1859 the church was dismantled and moved onto the "plank road" where it was used as a cheese factory until the 1880s.

The present church structure was erected in 1859. An inscription over the door reads " Salem, Ail Adeiladwyd 1859," "Salem, Second Was Built 1859." Inside, the new church had a balcony. The walls were papered with wallpaper depicting columns. This was intended to give the interior a grand look. To complement this, a large chandelier with seven kerosene lamps hung in the middle of the sanctuary. It was raised and lowered by weights so that the lamps could be lit. Unfortunately, after the church closed the chandelier was destroyed by vandals. In the front of the church a small organ stood to the side of the pulpit where William D. Williams held forth.

In the same year the new church was constructed, William D. Williams built his own home nearby. It still stands and is the second house on the right on Old Stage (formerly Winston) Road. There Rev. Williams resided until his death in 1899. It is presently owned by the Posher family.

Rev. Williams was a passionate preacher and held forth throughout Oneida County whenever he was required to supply. When he stepped down as pastor of Salem he was 80. In the years after his retirement Rev. Williams lived in the front room of his house surrounded by his vast library of Welsh books. His bookcase is still in the possession of his great-grandson.

Salem.
Salem Church is located on Church Road in Marcy.
This was the second church in this area and was erected in 1859.

After Rev. Williams retired, the church did not have a regular pastor. For many years, services continued to be held in the summer. The last minister to hold summer services was Rev. Gus Bathkey who was known for riding to church on his motorcycle. These services were discontinued in about 1925.

After 1925 the church held an annual Old Home Day service each Labor Day weekend, which Welsh descendants from around the area would attend. A covered dish supper would be held afterwards at the old homestead of William D. Williams, then owned by his grandson. These events continued until about 1950. Also during this time the church was used by "traveling evangelists."

After Rev. Williams' death, the pastor's son-in-law, Samuel Winston and his daughter Ann Williams Winston, were among those instrumental in leading the church. Their son, William D. Winston followed in their footsteps and was a trustee of the society for many years. In about 1942 his son, David Winston, became trustee, a position he has held for the last 50 years.

In 1950 the Board of Home Missions of the Congregational Church studied the feasibility of converting the church into a mission church. The study found no need for another Congregational church so near to Utica. Therefore the trustees had to find other uses for the building.

While David Winston was trustee, the chapel served various functions for the town of Marcy. In 1953 a decision was made to convert the church into a community center. The pews were removed and the sanctuary floor made level. Electricity was installed and the building was refurbished. At that time the church became the home to Boy Scout Troop 79. Other organizations such as the Women's Home Bureau also met there.

In 1963 the Boy Scout Troop became inactive. Later, in 1977 the church was used by the North Utica Arts Center. This use was short lived and for the past 15 years the building has stood unused.

Since services have been discontinued the cemetery has been maintained through bequests including ones from David Richards and William E. Lewis. These trust funds, however, were left solely for the maintenance of the cemetery. It has been through the efforts of David Winston that the church has been repaired, painted, and kept secure.

The cemetery was for many years maintained by the church. Recently the Town of Marcy, under the direction of town historian Raymond Ball, has assumed responsibility for its upkeep. Prisoners from the Mid-state Correctional Facility have removed damaged trees and painted the fence. Boy Scouts have repaired the fence and filled sunken graves. In 1990, Paul Pfeiffer of Troop 88 in New Hartford made a catalogue of all the cemetery's headstones for an Eagle Scout project.

The last person buried in the cemetery was Robert Evans who died in 1944; yet the cemetery is officially still active and can accept at least 30 more burials. It is estimated that 300 people are buried there.

The fate of the church structure is presently uncertain. In 1983, David Winston, being the sole trustee, appointed two of his children, great-great-great-grandchildren of Cadwalader Richards as trustees: Neal Winston, an attorney in Boston Massachusetts and Gaile Winston Lepper, a secretary at Plymouth-Bethesda Church. Dr. John T. Dizer of Marcy was made a trustee in 1989.

It has recently been proposed that the church be officially dissolved and the structure be transferred to the town. The town at one time considered moving it to a site adjoining the town offices and park. The town historian has dreams of converting the church into an historical society building and museum. However, in 1990, frustrated by the lack of support for his project by town residents, he asked in the town's newsletter, "Does anybody in Marcy care?"

Certainly the families of the original settlers have done their best to preserve their heritage. Only time will tell whether or not their efforts will continue to succeed.

Bryn Mawr

The Calvinistic Methodists also built a church in Deerfield. The church was located on West Davis Road, a road now split by Route 12. The church was located in the area between where East Davis Road ends and where Roberts Road intersects with West Davis Road. This road is now no more than a farmer's lane. The few stones which made up the cemetery are covered by brush and many are broken.

East Davis Road.
This farmer's trail leads to the remaining headstones of the Bryn Mawr cemetery. The headstones are hidden beneath the heavy brush.

The area and church were known as Bryn Mawr or "Big Hill." They were so named because the church was built where Deerfield Hill rises from Utica to Remsen and the north country. The Bryn Mawr Church was one of those churches which revolved around one person. In this case it was John Watkins who built the church on his farm. Mr. Watkins had come to Utica in 1831 and moved to Deerfield in 1832. The church was begun as a branch of the Calvinistic Methodist Church in Utica. Its first services were held in Mr. Watkins' log house. Then, in 1841, a small church was constructed. In 1855 the church was remodeled and enlarged.

During the Civil War, attendance declined and in 1868 John Watkins moved from the neighborhood. Without Mr. Watkin's presence the reason for the church was gone. In 1872 the church had 18 members and by 1878 was dissolved. During its existence Revs. John Hughes and Ebenezer Salisbury ministered there.

John Watkins had fourteen children, and many family members were buried in the church yard. Some of those buried were reinterred in New Hartford when Bryn Mawr's cemetery was abandoned. The chapel's communion set was given to a daughter of Mr. Watkins after the church closed. Deerfield's present county legislator, Phyllis Gates, is a direct descendant of John Watkins. All that remains of Bryn Mawr are the few broken headstones in the cemetery.

Marcy-Baptist

The first Welsh church erected in the town of Marcy, after it separated from Deerfield, was a Welsh Baptist church. It was erected in 1837 on land conveyed to the church from Owen Owens. It stood on the east side of Cavanaugh Road, opposite Kennedy Road.

Rev. John Stephens of Utica was the church's first pastor. Revs. Hugh Hughes and John Hughes, Baptist ministers who lived in the town, may also have served the church. Services were held until about 1860. Thereafter, an English-speaking Sunday School was conducted in the building by Rev. William Lane. Eventually the church was torn down.

Bethania

On April 8, 1836, Barnhardt Nelli and his wife conveyed a parcel of land on Luke Road (then known as Hutchinson Road) at the intersection with Fox Road to the Calvinistic Methodist Society of Marcy. The Methodists built their first church there in 1839. However, on July 28, 1840, they conveyed the property to John Ellis, a Congregationalist.

On September 15, 1840, Mr. Ellis conveyed the property to the First Welsh Congregational Society of Marcy. The society used the Methodist Church as their meeting house for a number of years. The Calvinistic

Methodists worshiped with the Congregationalists until 1848 when the Methodists built their own church. The remaining Congregationalists were not sufficiently strong to continue and the church was abandoned. Rev. James Griffith from Utica served as the church's first pastor. Revs. Hugh Lewis, Samuel A. Williams and William D. Williams all preached at the church.

In 1854 the church was reorganized under the direction of Rev. John R. Griffith who was ordained in the church. He was to remain the pastor for 14 years. He went on to serve the Congregational church in Camroden. He died in 1887 at the age of 70 and is buried with his wife Gwen in the Bethania cemetery.

In 1859 the original church had become too small for the congregation and therefore a new structure had to be erected. At this time it adopted the name "Bethania." This new church was constructed in the same year the present Salem Church was erected.

After Rev. Griffith left, the church relied on supply ministers to conduct its services. In 1872 it had a membership of 21 and a congregation of 40. In 1910 services were discontinued and the church was torn down. The lumber was purchased by Elmer Morris and used to build his home on the "main Utica road," on the east side, just beyond the Grange Road.

Bethania Cemetery.
"The First Congregational Church of Marcy" was erected immediately west of the cemetery which is maintained by the Town of Marcy.

An association was formed to take care of the cemetery. Burials continued for a time after the church was removed and approximately 100 persons are interred there today. Among those buried at Bethania was Kate Cotter of Fuller Road who was born in 1832 and died in 1917 at the age of 85. After her husband John's death Mrs. Cotter lived the life of a hermit. At the time of her death $800 was discovered sewn in her dress. Nearly $100 of that was in gold. Some of this money was brought to the post office in Stittville where its odor was so strong it had to be put out in the air. Some of the money had to be sent in for redemption because it was so musty. While her last name was Cotter, I am inclined to believe that she was of Welsh descent.

Today the cemetery is maintained by the Town of Marcy. Recently a new sign was erected by the Town of Marcy Democratic Club identifying the site. This is interesting as there is no evidence to suggest any Democrats are buried there.

Rehobeth

In 1839 the Calvinistic Methodists erected a church in Marcy, at the corner of Fox and Luke Roads, which shortly thereafter was conveyed to the First Welsh Congregational Society of Marcy. The two denominations worshiped together until 1848 when the Methodists removed themselves from the congregation and established their own church on David Edwards' farm on Marcy Hill, on the west side of Glass Factory Road.

The church was erected with the help of the local Presbytery and was called Rehobeth, a name originally given a well by the patriarch Isaac because, as he said, "now the Lord has made room for us, and we shall be fruitful in the land." The church erection committee of the Oneida (Welsh) Presbytery or its predecessor allocated $100 for the construction of the church on the condition that the building's cost would not exceed $250.

The first elders of the church were John H. Hughes and Joseph Hughes. John H. Hughes later entered the ministry and moved to La Crosse, Wisconsin. Sadly, he died in 1856 just seven years after his ordination at Bryn Mawr in 1849.

In 1858 Rev. William Rowlands became the pastor. He also shared his time with the church in Holland Patent. He remained there until 1864 when he became pastor of the Calvinistic Methodist Church in Utica.

In 1863 the church was destroyed by fire. One year later a new church was built across the road on land owned by Evan H. Morgan.

The church was always small and in 1872 had only 17 members. Between 1870 and 1890 Rev. Thomas T. Evans of Holland Patent frequently supplied the church's pulpit. It dissolved in 1900 and the structure was torn down one year later. Today nothing remains to mark the site of the tiny chapel.

Newport

Across the Herkimer County line from Deerfield is the town of Newport. There, for a brief period in the mid-nineteenth century, a small Welsh community flourished in the region known as Martin's Corners.

To get to this area from Oneida County, one takes Steuben Road East. Upon crossing the Herkimer County line, the road narrows. Soon it is barely more than one lane. Don't look for a sign welcoming you to Martin's Corners; there is none. Don't expect to see one of the three churches which once served the small community; they are gone. Don't expect the roads which are on the 1878 map to still be there. Bell Hill Road which once ran south now ends abruptly. Tanner Road no longer connects Steuben Road with Newport Road. Nothing is left of the community except a handful of farms.

Bryn Seion

In 1801 Thomas Thomas immigrated from Wales and purchased a farm on Tanner Road in Newport. In 1830 a society of Welsh Congregationalists living in the west end of the township organized and erected a church on Thomas Thomas' farm. For many years Rev. Robert Everett came from Utica to serve this church.

In 1839, the chapel known as Bryn Seion, or Mount Zion, was destroyed by fire, but in 1840 it was rebuilt. The first minister at the new church was Rev. Samuel A. Williams, who preached there for three years. Revs. John W. Williams, William Vincent, and David Hughes also served the church.

In 1870 there were 70 members of Bryn Seion, but by 1875 the members had moved away and the church was torn down. The Newport Welsh community had moved to the Cattaragus County Welsh settlement in the early 1870s, leaving only a few farmers behind to watch over the graves. The Bryn Seion cemetery was located near the church and was opened in 1831. Approximately 45 members, including Thomas Thomas were buried in the cemetery.

While at one time Tanner Road went from Newport Road to Steuben Road, today it begins at Newport Road in the town of Schuyler and then turns quickly to gravel. The gravel ends where the "no trespassing" signs begin. It is just before those signs that the Bryn Seion church was once located. The road continues as little more than tracks beyond the cemetery.

Bryn Seion Cemetery.
The headstones of Nathaniel and Mary Griffiths are among the best preserved in the cemetery. Many of the other stones lie broken in this graveyard located at the top of Tanner Road in Newport.

Approximately 45 people are buried in the cemetery, which is today "maintained" by the Town of Newport. Only a handful of the stones still stand. Thomas Thomas' headstone lies fallen and cracked in half, in the rear of the cemetery. Until recently two apple trees grew above the resting place of Mr. and Mrs. Nathanial Griffiths. Unfortunately a neighbor sawed the entwined trees down. At the same time many of the headstones were removed from their graves as the site was "cleared." One can only hope that someone will take the cemetery on as a project and restore the sanctity of the site.

Salem

Newport's Calvinistic Methodist Church was located on Steuben Road East and was known as Salem. On February 7, 1842 the Calvinistic Methodists decided to erect a church and opened a subscription for the construction of a small building. That same year construction began and the church was completed the next year. The church and cemetery were located on a one-acre plot which was officially conveyed to the trustees of the church on July 1, 1844. This plot was near what is known as Ferrell Corners, just before Steuben Road East turns north.

Rev. David R. Williams, who also served at Penygraig, was the church's pastor during the 1840s. The church was 20 x 30 feet in size and for the next 15 years served Newport's Calvinistic Methodists. By 1860, however, the census lists the church as having only six members and it was closed shortly thereafter. The chapel was used for a time by a society of Baptists, but in 1886 the building was torn down.

Salem Cemetery.
Within the grove of trees, pictured above, is the small cemetery which was used by Newport's Calvinistic Methodists. The site is now part of the Canary farm.

After the church was torn down the trustees of Newport Calvinistic Methodist Church continued to maintain the church yard and cemetery. At the turn of the century DeWitt Jenkins, the son of a former trustee, was in charge of maintaining the grounds. The cemetery contains 55 graves.

Today the property once owned by the church is part of the Canary farm. When the Canary family purchased the property in the late 1970s they restored the cemetery and maintained it. The grave yard soon became a favorite place for late night parties and for vandals. As a consequence, the brush was allowed to return and the cemetery is now hidden beneath a dense thicket.

Salisbury

Aside from the Newport churches previously mentioned, there were a few other Welsh churches in Herkimer County. Frankfort Hill and Ilion are discussed in Chapter IV, as they were outgrowths of the churches in Utica.

One of the other Welsh societies was located in Salisbury. Some Welsh farmers in Salisbury met in the Salisbury Academy in 1855 and for a few years thereafter. The church had about 15 members, but disbanded in the early 1860s.

There were also small churches in "Welsh Bush" and Little Falls, though without church buildings. These were both formed in the 1850s but by 1860 were gone.

Chapter III

Utica

WHILE THE WELSH SETTLEMENT was burgeoning in the Remsen-Steuben area, a similar community was forming in Utica. Unlike in Remsen, however, the Welsh in Utica were only one of many ethnic groups. Ethnic diversity has always been an important part of Utica's character. At the beginning of the nineteenth century, Utica was a melting pot with 12 different languages being spoken among a population of 250. Of these ethnic groups the Welsh were the second largest.

Today, Utica is a city of 65,000 and proud of its ethnic diversity. In East Utica one can find Italian traditions carried over from the old country. Every fall a statue of St. Rosalia is carried through East Utica, followed by La Banda Rosa, which stops to play the Italian National Anthem at every block as the faithful pin dollar bills to the saint's likeness. In West Utica a German Festival is held every year at St. Joseph and St. Patrick's Church, and each summer a brass band is brought to Utica from Germany to play at the Mannerchor festival.

Utica's ethnic diversity is particularly evidenced by its churches. There are Syrian, Russian, Ukrainian, Lebanese, Moravian, Polish, Italian, Lithuanian, Black and Hispanics churches, together with the various so-called main line churches, such as Lutheran, Presbyterian, Methodist, Baptist, Pentecostal, Congregational, Roman Catholic and Episcopalian. Many of these "main line" churches began by serving distinct local ethnic groups. Zion Lutheran, for example, conducted services in German for many years.

When the Welsh first came to Utica they settled in the "Second Ward" which was located between the Erie Canal (Oriskany Boulevard) and Whitesboro Street. Later they moved south into the Corn Hill area. Since World War II the Welsh have generally moved out of Corn Hill and into Utica's suburbs.

Vestiges of the Welsh churches exist today in the Plymouth-Bethesda United Church of Christ, Moriah-Olivet Presbyterian, Tabernacle Baptist and Central United Methodist churches.

First (Welsh) Baptist

Early Utica was described in 1802 by Rev. John Taylor from New Hampshire as a "mixed mass of discordant materials, its churches feeble and its people heathenish." At the time the first church was established in Utica, the village's citizens were known for their heavy drinking and gambling. Utica even had its own horse track.

Religious worship in Utica was first conducted in the village school on Main Street. All Saints Episcopal Church on Faxton Street can trace its roots to Trinity Episcopal Church which first began holding services in the school in 1798. Those services were erratic, however, and Trinity was not formally organized until four years later. In 1802 Rev. Taylor reported that Utica was made up of almost all religious sects, but the greatest part were of no religion. There were but a handful of people who had any regard for preaching. That handful must have been Welsh.

On September 12, 1801, 22 Welsh people met at the home of John Williams in order to establish the First (Welsh) Baptist Church of Utica. In Wales, the Baptists had the smallest membership of the four main denominations. However, when they immigrated to America, they quickly established a large number of Welsh Baptist churches. The first Welsh Baptist church in America was established in Swansea, Massachusetts in 1797.

In 1801 Utica was only a handful of log shacks centered around Main Street, near what became Bagg Square. John Williams' humble log cabin stood on the northerly side of the road from Utica to Whitesboro on what is now Court Street, across the street from the present State Hospital. At that time the site was about one mile outside the hamlet of Utica. When the Welsh organized the church, it became the first to be established in what is now the city of Utica.

After the church was organized, the Baptists met in a log house on Varick Street near the old Globe Mills. Both Welsh and English were used in the church, but Welsh was the predominant language. Those who organized the church loved the Welsh language, the purity of the gospel, and their freedom from the tithing which had been imposed upon them in Wales.

The first immigrants practiced and observed, with few changes, the same type of worship they had practiced in Wales. The church sought to make the worship service as "unconventional" as possible, consistent with dignity and reverence. In short, the church attempted to shun all rituals and symbolism.

The Baptists placed great emphasis on the doctrines of the faith. Candidates for church membership were examined in denominational tenets. Particular stress was placed on the candidate's conversion and how, when, where, and why it had taken place. If the candidate was not clear on this he was advised to wait before again seeking admission.

The sermon was doctrinal, sometimes seasoned with controversial arguments, and well flavored with denominational orthodoxy. The preacher never used notes and was a trained platform orator. Initially the preaching was in Welsh, but later was also in English to accommodate the non-Welsh speakers.

By 1806 the First Baptist Church had grown to the point that it was able to erect a frame church at what is now the intersection of Hotel Street and Oriskany Boulevard. In the early years Revs. John Stephens and James Harris, who both later preached in Steuben, served as pastors of the church.

After 1810 large numbers of English-speaking people from New England settled in Utica. Many of these new arrivals attended services at the Welsh church, even though they did not understand the language. Soon, those who did not understand Welsh sought to establish their own church.

One of the original members of the First Baptist Church, David Reed, eventually became a founder of the Second Baptist Church, also known as the Broad Street Baptist Church and later as Tabernacle Baptist. On October 7, 1819, 15 of First Baptist's members were dismissed so that they could form their own English-speaking church. David Reed experienced difficulty in obtaining a dismissal as he understood and spoke enough Welsh so that the original society saw no reason for him not to remain as a member. However, since his wife did not understand Welsh and sought to join the new church as well, Reed was allowed to leave. Rev. Stephens saw the church through this crisis and was the primary pastor in charge, on a somewhat irregular basis, until about 1836. During this period Abraham Williams served as an associate pastor. He later moved to Rome where he died on October 25, 1839. Also serving as pastors during the first decades of the church's history were Rev. David Griffith, Rev. Richard Roberts of Steuben, Rev. John Richards, and Rev. David Michael. David Griffith died in 1877 and had the distinction of being the first person buried in Utica's New Forest Cemetery.

In 1822 the construction of the Erie Canal forced the Baptists to move their building to the west side of Broadway, just north of Liberty Street, where the present Associated Textiles building stands. The original building eventually was replaced with a larger chapel, a structure the Baptists worshiped in for the rest of their church's existence.

In 1835 the Baptist Gymanfa of Oneida County, New York and Eastern Pennsylvania was formed to link the many Welsh Baptist churches in those regions. When the Pennsylvania churches withdrew to form their own association the Oneida County Gymanfa became the New York Gymanfa, an organization which endured until 1897.

In 1837 the First Baptist Church had 135 members. In that year Rev. William H. Thomas became the pastor. Revs. William T. Phillips, David Phillips, and Hugh Hughes served as pastors during the 1840s. William T. Phillips was the editor of the Welsh Baptist newspaper, *Y Seren Orllewinol (The Western Star)*, which began publishing in 1844.

By 1840 the Welsh Baptists in America had established 117 churches, including two in Utica. That same year an off-shoot of the First Baptist Church was established which held services in a building on the corner of Pearl and Broadway. By 1850 that group had returned to the fold.

In 1855 the state census listed 860 Welsh-born in Utica. The Welsh and their offspring represented ten percent of the city's population. The Baptists gained a share of the large influx of immigrants from Wales in 1850. During those years Revs. David Jenkins (1853-1858) and Morris J. Williams (1853-1858) led the church.

In 1859 Rev. J. Eldred Jones became pastor leading the church longer than any other minister. He first served until 1866. During that time the church was at its zenith with a membership of 283. This was the golden age of the church and was a period often longed for later.

Over the next few years various ministers, including Revs. David Jones, Joshua T. Morgan, H. C. James, and Owen Griffith, filled the pulpit. Rev. Griffith published *Y Wawr Americanaidd (The American Dawn)*, the national magazine of the Welsh Baptists.

When J. Eldred Jones returned in 1875, the church was already in a state of decline. It had been weakened by the deaths of many old members. Also, the young people were not learning Welsh and were attending English-speaking churches. Another reason for the decline was that most of the new immigrants were Calvinistic Methodists or Congregationalists, and therefore the Baptists did not receive an influx of new members like the other churches did.

Rev. Jones remained until 1882. He was followed by Revs. William M. Evans (1883-1884), John D. Roberts (1885-1887), Thomas Morris (1888-1890), and David Evans (1892-1893). The last full-time pastor was Rev. Allen J. Morton in 1894, a time when membership had declined to 75.

As the First Baptist Church entered its second century it began to feel the effects of an aging congregation and a change in its urban environment. As the city grew, the location of this church became unpopular; like the other Welsh churches it was situated in the Second Ward, where there had been a high concentration of Welsh during the nineteenth century.

By the turn of the century First Baptist found itself in an area that was predominantly Jewish. Moreover, the church which once could claim nearly 300 members and some of the area's most prestigious preachers had been without a regular pastor for quite some time. As a consequence, First Baptist, the oldest church in the city, decided to close its doors. On April 20, 1904, the trustees of the church voted to sell their building to Tabernacle Baptist Church. Tears openly flowed that night in a scene the local newspaper could only describe as "pathetic."

It was not initially known what would become of the building. Some suggested that it be used as a mission while others suggested the building be sold to raise money for the expansion of the Tabernacle Sunday School.

Ultimately the structure was sold by Tabernacle Baptist to a group of Jewish residents. A *Utica Daily Press* article from April 21, 1904 stated that "(t)he Church building is now in good condition and the auditorium is pleasant and inviting. It is a frame building and stands on a good sized lot. At the rear of the Church is a large shed where the farmers from the county drove and kept their horses while attending services and it is the only church in town, probably, that is fitted with such an appendage."

The structure was converted into a synagogue and was called The House of David, honoring King David not St. David. The date of the building's acquisition was placed above the door (1904). The House of David maintained that structure until 1950. Today the site is occupied by an industrial laundry, the building having been torn down years ago.

Tabernacle Baptist Church offered its sanctuary and chapel for the use of the former members of the First Baptist Church and it was suggested that a plaque honoring the contributions of the Welsh congregation be placed in the church. Many of First Baptist's members, however, elected to attend other Welsh churches. The money from the sale of First Baptist was used to fund the erection of the Thorn Memorial Chapel which stands at the rear of Tabernacle.

Today there are a number of families of Welsh descent who attend Tabernacle, but none trace their roots to a member of First Baptist. Nevertheless, vestiges of First Baptist continue to be visible in Tabernacle: the opening paragraph of Tabernacle's church history recalls the formation of the Welsh church, the Tabernacle choir occasionally joins with Moriah-Olivet's, Welsh Heritage Sunday is observed, and Welsh phrases such as "Bara Brith" are from time to time heard on the lips of Tabernacle's members.

Bethesda

At the same time the Baptists were establishing their church, a small group of recent Welsh Congregationalist immigrants began to meet in homes with the idea of forming a church. On January 1, 1802, fourteen of these immigrants met in a home on Main Street and formed the first Congregational church in Utica. It was only the third Welsh Congregational church in the Western Hemisphere. Eventually the Welsh Congregationalists established 229 churches in the United States.

Those first fourteen members entered into a covenant which began as follows:

> We, whose names are appended, in a strange land, and mostly strangers to one another, conceive that it is our duty and privilege to make known one to another our faith and order. "Can two walk together, except they be agreed?" Amos iii,3.

On September 6, 1802, the church called its first pastor, Rev. Daniel Morris of Philadelphia. The congregation, then numbering 28 members, was only able to pay its first pastor a small salary. Therefore, he continued to practice his trade as a bookbinder after his arrival in Utica in November of 1803.

For the next two years the society met in the homes of various members throughout the village and in October 1803 met to officially incorporate. At that time there were 33 members and John Nichols and John Roberts were chosen as Ruling Elders.

In 1804 a meeting was held to devise a means to build a church. That same year a small frame church was erected on the corner of Whitesboro and Washington Streets. It was dedicated on June 16, 1804 and was the first "finished" house of worship in Utica. The Trinity Episcopal Church had actually been started earlier, but the Welsh Congregational Church was the first to be completed.

Rev. Morris remained until the beginning of 1810. His most enduring contribution to the community came from his bookbinding business. When the church needed a hymnbook, he compiled and bound one himself. This hymnal was also used for many years by both Utica's Welsh Congregationalists and Baptists. Morris returned to the Philadelphia area before becoming pastor of the Union Welsh Church in New York City, where he remained from 1813 to 1817.

No permanent minister was immediately found to replace Rev. Morris. In the meantime, Rev. William G. Pierce, the pastor of Capel Ucha, traveled to Utica from Steuben once a month to preach. Two lay preachers, Rowland Griffith and Mr. Roberts, preached on the other Sundays.

Rev. Howell R. Powell (Powell Bach) served as pastor for three years (1810-1812). Powell came to Steuben from New York City where he had served at its Welsh Union Church from 1801 to 1807. In 1812 he went to serve a Calvinistic Methodist Church in Palmyra, Ohio where he was simply known as "Powell of Palmyra." He was replaced in Utica by Rev. Benjamin Powell, who came to the church directly from Wales. After serving from 1813 to 1820, he left to replace Rev. Evan Roberts in the pulpit of the New York City Welsh Church. He remained there until 1822.

For the next three years the church relied on supply pastors. Then in 1823, Rev. Robert Everett emigrated from Denbigh, North Wales. He had been educated at the University of Wrexham and later received an honorary Doctorate of Divinity from Hamilton College. He was a pioneer in the temperance movement and organized a society in Utica in 1830. Dr. Everett was also an abolitionist and was frequently criticized for his beliefs.

On one occasion, in October 1835, Dr. Everett was leading a prayer meeting at the church, when a great commotion was heard in the street. An anti-abolitionist mob had just destroyed the office of an anti-slavery paper located near the church. The mob was set to burn down the Welsh church because of Dr. Everett's abolitionist stance, but fortunately the crowd was dissuaded and the building was saved.

At the time of the above incident, Dr. Everett had already moved on to the Congregational Church in West Winfield, though he still remained a frequent preacher in Utica. Rev. James Griffith, from Carmarthenshire, South Wales, succeeded Rev. Everett in 1832. He led the congregation for the next 17 years, during which time a new church was built on an adjoining lot, purchased by the society, on the corner of Whitesboro and Washington Streets. This church was opened on January 1, 1836 and was large enough to seat five to six hundred people.

In 1837 a New York Gymanfa was established as an association of the Welsh Congregational churches in the state. This association continued until 1930.

In 1846 the first fragmentation of the church occurred. A splinter congregation built a small wooden church near the corner of Whitesboro and Hotel Streets. The Welsh Independent Church was served by Revs. William Jones and Tudor Jones. Its structure later became the home of the first synagogue in the city, Beth Israel, which was formed in 1848 and remained at that site until 1853. The splinter group soon returned to the fold, but it was not to be the last group to leave.

Rev. James Griffith left the church in 1849 after "trouble arose." He moved to Cattaragus County in Western New York which, at that time, had a thriving Welsh community. James Griffith was replaced by Rev. Evan Griffith from Llanegryn, North Wales (1850-1856) and David Price (Dewi Dinorwig) (1857-1864). It was said that Rev. Price had "passed his best days" before coming to Utica. In Wales he had been a first rank minister.

Rev. Griffith Griffith served from 1864-1866. He was born in Ffestiniog, Wales on March 15, 1824 and educated at Hackney College in London. He was ordained in New York City in 1853 and served in Wisconsin prior to coming to Utica. He later preached in Cincinnati and New Cambria, Missouri. He died in Ixonia, Wisconsin on December 9, 1899 at the age of 75.

By 1857 the church had 222 members. Seventy of these left in 1865 and formed the Second Congregational Church. They called James Griffith back from Cattaragus County to be their minister. The Second Congregational Church purchased the old Grace Episcopal Church at the corner of Broadway and Columbia Streets, which had recently been vacated. It appears that Rev. Griffith was the primary reason for the division as he was the only pastor the second church ever had. Frequently Welsh churches were driven by one pastor or one elder. Clearly it was the personality of Rev. Griffith which drove the splinter church.

It took the work of an extraordinary man to bring the two churches back together. Called in 1867 to unite the two societies was Rev. Rhys Gwesyn Jones. He was to remain pastor until 1901, except for the years 1879 to 1883, during which time Watkyn B. Joseph (Y Myfyr) was pastor. Under Rev. Jones' leadership the first church was sold to the public school district and the two congregations worshiped in the Columbia Street church. At that time the church had 250 members and a congregation ranging from 500 to 600.

In 1871 a new brick church seating 580 was erected at 108 Washington Street. In honor of the two congregations coming together the united church was given a new name: Bethesda. The name "Bethesda" came from the Bethesda Congregational Church in Merthyr Tydvil, Wales, from which Rev. Jones had been called. The old church on the corner of Washington and Whitesboro Streets was converted into a public school and later, in 1886, into a synagogue, The House of Israel.

During the 1870s the Welsh population in Utica was at its height. For example, the 1875 City Directory lists 75 residents with the name John Jones in the city. In 1879, Rev. R. Gwesyn Jones departed for Petaluma, California. No minister was found to replace him until 1881 when Rev. Joseph (Y Myfyr) came to Utica from Colwyn Bay in North Wales. Rev. Joseph, who was known as an exceptional poet, unfortunately passed away suddenly in 1882 at the age of 45. A tablet in his memory was placed on the front wall of the church.

Plymouth-Bethesda.
Plymouth Church was erected in 1906 on Oneida Square.
Bethesda joined Plymouth in 1963.

In the 1880s some of Bethesda's members became concerned that their English-speaking children would not be attracted to a Welsh-speaking church. On the 13th day of May, 1883, Rev. Edward Taylor of Binghamton, under the auspices of the New York Home Mission Society, began holding English language services in the common council chambers at Utica's City

Hall. These services ultimately led to the formation of the Plymouth Congregational Church.

Some church histories lead one to believe that Plymouth was a direct outgrowth of Bethesda. This is not entirely accurate: of the 47 charter members, only eight were from Bethesda. However, many Welsh-Americans from other churches such as Westminster Presbyterian and First Presbyterian were among its first members.

The Plymouth Congregational Church was formed on September 18, 1883. Originally the society worshiped in Dobson's Hall on Oneida Square. Later, it purchased a parcel on Plant Street near State Street and erected a small wooden chapel on the vacant portion of the plot. The society first occupied that structure on January 25, 1885. The congregation stayed in that chapel until the present stone church on Oneida Square was dedicated in 1906.

In the same year that the Plymouth Church was beginning, Bethesda searched for a new pastor. Rev. R. Gwesyn Jones, who left Bethesda in 1879 and moved to California, was invited to return to his former position. Although in ill health, Rev. Jones accepted the call and came back to Utica in 1883, remaining until his death in 1901. Despite his health problems, Rev. Jones is said never to have missed preaching on a Sunday from the time of his ordination until the end of his life. Rev. Lewis Williams also occasionally preached at Bethesda during this time.

In 1903-1904 a great religious revival in Wales sparked increased immigration to America. Many of these immigrants chose to settle in urban areas such as Utica instead of moving to rural areas such as Remsen. As a consequence, Bethesda received an influx of new members at that time.

Rev. Jones was succeeded by Rev. W. Caradoc Jones (1901-1915) and Rev. J. Vincent Jones. (1917-1923). During the tenure of Rev. R. W. Hughes (1927-1939) English was introduced to Bethesda, where for more than a century and a half, the ministry had been almost entirely in Welsh. Although language classes were held for the children and a Gymanfa Ganu was held each year, there was little the congregation could do to retain the use of Welsh for all worship services. By 1936, Welsh immigration had been almost completely cut off by the federal government and soon there were many young people in the church who did not understand the old language.

Although the church's children spoke little Welsh, they nevertheless made up the junior choir which sang every Sunday morning. Thirty boys sat on one side of the pulpit and thirty girls on the other. Often they would become restless during a long Welsh sermon, causing Rev. Hughes to tap on the pulpit and say, "Now, now, just a little longer." In 1936, Bethesda abandoned Welsh at its main Sunday service but did retain it for its evening service.

Rev. Hughes remained at Bethesda until 1939. That year he returned to Wales for a visit, but when the United States entered World War II it became impossible for Rev. Hughes to re-enter the country because he was not an American citizen. It was therefore necessary to replace him. Rev. Rees T. Williams was called to fill the position and he remained until 1951 when he left to serve a church in Oswego, New York. In 1946 Bethesda purchased the house adjacent to the church to be a parish hall.

Rev. G. J. Richards (1952-1959) succeeded Williams and was the church's last Welsh minister. When he left in 1959 the church ceased to be a "Welsh" church and all services thereafter were in English. Rev. Kenneth E. Roach, the church's first non-Welsh minister, came in 1960.

In 1963, faced with declining membership and urban renewal, Bethesda closed its doors. Like the Welsh Baptists the congregation joined with a daughter church, Plymouth, and formed Plymouth-Bethesda. However, unlike First Baptist, Bethesda, with its 242 members, was itself a vital church. Only about five families left because of the merger. In its final year as a separate church there were four infant baptisms: a Roberts, a Rahn, a Neenan and a Payne. It should be noted that the maiden names of the mothers of the last three named were Williams, Roberts, and Griffith, respectively.

The decision to merge with Plymouth was not made hastily and many options were explored. The possibility of merging with Plymouth had first been raised during Rev. Richards pastorate. Neither church, however, was prepared to give up its minister. Therefore, Bethesda actively looked for a place to relocate and almost purchased the Sayre Memorial Presbyterian Church in West Utica. When a rape occurred near that church those plans were quickly abandoned. The opportunity for a merger again presented itself when Plymouth's minister retired. Each church could now contribute to the merger: Plymouth could give its building and Bethesda, its minister. Thus was born Plymouth-Bethesda.

The members of Bethesda were deeply saddened to see their building torn down. Bethesda had an imposing brick exterior and beautiful interior. At the center of the sanctuary was the pulpit, on a raised platform. Behind the pulpit were the great ranks of organ pipes which formed an arch. The pulpit was flanked by the organ on the left and the baptismal font and choir on the right. A plaque honoring Rev. Watkyn B. Joseph was on one side of the pulpit and a plaque honoring R. Gwesyn Jones on the other.

In saying farewell to 160 years of ministry, Rev. Roach cited Philippians 3:13, "Forgetting the things which are behind I reach for the things which are before." Rev. Roach stated, "Our forefathers served their day in ways that were appropriate to their times and needs. We must carry on in the same spirit, determined to rise to the challenges of our generations and meet the needs of our day in the ways we regard best for us."

Bethesda brought to Plymouth its history and the symbols of its heritage. The stone plaques were brought to the new church and are in storage in the church's basement. The corner stone from Bethesda sits along the Plant Street side of the church. For many years the congregation alternated using each church's communion set and candles. Bethesda's baptismal font is now used in the main sanctuary. On the second floor of the parish house is a small chapel where the pulpit, organ, communion table, and pulpit chairs from Bethesda are still used. These physical reminders have kept Bethesda's traditions alive nearly 30 years after the merger.

Kenneth Roach remained until 1971 to serve the combined congregations. At that time the South Church congregation also merged with the Plymouth-Bethesda. Rev. John W. Morrau succeeded Rev. Roach and guided the congregation for the next twenty years. In 1992, Plymouth-Bethesda called a woman, Rev. Patricia Haddock Lawrence, to be its senior pastor. Today Plymouth-Bethesda has an active congregation of 340 which is committed to an urban ministry. Its members come from as far away as Poland and Sauquoit.

Moriah

When the Welsh Congregational Church in Utica was formed, it had both Congregational and Calvinistic Methodists members. With the organization of Penycaerau in 1824 the Methodists in Utica soon decided that they should have their own church.

The beginnings of Moriah can be traced to the arrival of Evan Roberts in Utica in 1822. He was a Calvinistic Methodist who joined the Congregational Church because there was no church of his denomination in the city. Shortly after his arrival he began inviting other Calvinistic Methodists to his home and there they discussed forming their own church.

On February 19, 1830, 12 members of the Welsh Congregational Church, all North Walians, had their memberships transferred to Penycaerau. The next day, at a meeting of that church, Rev. David Stephens was authorized to organize a church in Utica. This he did in March.

The church's first services were held in a schoolhouse on Bleecker Street and were conducted by Revs. David Stephens, Benjamin Davies, William T. Williams, and Morris Davies, all of the Remsen-Steuben area. Benjamin Davies, the first ordained minister of the denomination in

America, would walk the 20 miles from Remsen to Utica to supply the pulpit. Today, the trip from Remsen is easy and can be made by getting on Route 12 and driving south to Utica. In the 1830s it was anything but easy. Davies was a shoemaker by trade and weak in health, but would often leave Remsen on Saturday, walking through the woods and marking the trees as he went, preach twice in Utica on Sunday and then return to Remsen on Monday. For his efforts he was paid one dollar per week.

Three of the Utica church's first four supplies died shortly after it was formed. David Stephens passed away in 1835 and Benjamin Davies died one year later. Morris Davies, who had come to America in 1829, worked diligently with the Calvinistic Methodists of the area until his death in 1834.

In 1831 the society's first chapel was constructed on Seneca Street. Rev. Stephens was instrumental in raising funds for the construction of the building. He was the first pastor and was succeeded upon his death by Rev. Morris Roberts of Remsen. Roberts remained until 1837 and was the first minister to perform pastoral duties other than preaching. After that time Rev. David E. Davies was a frequent supply. Because the church did not have a regular pastor the leadership of the church throughout the 1830s was almost exclusively within the hands of the elders.

From 1841 to 1844 one of the most influential Calvinistic Methodist ministers of the day, Rev. William Rowlands, was pastor. Rowlands was considered to be the father of Calvinistic Methodism in America. In 1838 he had founded *Y Cyfail (The Friend)*, the Calvinistic Methodist monthly which lasted longer than any of the other Welsh denominational magazines. It even remained beyond the national church's union with the Presbyterian Church, ceasing publication in 1933. In 1844 Rev. Rowlands returned to New York City where he preached until becoming pastor at the Calvinistic Methodist churches in Holland Patent (Zion) and Marcy (Rehobeth) in 1858.

During Rowland's tenure the church flourished, so that by 1846 there were 190 members. Therefore, the congregation decided to tear down the first chapel and construct a larger brick structure. While waiting for the new structure to be completed, the church met on Catherine Street.

On January 28 and 29, 1847, the new chapel, with a seating capacity of 636, was dedicated. Upon its completion Rev. Thomas Foulkes was the first to preach there. He remained the pastor until 1849 when he moved to Wisconsin. The church called him back in 1852 and he served until 1855 when he again moved west.

During the three years (1849-1851) between Rev. Foulkes' terms, Enoch Samuel served as pastor and was soon joined by David Lewis. Both shared the preaching responsibilities. Sadly, Samuel died in 1851, just before he was to have been ordained.

In 1859, Rev. William Hughes (Llanwrst) came to Utica from Birmingham, England and was very popular at the Seneca Street Church, especially among the younger people. When he moved to Racine, Wisconsin shortly thereafter, the elders were criticized for allowing him to leave.

Seneca Street Church.
The Calvinistic Methodist Church was located in this building from 1847 to 1879. From 1879 to 1944 it was the House of Jacob Synagogue. Since then it has been known as the House of God: Church of the Living Christ.

Rev. William Rowlands returned to Utica in 1863 and served once again as pastor until his death in 1866. Rowlands was especially popular, as he could preach with great force in both Welsh and English, a skill attributable to the fact that he had been born in London. A man of medium stature, stockily built and physically strong, he was a preacher of exceptional ability and his passing was a great loss to the church. A large plaque honoring Rev. Rowlands hangs in the balcony of the present Moriah-Olivet Church.

In 1867 Ebenezer T. Jones of Johnstown, Pennsylvania came to the church's pulpit for one year, followed by Rev. Thomas B. Thomas (1868-1869). Rev. James Jarrett of Pwllheli, North Wales served from 1870 until he returned to Wales in 1875. Two years later Rev. William Roberts became the new minister for the Seneca Street congregation. Originally from Anglesey in North Wales, Roberts came to Utica from Bellevue, Pennsylvania. His son, William Henry Roberts, was Stated Clerk of the General Assembly of the Presbyterian Church in the USA for 35 years.

Between 1847 and 1877 the church did not grow and continued to have a membership of approximately 190. The reason for the 30 years of stagnation had much to do with the location of the church and the immigration routes of the Welsh. For example, the number of Welsh moving into Utica was equaled by the number who moved westward and out of Utica. Also, there had been a time when nearly all the Welsh lived in the Second Ward, that area on the north side of what was then the Erie Canal and which is now Oriskany Boulevard. In that relatively small area there were four Welsh churches. The first church to move out was the Second Congregational Church in 1865, followed by the new Bethesda Church in 1871.

The Second Ward was becoming almost completely Jewish, and as the Welsh moved uptown, into the Corn Hill area, many of the old churches were converted into synagogues. The move for Moriah began in 1873 with the purchase of a Sunday School, "The Corn Hill School," on South Street. This school remained open until 1882 when it merged with the Seneca Street Church's Sunday School.

The decision to move to a new structure did not come without controversy. The members who had moved out of the Second Ward wanted to have their church closer to their homes in Corn Hill. There were, however, "pillars" of the church who for years were opposed to the idea of moving. Those who were interested in building a new structure were responsible for calling Rev. William Roberts. He had been instrumental in overseeing the erection of new chapels in New York City and Pennsylvania and was known to be a good fundraiser. Upon coming to Utica he threw his support behind the move.

On December 29, 1879, T. Solomon Griffiths, one of the chief movers in the church and a leader of the Calvinistic Methodists on a national level proposed the following resolution: "That the board of trustees approves in the strongest way that the church sell the chapel on Seneca Street and build another one in place of it in a place more central and advantageous to the members of the congregation." This proposal was adopted.

As a lawyer, I took a special interest in the problems associated with selling the Seneca Street property. Apparently the deed to the property had contained a reversionary interest to the heirs of the transferror, Mr. Barnam, which vested upon the Calvinistic Methodists ceasing to worship on the site. Therefore, there are numerous quit claim deeds from Mr. Barnam's descendants filed in the Oneida County Clerk's Office, to clear title to the property.

With the title problems resolved, the church was sold to the House of Jacob, an Orthodox Jewish synagogue. The House of Jacob remained at that location until 1944 when it also moved. Since that time the Seneca Street Church has been the home of the House of God: Church of the Living Christ, a black church serving the almost entirely black population which now occupies what was once a formerly Welsh and then a Jewish neighborhood. The Washington Court housing project is situated at the end of Seneca Street and in recent years the neighborhood has greatly deteriorated. In 1993 the House of God moved uptown and opened a new church on Oneida Square.

The facade of the old Seneca Street Church has been altered over time. The square windows in the front were rounded at the top and later cemented over. An arched entryway bearing the church's new name, "The House of God," was also added.

At the laying of the cornerstone of the new church, the Hon. Ellis R. Roberts, the Postmaster General of the United States, asked the audience, "How many are present today who are able to testify about the warnings and the spirituality which they have felt through the actions of this church? How many families have been saved from destruction?" Mr. Roberts also noted that when their former house of worship was built, that part of the city was well kept and out in the country. How circumstances change!

It is interesting to note that during the period the church was located on Seneca Street it had only ten different elders. Robert J. Jones, Richard H. Hughes, and Evan Roberts were elected in 1830, Humphrey D. Roberts in 1854, David F. Jones, Evan Jones, and John T. Davies in 1857, Robert E. Roberts and David Anthony in 1867 and T. Solomon Griffiths in 1872. Of these, T. Solomon Griffiths was the most influential. A tailor by trade, he served as elder from 1872 until his death in 1914 at the age of 75. At various times he was presenter, treasurer, and secretary of the board. In 1910 he became moderator of the General Assembly. He also served as editor of *Y Cyfail* from 1899-1910. It was his leadership and foresight which was responsible for moving the congregation to its Park Avenue location.

The name given to the new church was "Moriah." It had been suggested in 1888 by Mary Williams, daughter of Robert ap Gwilym Ddu, a well-known hymn writer. The church was named after Moriah Church in Caernarvon, North Wales. A picture of Mary Williams hangs in the church to this day.

While the congregation awaited completion of its new chapel, it worshiped in the City Hall on Sundays and in Bethesda on Wednesday evenings. Finally, from September 23 through October 1, 1883, the new church was dedicated. With the new chapel came an increase in membership. In 1887, the year of Rev. Roberts' death, membership increased from 346 to 401. A plaque honoring Rev. Roberts hangs in Moriah's balcony near the one honoring Rev. Rowlands.

Peniel School.
This building was originally the Olivet Presbyterian Church.
It was used as a Sunday School building by Moriah from 1890-1924.
Today, it is the Pentecostal House of Prayer.

In 1890 church officials found it necessary to establish the Peniel Chapel on Miller Street, near Square Street. The Sunday School had 130 Welsh students and an English division of 30. The building had been the original Olivet Church and today houses the Pentecostal House of Prayer. The chapel served as Moriah's Sunday School for that area until 1924. Prayer meetings and children's services were conducted there for many years.

Rev. Robert Williams from Corwen, North Wales served the church from 1889-1891. He was forced to return to Wales on account of his wife's ill health. In 1894, when Rev. J. Hughes Parry became the minister, the church had a membership of 429 and was the largest Welsh church in the city. Bethesda was the next largest at that time with a membership of 238. Rev. Parry came from Holyhead, North Wales. His life ended tragically in

1899 when, because of a chronic obstruction of his bowels, he drank nothing but cold water for the last 47 days of his life.

In 1904 Rev. D. Morgan Richards came to the church from Llanberis, North Wales. He remained until 1917 when he assumed the pastorate of the Calvinistic Methodist church in New York City. Shortly after leaving Moriah he was married to the daughter of John Hughes Parry, his predecessor. During his ministry, membership increased to 666. At the same time the number of Welsh-born residents in Utica reached its peak at 1,188.

In 1918 Dr. John Davies from Racine, Wisconsin came to the church. He was forced to retire in 1923 on account of his health. He returned to Wales where he died in 1926.

In 1920 the Calvinistic Methodists united with the Presbyterian Church and a separate Welsh Presbytery was formed to govern the Welsh churches in Oneida county. In 1936 the Oneida (Welsh) Presbytery dissolved and Moriah became a part of the Utica Presbytery.

Moriah-Olivet.
Located on Park Avenue, this was Moriah Presbyterian Church until its merger with Olivet in 1989. The parish hall to the south was built in 1925.

Llewelyn Jones came to the church from Colwyn Bay, North Wales, in 1924. The next year the manse, which had been constructed in 1885 directly adjacent to the church in 1885, was torn down and a new parish house was erected in its place. The parish house replaced the Peniel School as it had a number of classrooms for the Sunday School. The parish hall also had a stage. Fifty years earlier theatrical productions in the church would have been unthinkable.

As Welsh immigration was cut off by new immigration laws the old Welsh institutions in the city began to fade. During the period of 1931 to 1947 only three new Welsh-born members joined the church.

In the 1920s Moriah undertook a variety of changes, both physical and spiritual. In the early days the church had been run by elders who called a minister. It was the elders who led the church and set church policy. By the 1920s, however, the minister had become much more influential as in other Protestant churches.

Also indicative of change in the church was the removal of the "set fawr" or "large pew," where the elders sat below the pulpit, from its place of prominence. The session also authorized a vested choir which became a regular part of the service in direct contrast to the Welsh tradition of congregational singing.

In October 1927 the session and board of trustees unanimously voted to recommend to the church that the evening service be conducted in English. The morning of the congregation's vote on the matter was filled with tension. Some believed a new era was beginning for the church while others thought the introduction of English would divide the congregation. Following the report of the balloting indicating the acceptance of the session's recommendation, Rev. Jones appealed to the congregation and offered a prayer which removed the tension. He asked that the Great Shepherd of the sheep that had watched over the church should lead it to nobler ideals and that the spirit of Christ should unite the church. His prayers were answered.

Rev. R. R. Williams followed Rev. Jones in the pulpit from 1932 to 1944. At the end of his tenure he returned to Llandudno, Wales. The period from 1945 to 1965 was the golden age of Moriah. Dr. R. Glynne Lloyd was called from Liverpool, England in 1945. At that time the church was vibrant and always filled to capacity. In fact, during his pastorate the church became so crowded that two morning services were required.

Between 1948 and 1958 the church admitted 300 new members. Some of these were former members of the Christ Reformed Church and Zion Welsh Presbyterian Church in New Hartford. Of these new members fewer than 70 were children who came to membership through the communicant class.

In 1956 and 1957 Moriah worshiped at the Christ Reformed Church while a new organ was installed, a new chancel constructed, and the entire interior of the church remodeled. These capital improvements were done in honor of the church's 125th anniversary. The new chancel was divided, the organ was moved from the front center to the right, and the pipes were placed behind it. Also, the communion table no longer had a Welsh inscription on it.

On January 20, 1957, Colin Miller, a Scotsman and chaplin at Hamilton College, conducted the service of dedication at the newly remodeled church. In 1958 the church had 534 members.

In the late 1950s a second service at 9:30 was introduced to help attract young families. The Sunday School was moved to Sunday morning to attract more students. In 1963 the congregation voted to conduct another series of church improvements including modernization of the kitchen and restrooms.

In 1964 Dr. Lloyd became ill and it was at that time that I first began attending Moriah. My father, Dr. Jay G. Williams, was invited to be a supply pastor and then, after Dr. Lloyd's passing, he served as an interim pastor until a new pastor was chosen. In 1966, my brother, Daryl Williams, was the last infant baptized by Dr. Lloyd. Although Moriah was not the church I normally attended, from that time on I attended services at least a few times per year until the mid-1980s.

One of my earliest memories of Moriah was of a choir rehearsal, held in the parish house prior to its renovation and the creation of the small side sanctuary known as the Lloyd Chapel. I was three or four, and had been brought there with my parents because they could not find someone to watch me. While I do not remember the details, I was probably placed at their feet with crayons and paper to amuse myself while they sang. "We need someone else to sing tenor," said the conductor. "I will," I volunteered from my seat below the chairs. My offer was met with uproarious laughter, though at the time I did not grasp the humor of my suggestion.

At another rehearsal choir members inexplicably began to slip out the back one by one until most of the choir was gone. Upon investigation it was discovered that Elizabeth Taylor, who was at that time married to Welsh actor Richard Burton, was being interviewed on television. The missing choir members were found in the sexton's third floor apartment watching the program. It should be noted, however, that at least one choir member had a legitimate reason for her interest. Mair Lloyd, widow of Dr. Lloyd, is a cousin of the late Richard Burton.

Of all my memories of Moriah, it was that joy and laughter which I will always remember most about the church. Years later I had the opportunity to represent a lady at a closing when she sold her house. She was the woman with whom I would always sit while my father preached and my mother sang in the choir. This bit of history she insisted on relating to the other attorneys and everyone else at the closing.

I also have fond memories of attending Sunday School with Ellen Roberts, Allison Weaver, and Jeff Adams. Our names are all memorialized in the guest book in the front of the church.

Through the years Moriah attempted to maintain its Welsh heritage. Until the 1970s the Welsh National Gymanfa Ganu Association's hymnbook was kept in the pews. One verse would be sung at each service as an approach to the pastoral prayer. A St. David's Day service was also held annually on the first of March.

In 1967 the church called its first non-Welsh pastor, Rev. Richard Weld. He remained until 1969. Rev. Weld was followed by Rev. Thomas O. Williams, a Welshman who had been in charge of a church in Canada. His tenure at the church was a troubled one. Numerous problems led to his departure in 1978 and he returned to Wales.

By the early 1970s Moriah's location had also become a problem. The Corn Hill area, where many Welsh had located earlier in the century, became run down while its Welsh residents became more affluent and moved to the suburbs. By 1971 only 15% of Moriah's membership still lived in Corn Hill and today almost no one in the church resides in the neighborhood. The area's decline has often made the older members of the parish afraid to come to the church after dark. Therefore, the church's night-time functions have been greatly curtailed.

Rev. Williams was followed by Rev. Arden Coe, a former minister of Olivet Church. He retired in 1981. In that year Rev. Davis Robinson was called as pastor from a church in Buffalo.

In 1980 Moriah celebrated its sesquicentennial. Richard Lloyd, son of the late pastor, composed the music for a special hymn for the occasion. His brother David Lloyd, now a profesor at LeMoyne University, wrote the hymn's text. It was a time for looking back at the church's achievements. However, the most difficult decade was ahead for the church. No longer were there children for a junior choir. New members were few and far between. The church's population had aged greatly. Many of the church's members were confined to nursing homes. On an almost weekly basis a member's name would appear in the obituary column of the local newspaper.

During the 1980s many of the church's most faithful members stopped attending services. Many families began attending other churches after generations as members of Moriah. The struggles and problems which befell the church are too recent to discuss as even their mention might open the deep wounds felt by many. Suffice it to say a cloud of sadness and regret had fallen over the church.

In 1988 Moriah merged with Olivet Presbyterian Church. For many years the two churches had shared the same minister and had joined together for summer services. Olivet was also located in the blighted Corn Hill area. While it had not been a Welsh church, many Welsh names appeared on its honor roll plaques. After years of encouragement from the Presbytery, a merger was effected and Moriah became Moriah-Olivet. The Park Avenue structure, the former Moriah Church, became the home of the merged church. With the Olivet congregation came its plaques which were placed on the walls of the church. Olivet's sons and daughters are now memorialized at Moriah-Olivet.

Before the merger took place the average congregation numbered 60 at Moriah. By 1992 the congregation was still at 60, but with the congregations of both churches. The congregations of the two former churches, set in their ways, tended to stay with their own, so that sometimes it seemed as if there were two churches meeting under one roof.

Dr. Robinson retired at the end of 1992 and the search has begun for a new pastor. Revs. Jean Anne Swope and James L. Mechem, a husband and wife preaching team, were called to serve as interim pastors. They accepted the call on the condition that the church reach out to the neighborhood surrounding it. They have worked hard to bring the two congregations together and to revitalize the church. As a result, many people who left during the 1980s have returned. Nevertheless, 80% of the congregation is over 70, and whoever is selected as the new pastor will face an undaunting challenge. In June, 1993 Paul Lent became interim pastor.

Other visible aspects of revitalization include painting of the church by inmates from Mid-state Correctional Facility, institution of a special Sunday evening service for people involved in 12-step programs, introduction of Bible study classes and renovation of the nursery by the Rainbow Circle to help attract families with young children. To this day there is a chair in that nursery bearing a plaque with a Welsh inscription honoring T. Solomon Griffiths.

Despite the declining numbers and increasing age of the congregation, the singing at Moriah is still amazing. It far exceeds the singing in a church three times its size. Evan Gwyndaf Roberts, who has served as organist at Moriah for many years, keeps alive the Welsh heritage of music. For example, during communion he often plays the old Welsh melodies so that not only does the congregation hum along but so too a cloud of witnesses heard quietly in the distance.

Coke Memorial

On July 1, 1849, 27 Welsh Wesleyan Methodists met to form a chapel of their own denomination. It was organized under the direction of Rev. Isaac Foster of the State Street Methodist Church.

For the first eight months, services were held in the old Cambrian Hall on the lower side of Liberty Street between Hotel and Seneca Streets. During the first year Revs. Reese Davies and Thomas Hughes led the congregation.

On May 1, 1850 the society purchased an old school on Washington Street known as the "Commercial Lyceum" and converted it into a house of worship. The building made a small but convenient chapel. The first two pastors in the new building, Revs. David Hughes and John Jones, preached on alternate Sundays until September 15, 1852. Rev. Hughes left at that time and John Jones continued alone until December 1853.

From 1854 to April 1860, Rev. R. L. Herbert from Liverpool, England was pastor. During his tenure, the church was enlarged, measuring 28 by 44 feet. While he was pastor an additional 33 members were received on probation, 43 were received by letter from another church, seven "backslided" and seven died. Rev. Herbert went on to minister to the Welsh Wesleyans of Fair Haven, Vermont.

In March 1860 Rev. Thomas Thomas came from Ironton, Ohio and in April was appointed pastor. Rev. Humphrey Humphreys followed from 1863 to 1867. Thereafter, Revs. David T. Davies and Reese Davies supplied the pulpit until Rev. Isaac Thomas came to the church from Wilton Park in the north of England. He remained until 1871. At the time he left, the church had 60 members.

D. T. Davies returned to the pulpit in 1871 and remained until 1873 when Humphrey Humphreys returned to Utica from St. Louis. He remained until 1878 when he resigned.

The church was briefly under the charge of Rev. L. D. White. He was not Welsh-speaking so various Welsh-speaking pastors in the area would actually conduct the services. In 1878 David Williams came to the church from Pottsville, Pennsylvania. At that time the church had a membership of 85 and a congregation of 100.

In May 1885, during the pastorate of Rev. William R. Griffith (1882-1889), the society sold the old church property on Washington Street and purchased a lot on the corner of Hopper and Union Streets. In the spring of 1886 work began on a new structure and the cornerstone was laid in August 1887. At the dedication the name Coke Memorial was adopted in honor of Bishop Thomas Coke. Bishop Coke was the first Methodist Bishop sent to this country and was also a Welshman.

Soon thereafter, in 1889, Isaac Thomas returned as the church's pastor for one year. In 1890 Rev. J. L. Davies, a professor at the Genesee Wesleyan Seminary in Lima, New York, became minister and remained for a few years. In 1894 the church had 88 members and was led by Rev. Thomas Roberts.

Coke Memorial.
This church was erected in 1887 and was a Welsh Wesleyan Methodist church until 1918. Today the structure houses an office supply store.

Coke Memorial Church was well known for its fine suppers; it had a large kitchen and dining room in the basement. A supper was held at the church each year to sustain the participants at the Utica Eisteddfod. The Eisteddfod was held for many years at the Armory on Rutger Street, near the church. The annual competition began in 1856 and lasted for 100 years.

One of the last ministers of the church, David Davies, came to Utica from Anglesey in 1903. He was not ordained but was a lay preacher. Each Sunday he preached in Welsh. His daughter Ceinwen Davies Wall still lived in Holland Patent in 1992. Other ministers who served in the twentieth century include Revs. E. Eurog Jones, A. Harris, Evan Evans, and D. C. Roberts.

In 1916 the South Street Methodist Church raised enough money to build a new chapel. Shortly thereafter First Methodist and Coke Memorial decided to merge with the South Street Methodist Church. John D. Lloyd and William Davies represented Coke in merger discussions.

In 1918 Coke Memorial officially dissolved. The society had never been very large, and with the halt of immigration from Wales, it could not survive. Many of its members did join with Central Methodist Church, located on the corner of Court and Broadway. Of those who did not, only a few went to the other Welsh-speaking churches, whereas many did join Plymouth Congregational.

Coke Memorial's large steeple and bell tower were removed after the sale of the building. Today, the former church is the home of Hummel's Office Supply Company. Down the street, at Central Methodist, there is a chapel named after Coke Memorial Church. In a glass case located in the hall outside of the chapel can still be seen the communion set of the old Welsh chapel, along with the sets from the other Methodist churches which have joined to make up Central Methodist Church.

Welsh Episcopal Church

The Welsh who immigrated to America tended to belong to denominations which "dissented" from the established church. Nevertheless, the established "Church in Wales" does have a sizeable membership in Wales. It is a part of the Anglican Communion, as is the Church of England and the Episcopal Church in America.

There were few Welsh Episcopalian churches formed in the United States. In fact there were only six other Welsh Episcopal Churches, all founded in Pennsylvania during colonial times. They were St. David's (1700) in Radnor; Trinity (1711) in Oxford; St. James (1715) in Perkiomen; St. Peter's (1720) in Great Valley; Bangor (1732) in Churchtown; and St. Thomas (1756) in Morgantown.

In the 1850s an Episcopal priest, a Rev. Humphreys, lived in Remsen, but there is no record of a Welsh Episcopal church being formed at that time.

From 1896 to 1899 a Welsh Episcopal Church existed in Utica. The congregation worshiped in the chapel of Grace Episcopal Church on Genesee Street in downtown Utica. Rev. R. W. Prichard, who led the services, was a frequent contributor to *The Cambrian* and his sermons were reprinted in that publication on a number of occasions. After 1899 there is nothing more written about this small society.

Chapter IV

Utica's Suburbs

SURROUNDING UTICA are a number of small suburban towns, many of which once had Welsh churches. In these towns the Welsh were clearly in the minority and, as a group, had little influence on the communities as a whole. These societies were frequently outgrowths of churches in Utica and looked to the city for support.

In this chapter, the churches of New York Mills, New Hartford, Frankfort Hill, Ilion and Clinton will be examined. While none of these communities has either Welsh churches or Welsh organizations today, New Hartford, Clinton, and Whitestown (of which New York Mills is a part) are the home of many Welsh-Americans.

New York Mills

It is difficult to distinguish the former Welsh Congregational Church from the other houses along Main Street in New York Mills. It is located at the north end of the village in the town of Whitestown, an area known at the time of the church's formation as the Upper Mills.

Salem
This former church is located on Main Street in New York Mills. It was the Salem Congregational Church from 1849 to 1954.

Today New York Mills is primarily Polish in ethnic composition. However, when the New York Mills Cotton Manufacturing Company first opened, many of its workers were Welsh. In addition, Welshmen Thomas Ellis Esq. and William Roberts Esq. established a large pail factory which also attracted many Welsh to the village.

The first meeting held for the purpose of forming a Welsh church in New York Mills was conducted in the village schoolhouse on June 1, 1847. At that meeting it was decided that the Welsh of the village needed a place where they could worship in their own language. At a subsequent meeting, the Congregationalists extended an invitation to the Calvinistic Methodists and Baptists to form a Congregational or Independent Church.

The Welsh Congregational Church was organized under the direction of Rev. William D. Williams on September 23, 1847. At that time the name "Salem" was selected. The first trustees of the church were David Jones, William Roberts, Owen Griffith, Ellis Ellis and Benjamin Walcott. Mr. Walcott was not Welsh but owned the largest mill in the village and was one of the most successful mill owners in the country.

After a suitable place to worship was erected in 1849, several pastors served the congregation, namely, Mr. Owen Baxter and Revs. Edward Davies and John R. Griffith.

I recently received a letter from a woman in Wales whose great-great-great-grandfather was Owen Baxter's brother. She related that Owen Baxter was born in 1814 on the Penarth farm in Llanfaircaereinion, Montgomeryshire, and was a descendant of Richard Baxter (1615-1691), the Protestant divine who was imprisoned several times for preaching religious tolerance. Owen Baxter later moved to Waterville, where in 1852 he was involved with the establishment of that village's Welsh Congregational Church.

In 1856 the young Thomas W. Roberts was ordained to be the church's full-time pastor. However, he soon left for Auburn College where quite unexpectedly he died. A Rev. Morgan served Salem until 1859 when the pastorate was filled by Edward W. James, who remained until his death in 1869. In May of 1870, Rev. Thomas M. Owen of Llanwst, Wales assumed the pulpit. Rev. Owen later went on to minister to the Welsh in Turin.

In 1870 the church was refurbished. Its membership at that time was between 55 and 65. Later in the 1870s, Rev. Rhys Gwesyn Jones served the church. After a brief absence of four years, he returned and remained the pastor from 1883 to 1901. During this same period his primary responsibility was to Bethesda Church in Utica.

Rev. Jones was succeeded by Rev. Richard Hughes who began his tenure in May of 1901 and remained for 28 years until his death in May of 1929. During those same years he was also able to serve Holland Patent's Welsh church, as he was a resident of that village.

While Rev. Hughes was pastor, further renovations were made to the church. In 1926 a new wall was built underneath the church to raise the structure. Inside, an auditorium which could seat 250 persons was constructed. Upon Rev. Hughes death a large plaque in his memory was placed in the sanctuary, honoring his years of service.

In the 1930s membership began to decline at Salem Church to the point where the congregation could no longer support a regular minister. During the final years of Salem's existence, the congregation relied almost entirely upon supply pastors. In 1954 the church was closed. The property was sold to a Mr. Landers and it has been in his family ever since. Today the former church is a two-family home.

New Hartford

Farmers living outside the city limits had difficulty attending Sunday morning services in Utica, first because of their farm responsibilities and second because of poor modes of transportation. To help accomodate the needs of Welsh farmers who lived in the adjoining town of New Hartford, a "Fellowship Meeting of the County" was held once every three weeks at Moriah in Utica. The "County Meeting" provided a more convenient time, generally on a weekday evening, when people from the outlying regions could attend services.

In 1888 the "County Meeting" was discontinued and 40 members of Moriah removed their letters to Zion, a new Welsh Presbyterian church in New Hartford. The group first met in the home of Enoch Morris. It then moved to larger quarters, meeting upstairs in what was to become the First National Bank building. Rev. D. Charles Edwards, who also supplied at Moriah, was the first minister for Zion.

In 1895 the membership was large enough to warrant construction of a church building on Pearl Street. At that time Rev. John J. Williams was pastor, serving from 1894 until 1899. In 1915 a small pipe organ was purchased and Olwen Humphreys served as organist for many years.

Although Zion's membership was relatively small, it nevertheless supported several organizations. For example, a men's club met once a month, at which time the history of a different Welsh county would be discussed. Similar organizations existed for the women.

As the church was frequently served by pastors from Moriah and was attended by many farmers, services were usually held on Sunday afternoons. Prayer meetings were conducted Thursday evenings. The men often tried to outdo each other with longer and more fervent prayers. It was not uncommon for loud "Amens" to be shouted and the effectiveness of the prayer was often judged by the number of "Amens" it received.

The church also had a Sunday School and, like all other activities at Zion, it was in Welsh. The Sunday School was necessary for the preservation of the Welsh language, because there the children not only learned their religious lessons but they were also taught their Welsh ABCs.

Rev. William R. Williams, who also preached in Ilion in the evenings, served as pastor from 1917 until his death in 1926. A similar arrangement was maintained between the two churches when Rev. John R. Evans succeeded him. Evans remained into the 1930s.

In 1941 the church found its membership declining. At the same time the Masonic Temple on Oxford Road was unable to maintain its ornate structure. Hugh G. Humphreys, who was a leader of the Masons as well as a trustee of Zion, was instrumental in having the Welsh church convey its building to the Amicable Lodge, F. & A. M., thereby resolving both organizations' dilemmas. Zion was allowed to continue using the building for services for as long as the congregation continued to meet. In the 1940s there were still 25 members.

Zion.
New Hartford's Welsh Presbyterian Church was located on Pearl Street from 1895 to 1958. Today it is the village's Masonic lodge.

During Zion's final years, Dr. R. Glynne Lloyd of Moriah conducted services. By 1955 only ten members remained to attend the Sunday afternoon services and in 1958 services were discontinued, with the remaining members joining Moriah. Today the building remains New Hartford's Masonic Lodge.

Over the years New Hartford has been the site of many activities for the local Welsh community. While Zion was active, Hugh G. Humphrey's farm on Tibbitts Road was a frequent location for such events. For example, in the winter, sleigh rides for church members were held there. During World War II a Welsh-American Days celebration was held on the farm as well. Today the Humphreys farm remains one of the most successful in the county.

A number of Welsh farmers lived south of the village of New Hartford, in and around Washington Mills. Further down Oneida Street in the hamlets of Willowvale and Chadwicks, an annual Welsh gathering was held in the local community hall. That tradition continued well into the middle of the twentieth century.

It is interesting to note that as time passed, many of Moriah's members moved to New Hartford. Of these, the majority joined New Hartford's Presbyterian Church. Today that church is the site of the St. David's Choir's rehearsals and the St. David's Society of Utica's annual Welsh-American Days and Gymanfa Ganu. Even the annual Welsh picnic is held in New Hartford at the town park. One hundred years after the establishment of Zion, New Hartford has become the center of Welsh activities in Oneida County.

Frankfort Hill

On Higby Road, which runs from South Utica to the town of Frankfort, there is today a large water works facility. Located just before that facility and immediately beyond the intersection of Higby and Graffenburg Roads is an area known as Frankfort Hill, where once stood a small Welsh chapel.

When Welsh-speaking Calvinistic Methodists first settled on Frankfort Hill, they regularly attended Sunday morning worship services at the Seneca Street Church in Utica. They, however, preferred to hold Sunday School in various homes in their neighborhood. Since the weekly trip into Utica was long and arduous, it is not surprising that one of the Frankfort Hill Welsh decided to found a local church.

Although the Utica church believed that the Welsh at Frankfort Hill should come into the city for services, Hugh Davies, an immigrant from Penmachno in North Wales held a different opinion.

On March 25, 1849 Davies organized a society comprised of his wife, Samuel Samuels, Owen Evans and his niece Sarah, one other person and himself. Since Hugh Davies had been an elder in Wales he felt capable of assuming the same position in the newly formed church.

With Hugh Davies as the driving force behind the society, land for building a small chapel was readily obtained in 1858. He personally solicited subscriptions from both Welsh and non-Welsh residents of the area. This was an impressive accomplishment as Davies spoke no English. It is said he learned two important words: "dollar" and "church." This bit of linguistic knowledge and his ability to gesture and point to the site of the new church helped him create a substantial subscription list.

The Frankfort Hill church was so connected with Mr. Davies it often was referred to as "Hugh Davies' Church." He was instrumental in getting preachers to come to the small chapel. Often its congregation was too small for its collection to cover the cost of the minister, so Davies would make up the difference. In 1872 the church had 30 members. Other Welsh denominations from time to time would invite preachers to the area but there were no other Welsh chapels erected.

Secure in the knowledge that his small church was firmly established, Davies moved to Utica. Here he was immediately asked to be a church elder and he accepted. Hugh Davies passed away in June, 1878. After Davies left the Frankfort Hill area the church continued until 1920 when it was dissolved.

Ilion

The Welsh immigrants to this country often sought employment in fields with which they were familiar. For many, this meant working in one of the slate mines in Eastern New York or Vermont. For their part, mine operators in those areas were anxious to obtain skilled workers and actively encouraged the Welsh to settle near the mines. Large Welsh communities grew around Granville and Middle Granville in Washington County, New York and in Fair Haven, Poultney, South Poultney and West Pawlet in Vermont.

In the early part of this century, many of the slate mines in New York and Vermont were mined out, causing the Welsh to look elsewhere for employment. When World War I began, many of these unemployed Welsh slate miners moved to more industrialized areas where factories were meeting the needs of the war effort. One of these areas was Ilion, where the Remington Arms plant was operating around the clock, producing firearms.

Not only was work in Ilion plentiful; it was profitable, as workers at the plant were paid very good wages. Ilion was also attractive to the Welsh, because Utica, with its large Welsh population, was nearby. As a result, many Welsh came to Ilion during the First World War.

At first the Welsh in Ilion attended services in Utica. As the Welsh population in Ilion increased, Moriah's session authorized the establishment of a Welsh Presbyterian church in the village. The Ilion church was simply known as "Y Capel Cymraig" or the "Welsh Church." The society was organized in 1914 and met above a firehouse adjacent to the Remington Arms plant on Oswego Street, at the intersection with Second Avenue. During those early days Rev. Owen Davies served the church. Rev. William H. Davies also served the church.

In 1919 the church called its first regular pastor, William R. Williams of Utica. He became a candidate for ordination in that same year, and one year later was ordained. Rev. Williams had been an elder at Moriah in Utica prior to entering the ministry.

Rev. Williams was an older man at the time of his ordination, fulfilling late in life a long-held desire to enter the ministry. Each Sunday afternoon he would take the trolley to Ilion from Utica, after having preached a morning sermon in New Hartford where he was also pastor. Services in Ilion were held from 7 to 8:30 on Sunday evenings. Children enjoyed this arrangement because they could justify staying up late on Sundays. Parishioners would give the minister baked goods and the like to take home with him on the trolley after service.

Rev. Williams remained in this pastorate until his death in March 1926. He was followed by Rev. John R. Evans. Like his predecessor, Rev. Evans commuted from Utica on the trolley, and like Rev. Williams, he was also elderly. Because of his advanced age he was known for being very slow and his services were very long. Edna Williams Gorney recalls that her brother's wedding, on June 23 1930, was so long that no one doubted the couple was married by the end of the ceremony.

"Y Capel Cymraig."
In this old firehouse on Oswego Street in Ilion,
Welsh of the village worshipped from 1914 to 1935.

At its height, the congregation numbered about 50. A piano provided the accompaniment for the church's long singing sessions. In later years, the youth of the church left to join the English language churches of the village. In 1935, when the Oneida (Welsh) Presbytery was in the process of dissolving, its member churches joined the local English-speaking Presbyteries. In that year the church closed and the remaining dozen members transferred their memberships to the Ilion Presbyterian Church.

Clinton

The village of Clinton is located nine miles southwest of Utica and is the home of Hamilton College. It briefly had a Welsh religious society from 1886 to 1887, known simply as "The Welsh Church." Its meetings were first held in homes of various Welshmen in the village. In November of 1886 the church needed a larger meeting place, so it held services on the second floor of the Sherman Block, which was located for many years on North Park Row until a fire on July 4, 1989 destroyed the entire building.

The second floor of the Sherman Block contained the office of H. W. Mahan. Mr. Mahan had originally owned a shoe store on the first floor, but by 1886 he had become a hops dealer. In that capacity he was well acquainted with the Welsh hops farmers of southern Oneida County and allowed them to meet in his quarters.

On February 18, 1887 a benefit for the Welsh Church was held at the Methodist Episcopal Church on the village green in Clinton, in a building that now houses the Kirkland Art Center. It is possible, therefore, that the Welsh Church was of the same denomination.

The benefit cost 25 cents admission and it was reported that $70.25 was raised for the cause. The festivities included a dinner and speakers in English and Welsh before and after the meal. Rev. George Godwin acted as moderator for the evening and Rev. William Ashforth of Boston spoke. The entertainment that evening included singing by William J. Jones of Clinton, accompanied by Mrs. E. H. Thomas. The Clinton Welsh Quartet also performed.

Later in the evening Rev. I. A. Best and H. W. Mahan gave "spicy" addresses. Rev. William Price of Hanover Green in the town of Marshall also assisted in the event.

After this benefit there appears to have been no other church activity. By October of 1887 the Welsh Church was no longer listed in *The Clinton Courier* as one of the Clinton churches.

Today many descendants of the Welsh from Utica and Remsen reside in Clinton and the town of Kirkland, but no trace remains of Clinton's Welsh Church.

Chapter V

Southern Oneida County

IN THE SOUTHERN PORTIONS OF THE ONEIDA COUNTY there were a number of Welsh communities. While the Welsh living north of Utica in the Remsen-Steuben area were primarily dairy farmers, those to the south generally operated hops farms. This is especially interesting in light of the strong temperance views of the Welsh. Societies in southern Oneida County were formed at Waterville, Paris, and Bridgewater. Plainfield Center, in northern Otsego County, should also be considered when discussing this group of Welsh churches, as it is in close geographic proximity to the other towns.

Waterville

The Welsh Congregational Church in Waterville was formed in 1852. The congregation purchased the old Episcopal Church when the Episcopalians moved to their present building. The Episcopal priest, Rev. Hughes, was instrumental in conveying the old church to the Welsh. This explains why the Welsh church has a very Anglican look to it.

Congregational Church.
Waterville's Village Hall was the village's Welsh church from 1852 to 1926.
Prior to that time it was the home of Grace Episcopal Church.

The church's first minister was the Rev. Edward Davies. He remained for 16 years until 1869 when he left to minister to English-speaking Congregational churches at Oriskany Falls and Deansboro. He later preached in Remsen and Steuben while serving as editor of *Y Cenhadwr*.

Davies was known as an ardent supporter of temperance, often casting the Prohibition Party's sole vote in the town of Sangerfield, a town whose livelihood depended upon the production of hops. Davies' neighbors wondered "what he voted for," and what good could come from the lone ballot that he cast. He, however, felt that he was registering his conviction as to what was right.

John Owen of Carmarthenshire, South Wales followed Davies in 1870, but unfortunately he passed away the next year. The church had 63 members in 1872. Later the church was ministered to by pastors from neighboring towns including Rev. Caradoc Jones of Utica and Rev. Thomas Jenkins of Madison.

In 1926 the church closed its doors and in 1931 the church became the Waterville Village Hall and remains so today. The Waterville cemetery is the final resting place for many of the Welsh of Waterville and the surrounding area.

Paris

Most of the Welsh who attended the Waterville church did not actually live in the village. They lived on nearby farms and would generally travel to Waterville for services. As the Welsh population grew in the nearby town of Paris many of the farmers wanted to have their own church.

The Welsh generally settled in the southwestern portion of the town of Paris, northwest of Cassville. This is the area identified today as Paris Station.

Rowland Morris Farm.
The Morris farm was the site of many early meetings for the Calvinistic Methodists of both Paris and Bridgewater. It is located on Canning Factory Road near Paris Station.

There were three Welsh religious societies in the town of Paris: Wesleyan, Congregational, and Whitefield (Calvinistic) Methodist. These Welsh were attracted to the Paris Hill area because of its wonderful farm land. My great-great-grandfather initially settled in Paris in 1850. For the first years of his life in America he worked as a hired hand on a farm in the area until he could afford his own farm in Plainfield. This may have been the path taken by many other new immigrants to the area.

The Paris Wesleyans were the first to establish a Welsh church in the region. In 1858 the Wesleyans or Methodist Episcopalians purchased land and constructed a chapel. This was located next to a country schoolhouse at the intersection of Larson and Canning Factory Roads. They were ministered to by Rev. Humphrey Humphreys of Utica. Among the church's elders were David Parry, Solomon Lewis, Cadwalader Jones, and Thomas Hughes.

The Calvinistic Methodists met at the home of Rowland Morris on Canning Factory Road, among other places. The Calvinistic Methodists were listed in church records as having established a church in Cassville, although no church was ever erected. In as much as Rowland Morris had been influential in forming the Calvinistic Methodists' church in Bridgewater, members of that church may have at one time worshiped with the Calvinistic Methodists in Paris.

Of the three societies, the Congregationalists' was the smallest. There are no records regarding the society and, when the three churches merged, it did not have a representative involved in the purchase of the property.

The three societies, all being rather small, joined together to form a union church in the Wesleyan chapel. The property was purchased from the Wesleyans by David Parry and Rowland Morris and their wives, who immediately conveyed the property to the union church for $400. Interestingly, the deed from the Parrys and Morrises to the union church was recorded before the deed from the Wesleyan church to them.

The union church was formed in 1868, but as early as the 1870s this union may have dissolved, with the Congregationalists going to Waterville and the Calvinistic Methodists going to Bridgewater. The Wesleyans apparently remained into the early part of the twentieth century. The small church was given the name Bethany.

As time passed, the old church closed and was torn down. However, the property remained in the hands of the "church." In the 1940s, the heirs of the original owners of the site conveyed the land. As title was vested in the church, however, the prior owners had no right to transfer the property. Therefore, to give the new property owners clean title, a group of twelve former members living in the Waterville area signed a deed as well.

Today, the old schoolhouse which stood next to the church has been converted into a private residence. Nothing remains of the church.

The most telling reminder of the Welsh influence in the town of Paris is the Lincoln Davies General Store at Paris Station. For years the store has served that rural area of the county. It was founded in 1878 by David J. Davies. "If we don't have it, you don't need it," the cashier told me, and indeed it's true. The general store contains hardware, auto parts, kitchen supplies, groceries, lumber and farm supplies. Its wide board floors give one the feeling of being transported to the days when Welsh farmers would come to the store for supplies.

Lincoln Davies Store.
Founded in 1878, this store serves Paris Station and the surrounding area.

Bridgewater

The Welsh settlement in the town of Bridgewater was three or four miles south of Paris Station. As with so many other communities the Welsh did not establish their church in the village center, but in the outlying hills.

On Hardscrabble Road, just north of the village, the Calvinistic Methodists established a church known as Bethel. Edward Jones, John J. Williams and Rowland Morris were the "heads" of some of the early Welsh families in Bridgewater and Paris. These families first assembled in a barn on the farm of Rowland Morris in Paris and organized a church in 1851. Rowland Morris was later instrumental in the formation of the Welsh society in Paris.

John J. Williams and Edward Jones were Bethel's first elders. In 1857, Rev. John Davies of Bridgewater was accepted as the church's first pastor.

He, however, died one year later. The church was probably served primarily by supplies throughout its history, including the Rev. Thomas T. Evans.

In 1858 a church was built on land formerly owned by John E. Jones. In 1872 the church had 37 members. It continued until the turn of the century when it was dissolved.

Today nothing remains of that church. The area is desolate, with a number of abandoned homes. The paved portion of the road turns to gravel as it winds into the hills where some new homes have been constructed. Hardscrabble Road eventually becomes a seasonally limited road. It seems almost obligatory that Welsh churches be located on such gravel roads.

I stopped my car near the area where the church had once been and got out to look around. A man came out from a yard strewn with abandoned cars looking suspiciously at me. "Ever heard of a church having been up on this road?" I called. "No, there's never been any churches out here, you'd have to go into town," he replied. How quickly the past is forgotten.

Plainfield

Traveling south on Route 8 from Utica, one passes through New Hartford, Paris and Bridgewater. A few miles east of Bridgewater on Route 20 is a sign pointing to Unadilla Forks. This area is at the intersection of three counties: Oneida, Herkimer, and Otsego. Unadilla Forks is a small collection of neat homes, a Baptist church, a war monument and a cemetery, and is located in northern Otsego County.

Traveling east of that hamlet, one can see large hills which look to have been left behind by a gigantic glacier. These rocky and steep hills are where the Welsh settled in Otsego County. High in those hills is the hamlet of Plainfield Center.

At one time Plainfield Center was a thriving community, being located on the Skaneateles Turnpike which wound its way across the state. The turnpike was the main road between Albany and Auburn. In its hey-day the road was used to herd turkeys to slaughter. Two hotels were located at Plainfield Center to accommodate the road's travelers. There were also several shops, several cheese factories and a charcoal kiln. Today the Skaneateles Turnpike is a narrow road, portions of which have been abandoned.

Originally the town was settled by English-speaking settlers, many of whom are buried in the lower portion of the Plainfield Center cemetery. The first Welshman to settle in the area was Edward L. Morris of Meifod, Montgomeryshire, North Wales, who arrived in 1853. A number of other Welshmen arrived soon thereafter including my great-great-grandfather

Moses Davies. Like his neighbors, he found the land too harsh for dairy farming and therefore grew hops.

Plainfield Cemetery.
This cemetery is the final resting place of both the
early Yankee settlers as well as the Welsh.

Today, much of the area on which the Welsh farms sat has been transferred to New York State for a forest preserve. Many of the roads in the town are rough and open only in the summer. Even then they are primarily used by loggers. The Moses Davies farm is now covered by forest. Deep in the woods behind the homestead's foundation one can see where the hops barn once stood. Deeper still there are the remains of the first log cabins, constructed when the family first arrived, together with the graves of their young children who died shortly after moving to the farm. Similar remains of the once flourishing community can be found throughout the township.

Calvinistic Methodist

South of Plainfield Center there is a hill which rises above the others. At one time this area was known as Welsh Hill, though a modern map refers to it as Noah's Rump.

It was on Welsh Hill that the Calvinistic Methodists met in the McCauley schoolhouse in 1855 and organized a church. Moses Davies was instrumental in the church's formation and became an elder. Rev. E. J. Hughes was called as the church's first pastor in 1857 and services were conducted in the school.

The first church structure was not erected until 1869 and was 26 x 29 feet. It sat on Mason Road, near its intersection with Adams Pond Road, across from the McCauley schoolhouse. It served a membership of 32 with a congregation of 62. The Rev. John S. Adams succeeded Rev. Hughes as pastor and served until 1871. Many of Rev. Adam's relatives still live in the area. He made his home in Plainfield but also served as pastor for churches in Nelson and other villages. Adams Pond Road is named after both him and his family. His son lived on Welsh Hill for many years.

Rev. Adams was succeeded by Rev. T. H. Griffith who had been ordained in 1870 and remained in Plainfield for three years before leaving to serve an English-speaking church. It is unclear whether John Adams returned to the church's pulpit. Adams died in 1886 in Wales, where he may have gone on a visit. In 1888 Robert T. Jones came to Plainfield from Wales to assume the church's pulpit.

While the Welsh population in most of Central New York's rural areas declined in the mid-nineteenth century, Plainfield and Nelson in Madison County were exceptions. These rural Welsh centers reached their peak in about 1890. Shortly thereafter, however, they too experienced a decline in their populations.

In the 1890s John Davies was the pastor and was probably the last minister to serve that Plainfield church. In 1892 Moses Davies passed away, having been an elder of the church for 37 years. Shortly after his death the church closed and its members transferred to the Plainfield Congregational Church.

The church was used as a carriage shed by a neighboring farmer, John Mason, who moved the structure to his farm. The Mason homestead was located nearby and its chimney can still be seen in the brush. Many curious people have thought the chimney was once connected with the church. There is, however, no longer any trace of the Welsh church, although Donald Davies of West Exeter has the church's pulpit chairs in his garage.

The small church has almost faded from the memories of area residents. Welsh Hill has become part of the forest preserve, the state having purchased many of the farms. Most of the people I spoke with did not know that Plainfield had two churches and could only recall the one located at Plainfield Center.

Shiloh

In the Bible, Shiloh appears in connection with several different events. It was the place where Joshua cast lots to apportion the land to the people of Israel (Joshua 18:8). It was here that the congregation of Israel met and sacrifices were made to God (Samuel 1:3). It was also at Shiloh that the ark of the covenant was destroyed by the Philistines and thus, it is said, was forsaken by God (Psalms 78:60). It also refers to the Davidic Messiah coming to rule (Genesis 49:10) Whether any of these biblical connotations influenced the selection of the name for the Plainfield Center church is not known. What is known is that Shiloh was the name given to the Congregational Church.

In 1861 the Congregational Church was organized. The congregation first worshiped in the upstairs ballroom of an old hotel which the church had purchased. This hotel had, at one time, served travelers on the Skaneateles Turnpike. In the summer of 1869 the congregation built a chapel 40 x 30 feet in size. Its membership was then 88 with a congregation of 160. Rev. Hugh R. Williams began ministering to the church on July 4, 1868 and continued for over a decade. He had previously been instrumental in organizing the Congregational Church in Prospect.

During the nineteenth century Rev. Richard Williams and Rev. Holmes served the church. In the 1890s Rev. Henry Hughes was pastor. Later, Rev. Morien Mon Hughes supplied on occasion.

The Congregational Church was the center of both religious and social life in Plainfield. On Sundays a worship service was held at 11:00, followed by Sunday School, and in the evening a Christian Endeavor meeting was held. On Wednesday evenings there were prayer meetings.

The parsonage next to the church served both as a residence for the pastor as well as a parish hall. The second floor contained dining and meeting areas which were used for many church events. The large barn behind the church was frequently filled with horses and buggies from members attending one function or another.

Each year an Eisteddfod was conducted at the church. This was the time for children to stand before the community and sing a song or recite a poem they had memorized in hopes of winning a prize.

The highlight of the year in Plainfield was the Gymanfa Mawr or Big Meeting. This was held at the church each fall and lasted for three days. All the ministers in the area would take a turn in the pulpit preaching to a capacity congregation. The Welsh from throughout Central New York would attend, with many traveling from Utica. Large suppers were put on for those attending and people who had come a great distance would be put up in homes of local residents. These "big meetings" continued until after World War I.

In about 1910 Rev. Isaac T. Williams of Slatington, Pennsylvania succeeded Rev. Hughes in the pulpit. During I. T. Williams' tenure the church was full almost every Sunday. Williams moved to Cleveland and was followed by Rev. Abraham Jones, also of Slatington, in about 1913. Rev. Jones remained at the church until about 1920.

Parsonage.
This house, at the four corners in Plainfield Center, served as the parsonage for the Congregational Church which stood to its north.

After Rev. Jones departed, the big meetings stopped and the Eisteddfod was discontinued. Many of the Welsh moved away from Plainfield. Some went to one of the neighboring hamlets such as Unadilla Forks or West Exeter. Others moved to Utica and its surrounding towns. For example, of the children of Moses Davies, Robert H. Davies moved to Waterville, Caleb E. Davies moved to Utica where he became an elder in Moriah, Elizabeth Davies Williams moved to Rome, and Sarah Davies Roberts moved to Minnesota. Only one son, Joseph Davies, remained in Plainfield on the family farm.

In about 1915 or 1916, many of the descendants of the early Welsh settlers realized that the area was in decline and that few would remain to watch over the graves in the old cemetery. For that reason, over a three-day period, many of the settlers who had been buried in Plainfield Center were exhumed. Their caskets were placed on wagons and they were taken to Unadilla Forks for reinterment. This caused the local children to become frightened at the thought of the dead being raised and left a lasting impression on many.

John Griffith, John Williams and Francis Griffith served as elders of the church for many years. The elders would sit in the front of the congregation facing the pulpit. However, when a hymn was sung they would turn and face the congregation. Evan and Ellen Griffith were also great workers in the church. For many years Ellen Griffith was in charge of the Sunday School.

Shiloh Monument.
This marker was placed on the site of the Shiloh Congregational Church in Plainfield Center. The church stood there from 1861 to 1942.

The last person to serve as pastor was Rev. J. T. Williams. He came to the church in 1920 and remained until it closed in 1941. Welsh continued to be used at this time, but every other week was "English Sunday." In the summers the church joined with other local churches for worship in English. During the final years membership dwindled to about 20. When Rev. Williams retired it was impractical to hire a replacement. Moreover, it was no longer possible to find a Welsh-speaking minister to live in the remote hamlet.

With much sadness the church was taken down and removed to Syracuse and the land was sold. A stone marking the site of the Shiloh Congregational Church was erected and the church site became the side lawn for the former parsonage. Rev. Williams moved down the road to an old schoolhouse which he converted into a home. There he lived with his daughter for many years. The remaining members were given letters of transfer signed by the deacons, Griffith Jones and John D. Jones. Some transferred their membership to the church in West Exeter while others went to the Congregational Church in West Winfield, now part of the West Winfield Federated Church. For a time in the 1830s Dr. Everett of Steuben served as pastor of that West Winfield church in which there was a window dedicated to his memory.

On Crumb Hill Road, behind the former parsonage, remains the old cemetery. In the summer tall grass obscures the graves of the Welsh and English settlers alike. The original settlers are buried near the road while the Welsh are buried on the hill. A John Williams, possibly a former elder in the Calvinistic Methodist church, lies there. Through the waving brown grass his epitaph still can be seen: "You shall not be forgotten."

Chapter VI

Madison County

MADISON COUNTY is located to the west of Oneida County and south of Onondaga County and Syracuse. It is rural in nature, and its Welsh settlers were primarily farmers. The greatest concentration of Welsh settlers was in the town of Nelson, although there were also many Welsh farmers in West Eaton. The village of Madison may have had a small Calvinistic Methodist society as well.

Nelson

As one drives west on Route 20 from Sangerfield, through Madison and Morrisville, one comes to Nelson. The town is located immediately east of Cazenovia and is a patchwork of small farms. Before reaching the hamlet of Nelson one passes a small wooden sign with a replica of a chapel on it. This sign points to East Nelson and the old Welsh Church. In fact, the road intersecting with Route 20 at the sign is known as Welsh Church Road.

In the 1840s, or maybe even earlier, the Welsh began to come to Nelson. In fact, the first Welsh burial in the Nelson cemetery occurred in 1830 when Samuel Jones died. At first glance it is hard to understand why Nelson's Welsh churches were constructed where they were, for today they are in a remote area, away from the main highways. When they were built, however, they sat on the Cherry Valley Turnpike. When the turnpike was constructed in 1806, it connected much of upstate New York. It was a stagecoach route along which businesses sprang up to meet the needs of travelers. Also, during its early years, the turnpike was fenced in, as droves of cattle, sheep, hogs, horses, turkeys and geese were herded along the road to market in Albany. Stagecoaches frequently were delayed by these droves and as a result spicy remarks would fill the air.

Capel Bach

Around the year 1845 the Welsh began holding services in private homes. By 1850 they had erected a meeting house and called their first minister. For unknown reasons, this minister began to preach in English instead of Welsh. A man named Samuels, a staunch advocate of tradition, was so incensed at hearing the word of God preached in a "foreign tongue" and feeling the services were being corrupted, set fire to the church and burned it to the ground.

Capel Bach.
This photograph was taken of the former Calvinistic Methodist Church shortly before it collapsed in 1992. It was a church from 1850 to 1930.

Thereafter, Congregationalists and Calvinistic Methodists, who had worshiped together in that first church, began holding services separately in private homes. The Calvinistic Methodists removed themselves from the church and in the latter part of 1850 decided to build their own structure. To expedite the process, John E. Richards took trees from his woods to a nearby saw mill and turned them into lumber for the little church. Other men in the community contributed material and soon a suitable structure was completed. Services in the newly constructed church were held in Welsh and before long the church soon became known as the "Little Welsh Church" or "Capel Bach."

In 1851 David D. Hughes and Edward Richards, the father of John E. Richards, became elders of the church. David Hughes continued to be an elder until his death in 1902. It is interesting to note that Mr. Hughes' son, David D. Hughes, Jr., married Edward Richards' granddaughter. The church was certainly a tight knit community.

Rev. John S. Adams, who also served the church in Plainfield, was the church's first pastor. Rev. Adams died in 1886 in Beaumaris, Anglesey, North Wales. It is said he expired in the pulpit just after he had finished preaching.

Rev. Ebenezer T. Jones followed Rev. Adams and was the minister in 1872. At that time the church had 50 members. Rev. Jones was also at one time the pastor in Prospect.

Rev. Jones was succeeded in the pulpit by Rev. Benjamin D. Davies who came to Central New York in 1887. William E. Morgan also served the church during the late 1880s. In 1895, Thomas E. Jones came to Capel Bach. The church's last regular minister was D. T. Davies. Rev. Davies had been a Wesleyan minister and had served at Coke Memorial Church in Utica. In 1898 he was ordained as a Calvinistic Methodist minister and served Nelson and other churches.

In 1917 the church officially dissolved. However, services were continued after the dissolution and the church was kept open for Sunday School even though there was no regular pastor. The congregation often had the minister from the Welsh Congregational Church come to preach in the afternoons. If there were no preacher available, then a Bible study or prayer meeting would be led by a member of the congregation. One of those members, Clarence Wakely, was received as a candidate for ordination from the church in 1922.

In 1930 David D. Hughes, Jr. passed away and the little church closed its doors forever. As his granddaughter May Hughes wrote, "the last faithful 'door keeper' of his Father's house on earth had gone to his Father's house in a fairer land."

In the summer of 1930 the Oneida Presbytery sold the church. Idwald Roberts of Utica had been brought up in the church and feared that it would fall into the hands of people who might put it to evil use. He therefore purchased the property and turned it into a little home for his widowed mother, Mrs. John Roberts. The horse sheds were removed from behind it and its double door was made into a single house door. Even after Mrs. Roberts' death, the home remained in the Idwald Roberts family.

The brown shingled house which once was Capel Bach, located on the Old State Road just opposite Hughes Road, recently fell into disrepair and then collapsed. In the winter of 1992 the roof was removed and by summer the structure was reduced to a pile of bricks and lumber, a faint reminder of the past.

Peniel Church

The Welsh Congregationalists formed their own society in Nelson on June 22, 1850. The rise and decline of this church was directly tied to the rate of Welsh immigration to the area. The following were the number of persons born in Wales living in the township:

1850:	51
1861:	48
1871:	83
1891:	26
1915:	57

The East Nelson area had been settled first by the English-speaking people. In 1813 a Presbyterian Church was built on the site of the present Welsh Congregational Church and many of its members are buried in unmarked graves in the church cemetery. Other churches in East Nelson in the early nineteenth century included a Free Methodist Church on Larson Road, and Presbyterian and Baptist churches.

In 1848 the English-speaking Presbyterian Church sold its building to a Baptist society and moved into the village. "The First Free Baptist Union Society," organized in 1839, took over the vacated Presbyterian building and used it until their membership became too small to operate it.

In 1853 the Baptists signed the church over to the Welsh Congregationalists for one dollar in consideration for repairing the structure. The Baptists, however, reserved the right to hold funerals in the building.

The inspirational leaders of the Welsh church were David E. Davies, Robert R. Jones, their wives and Esther Williams. They joined with others within a 14-mile radius to form the Welsh Congregational Church, which had 27 members when it was organized.

In 1851 John Lloyd was called as the church's first pastor. Since the congregation was small, it could not sustain a pastor on its own. Therefore,

*Peniel Church.
Nelson's Congregational church was built in 1876.
Summer services are still held here and its annual
Gymanfa Ganu always fills the church.*

John Lloyd also worked as a shoemaker in the village of Nelson. He remained until 1860 when he moved to Palmyra, Ohio. Rev. Cadwalader Jones ministered there for two years, before moving to Cal Valley, Illinois. In 1862 Rev. James Williams of Minersville, Pennsylvania was ordained to minister to the church.

By 1876 the church had outgrown the old meeting house. Rev. Griffith Jones, who was then the pastor, had a reputation for raising funds to build new churches, having done so in other parts of the county. Under his direction a new church, 55 x 34, was built immediately adjacent to the old structure at the cost of $6,000 and was known as Peniel Church. Peniel was the place where Jacob wrestled with God (Genesis 32:30).

The former church was converted into a private residence which it remained until destroyed by fire on March 28, 1946. Pictures of the old church can be seen in the present church's basement.

Peniel Church rests on the stone foundation erected by James T. Jones (1826-1912) who is buried in the church yard. On a small stone at the rear left-hand side of the building is chiseled "1876–J T J." The new church had kerosene lamps for lights, sturdy wooden pews, and an elaborately bound Welsh Bible which sat on the pulpit. Four stained-glass windows graced the sides of the sanctuary and on the ceiling were two panels with paintings, one of the Holy Bible opened and the other of the ten commandments. In the basement were other pews and an organ where club meetings were held around a wood stove.

Griffith Jones was succeeded in the pulpit first by Rev. John Lally who served seven years, then by Rev. C. D. Jones who remained 18 months, and finally by Rev. Benjamin H. Williams who stayed for seven years. During these pastorates the church had approximately 200 members.

In November, 1891 Rev. Richard Hughes assumed the pulpit. He had been born in Anglesey, North Wales in 1861, and immigrated to America in 1883. Prior to coming to Nelson, Rev. Hughes had been pastor in Holland Patent and Trenton.

Rev. John M. Jones came to the church from Newfoundland in 1903. At the time of his ministry the church had a membership of 136, with 54 children in the Sunday School.

The members of the church came from great distances for the services which took place both in the morning and evening. In the winter months, on Wednesday afternoons a literary meeting was held at the church and on the Friday afternoon before a communion service a preparatory meeting took place. Prayer meetings were also held during the week at various members' homes.

John M. Jones remained as pastor for a number of years. The ministers who followed him included Revs. John M. Pritchard, W. Alun Roberts and John Roberts.

Beginning in 1919 the church abandoned the use of Welsh in its services. Despite the use of English, membership continued to decline, so that by 1930 there were but a score still attending. In 1925 the Cemetery Association was officially incorporated so that an organization could maintain the graves should the church not survive.

Two of the most important events in the church's year were the Eisteddfod and the Gymanfa Ganu. The Eisteddfod took place once a year in the fall. Prizes were given for the best solos, duets, instrumental music, choir singing, and literary efforts. This annual event was discontinued in the mid 1920s.

On August 9, 1931 during the pastorate of Alun Roberts, the first Old Home Day was observed. Old Home Day is a time when relatives of those buried in the cemetery and others return to remember their loved ones. The guest speaker on that first Old Home Day was a former pastor, Rev. John M. Pritchard, assisted by Rev. R. W. Hughes of Bethesda Church in Utica. After 1931 services were only held during the summer.

In the early 1930s Rev. Davies was the last regularly installed minister to serve the church. When Davis moved to Iowa, the pulpit was supplied for a time by Rev. Alun Roberts and then by Rev. Lewis Powell, pastor of the United Methodist Church in Morrisville.

In 1950 the church became a community church, serving the neighborhood and surrounding environs during the summer months.

In the mid-1950s the old kerosene lamps were removed and replaced with electric lights. Other renovations were also performed at that time. The church's preachers included Dr. R. Glynne Lloyd and Rev. Robert J. Thomas.

Over the last 20 years or more Rev. Robert J. Knapp, now pastor of the Madison Baptist Church, has preached at the annual Old Home Day service. Even during the years he lived in the southern part of the state he would still return for the event. The Old Home Day service culminates the summer services held at the church. It is always held on the Sunday following Labor Day. A church supper prepared by the women of the church is served in the basement following the service.

One of the most bizarre incidents I have ever experienced occurred at an Old Home Day service during the late 1980s. My father and I arrived at the church to find a number of anxious women from the St. David's Choir standing on the steps. "There's a lady who's taken ill," said one. "We're waiting for the medics," said another.

Inside, the church was full, but an elderly lady lay motionless on a pew as a man attempted to perform CPR on her. A concerned daughter looked on. All around this tragic scene people chatted, seemingly unaware of the gravity of the situation, waiting for the service to begin. After more than 15 minutes, two men from the local fire department arrived dressed in full firefighting gear, including rubber boots and fireproof jackets. The firefighters had to excuse themselves past the chatting churchgoers, some of whom looked slightly annoyed at being asked to move. After the motionless woman was removed and a moment of silence was observed, the service began. It was an Old Home Day I shall never forget.

West Eaton

At the same time the Welsh settled in Nelson, some also settled in West Eaton in the town of Eaton, which immediately adjoins Nelson. West Eaton was at one time also known as Leeville, named after Philip Lee who operated a tavern there, perhaps the tavern built in 1831 which still stands in the center of the hamlet.

Many of the Calvinistic Methodists worshiped with the Congregationalists in the village in a "union church." They did not have an actual church structure; instead they met in private homes. The Calvinistic Methodists withdrew from this arrangment in 1851 and joined Capel Bach in Nelson. It should be noted that the Welsh population of West Eaton during the 1850s was equal to, if not larger than, that in Nelson.

West Eaton's Welsh Congregationalists were ministered to for a time by Rev. John Lloyd at the home of Edward Lewis. Thereafter this small congregation dissolved. There was also a settlement of Welsh around Williams Corners in the town of Eaton. These Welshmen also preferred to attend services in Nelson.

Chapter VII

Rome and Vicinity

WILLIAM FLOYD, a descendant of seventeenth-century Welsh immigrants, was a signer of the Declaration of Independence and a large landowner in Oneida County. He resided in what is now the hamlet of Westernville until his death in 1821. Despite his vast holdings and his heritage, Floyd did not attract many of his fellow countrymen to settle on his land surrounding the city of Rome. In fact, the Welsh did not begin to settle in Rome until the mid-nineteenth century.

The Welsh community in Rome was predated by the settlement in nearby Camroden, located in the town of Floyd (named for William Floyd). Welsh settlers of both Rome and Camroden are buried in the Wright Settlement Cemetery which is situated between the two communities on Wright Settlement Road.

Once established, Rome's Welsh community provided assistance to the small rural Welsh churches which had sprung up north of the city. These were established at Delta in the town of Lee, and on Quaker Hill, Mullen Hill, Webster Hill, and Western Hill—all in the town of Western. To the southeast of Rome, the small Calvinistic Methodist church in Oriskany was connected, at various times, with both Rome and Camroden.

For many years Rome had both men's and women's lodges of the Order of American True Ivorites, a Welsh benevolent organization. A St. David's Society also existed there for many years. Today, while there are no longer any such organizations in Rome, there are many who are of Welsh descent and who are now members of the St. David's Society of Utica.

Camroden

One of the Welsh chapels which has always intrigued me is the "Little White Church on the Corner" in Camroden. It was here that my grandfather began preaching while he was a Hamilton College student. It was also here that I attended one of my first Gymanfas at a Welsh Day service.

I will never forget one fall day, when I was a Hamilton student, leaving the bustle of the college campus and driving toward the town of Floyd for a Welsh Day service at Camroden. It was a gorgeous fall day and the leaves were at their peak. Not knowing where Camroden was located, except that it was in the town of Floyd, I headed for the countryside looking for signs to direct me to the small hamlet. As it became later and later, my speed increased until I was flying across the rolling countryside. Then, suddenly there it was, the "Little White Church" surrounded by cars parked along the highway. I slipped into one of the hard back pews. The red leaves waved at the window as we sang old hymns, our voices carrying us back 100 years to the time when the church was the center of a small vital hamlet.

Three churches once stood within a mile of Camroden. There were two stores, two sawmills, a post office, a blacksmith shop and a large tannery. The hamlet, located three miles north of Floyd Corners, had originally been known as Bacon's Hill. Over time the Welsh began to settle on the hill, while the English Yankees settled in the hamlet of Floyd. The first Welsh settlers in the area were Nathanial Davies and his wife from Carmarthenshire. They arrived around 1800. In 1830 Owen Evans settled in the area along with many other Welsh immigrants. He suggested that the name be changed to Cymmrodorian, which means the place of Welsh comrades. Over the years the name was corrupted into Camroden.

Congregational Church

Camroden's "Welsh Hill" was a very closed society. The Welsh settlers attempted to keep the area solely Welsh so that their traditions and language would be maintained. The new immigrants had no desire to assimilate.

The first church in the area was an English language Baptist Church founded in 1807. As the Welsh were not inclined to worship in English, many traveled as far away as Utica for services.

In 1834 a Welsh union church was erected north of Camroden's "four corners." It was located on the west side of the Floyd-Camroden Road below the intersection with Price Road. All the denominations worshiped together in this church, which was painted red and thus was known as Capel Goch or Red Chapel. In 1839 both the Congregational and Calvinistic Methodist Churches were formed out of this union church, with the Methodists moving down the hill to the four corners.

During the 1830s and 1840s the Congregational Church was served by Revs. Hugh Lewis, Edward Blunt and John Edwards. In 1855 the Congregationalists moved to a new building slightly south and across the street from the old structure. Their church was referred to as the Upper Church to distinguish it from the Methodist Church at the foot of the hill.

Rev. R. D. Thomas (Iorthryn Gwynedd) was pastor of the Upper Church in 1856 and 1857, the same year he also served the Welsh Congregational Church in Rome. I recently received a letter from Gwawr Jones of Bangor, North Wales, who is related to both Owen Baxter of the Salem Church in New York Mills and Rev. R. D. Thomas. She indicated that Rev. Thomas had come to America in 1855 with his wife Sarah Roberts Thomas and their children. During his stay in Oneida County two of his children died and they are buried in the Wright Settlement Cemetery. When he left Oneida County he went to New York City to take the pastorate of its Welsh Congregational Church. He also served at Congregational churches in Mahanoy City, Pennsylvania, Knoxville, Tennessee, and in Columbus, Ohio.

After Thomas, Rev. Edward M. Jones was the next pastor. Rev. John R. Griffith, who resided in the hamlet, succeeded Jones in 1868 and served until his death in 1887. During the 1870s the church had a membership of 64 and a congregation of 108.

The Congregational Church survived until 1920 when it was disbanded. At that time, some of the remaining members joined and revitalized the Calvinistic Methodist Church.

It is interesting to note that the second structure erected by the Congregational Church looked identical to the present Presbyterian Church located at Camroden's "four corners." Obviously, the latter structure, built in 1863, was an attempt by the Calvinistic Methodists to copy the Upper Church.

Calvinistic Methodist

The Calvinistic Methodist Church was organized in 1839 out of the union church. Rev. Henry Rees and Rev. Moses Parry, commissioners from the church in Wales to the church in America, were present at the organizational meeting held at the home of William Owens. Rees and Parry, two prominent ministers from Bala, North Wales, had been sent to America to strengthen and encourage Calvinistic Methodist churches in this country. They witnessed 12 persons join together to form the Calvinistic Methodist Society of Camroden.

The Society erected its first church in 1840 at Camroden's "four corners," on the site of the present structure. In the late 1840s Hugh Roberts of Wisconsin became pastor. He later moved to Radnor, Ohio. In 1850 the New York State Gymanfa meeting was held at Camroden, but since the church was so small, services had to be moved into a nearby field.

Original Calvinistic Methodist Church
The Calvinistic Methodist Church in Camroden was erected in 1840. It was moved to its present location in 1863 and was a post office for many years.

One of the most important citizens of Camroden during the mid-nineteenth century was John Edwards (Eos Glan Twrch, or Nightingale of the Vale of Twrch) a renowned Welsh-American poet. Edwards was born in North Wales in 1807 and immigrated to America in 1829. After living in both New York City and Utica he purchased a farm in Floyd in 1842. He was a good friend of Dr. William Rowlands and helped him form the Calvinistic Methodist Church in Rome.

Edwards died in 1887 and is buried in the Wright Settlement Cemetery. Though one of the greatest Welsh-American poets, he has been all but forgotten because his writings are in Welsh. His great-granddaughter still resides in Rome.

Rev. Thomas T. Evans began to preach in Camroden in 1855. He had previously been associated with the Congregational denomination. He remained until 1870 when he moved to Holland Patent to assume the pulpit of its Calvinistic Methodist church. It was during his tenure at Camroden that the church's membership was at its height.

By 1863 the congregation, which numbered some 200 people, had outgrown its 1840 church. The old church was sold to Richard M. Williams, the postmaster, who then moved the church to land east of the present church where it became a post office in 1872 and remained so for many years. The building has now been converted into a private residence.

The present church was constructed in 1863 by Humphrey Williams and John J. Vaughan of Remsen. The new structure, which had a balcony, could hold 200 people. Whether or not the interior of this church was identical to that of the Congregational Church I do not know. During this time (1856-1867), Camroden and Rome shared a minister. In 1857 Richard W. Jones was ordained at Rome. He supplied the churches in Camroden and Holland Patent as well as Rome.

By the early 1870s the congregation had declined to 100 with an actual membership of just 37. From 1877 to 1883 Rev. David M. Jones was the minister before he moved to Wisconsin. During the latter half of the nineteenth century, Camroden shared its pastor with Oriskany. The preacher would conduct services in Oriskany in the morning and in Camroden in the afternoon. Rev. Benjamin D. Davies was the last person to divide his time between these two churches.

Rev. J. Rhiwen Williams, the minister at the Calvinistic Methodist Church in Rome, also served in Camroden for six years from 1898 to 1904. By 1910 the church had only 23 members. Rev. Benjamin D. Davies returned as pastor from 1912 to 1914, followed by Dr. Robert T. Roberts of Rome from 1915 to 1921.

In 1922 my grandfather, Jay Gomer Williams, was a junior at Hamilton College. He was a slightly older student, having decided to attend college after serving in World War I. He did so for the express purpose of entering the ministry. His college yearbook notes that he was "another of those who worry about the souls of their roommates."

Jay Williams was called to his first ministerial assignment at Camroden in 1922. At that time membership had declined to six. From June 1922 through September 1923 he preached at Camroden, breathing new life into the church. Part of his success was that, although he was fluent in Welsh, he preached in English. He also organized the Sunday School and attracted children of recent Polish immigrants who had settled in the area.

In September of 1923 Robert T. Roberts returned briefly. He and my grandfather arranged to have Rev. William T. Griffith hold services in English on Sunday afternoons. Rev. Griffith was the father of Emlyn Griffith, who is currently a Rome attorney, a New York State Regent, and a past President of the National Welsh American Foundation. Prior to Rev. Griffith accepting the assignment, my grandfather insisted that he promise to continue to conduct services in English.

During the 1930s the church had a special member of the congregation. The Evans family, who lived nearby, had an old collie named Skip. Regardless of whether or not the Evanses attended on any particular Sunday, Skip would enter the church each week, walk one third of the way down the left aisle and lie down. Surely this was the most pious dog in the county.

Rev. Griffith yoked the Camroden and Westernville parishes and continued conducting services for the next eighteen years. Mr. and Mrs. Griffith organized the ladies' "Helping Hands Society" which aided both the church and community, especially during World War II.

Rev. David C. Davies succeeded Rev. Griffith and served until August 1957. The end of his ministry was marked by a decline in the church. The church school ceased to exist because of a lack of students and services were limited to the summer months. By the beginning of 1962, the Utica Presbytery was ready to close the church, but Rev. Charles Leport of the First Presbyterian Church in Rome and Rev. Griffith joined togther to bring the church back to life. Rev. Griffith came out of semi-retirement and on Easter Sunday in 1962 the church held its first service in months. Slowly, the average attendance rose from 20 to 40 and the church school was reorganized.

In the summer of 1962 electricity was installed in the church along with a new furnace. Bathroom facilities were also constructed. In the sanctuary the ceiling was lowered and the balcony was sealed off. The two large cast iron stoves which had been in the sanctuary were removed. To the east of the church a dining facility was built. Mead Hall was officially dedicated on October 14, 1963. These many renovations were of course very costly and could not have been accomplished but for a donation of $10,000 from Bethel Presbyterian Church in Rome.

On October 6, 1963 the "Little White Church on the Corner" celebrated its 125th anniversary as a revitalized church. During the next 25 years the church continued, occasionally having Old Home Days or Welsh Day services in October. Throughout that time, Mr. and Mrs. William K. Henry were influential members of the congregation and instrumental in keeping the church going.

It was at one of those Welsh Day services in the mid-1970s that I last saw Rev. Griffith, shortly before his death in 1978. He had preached at least once every month until he was 91 in 1975. On that Sunday he was honored with a portrait which still hangs in the parish hall. The distinguished gentleman rose in his seat and addressed the congregation, proud in his accomplishment of saving the small church.

Camroden Presbyterian Church.
The "Little White Church on the Corner" was erected in 1863.
It is one of the few former Welsh churches still active in Oneida County.

In 1987 the Camroden Presbyterian Church, as it is now known, observed its sesquicentennial. This event featured the St. David's Choir from Utica. Also, a hymn which I composed for the occasion entitled "Camroden" was sung. Emlyn Griffith spoke about the church's history.

At this celebration, a number of descendants of former members returned. Descendants from the original twelve families and my family were each called outside in turn to have their picture taken by Bill and Jim Griffith, grandsons of Rev. Griffith. The organist that day was Clarice Koziara, a sixth generation member of the church. Edwin C. Evans, great-grandson of Owen Evans, who named the hamlet, was present as well.

In 1987 Rev. JoAnn Watson was pastor and conducted Sunday evening services. David Loper, (husband of Susan Loper, the last minister of Capel

Cerrig) served the church for a time, yoking it with the Presbyterian church at North Gage. Today the church's congregation is very small with only about a dozen persons attending the weekly summer services. Winter services have again been discontinued.

The original Calvinistic Methodist Church has been converted into a house and stands adjacent to the present church. For years Humphrey Morris lived in the house. He was the nephew of a prominent Welsh businessman in Rome and was well known in the hamlet. The old man never had a car and was famous for walking everywhere. Recently, it has been said that the old man, now long deceased, has been seen walking silently up his driveway. As with so many of the Welsh communities of Central New York, it appears that soon all that will remain of Camroden will be its ghosts.

Rome

Bethel

The Welsh community in Rome has always been special to me, because it was in Bethel that my great-grandfather was an elder and lay preacher, and my grandfather was an organist and later ordained into the ministry. Many of my Williams relatives still live in Rome.

The Rome Calvinistic Methodist Church was organized by William Williams when there were only two Welsh families in the city: those of William Williams and Hugh Williams. The church began when the two families joined to worship at the William Williams' home altar. On December 6, 1841 ten people were present when Rev. William Rowlands first preached to the congregation. In that year, the church was formally organized and William Williams and William N. Jones became the first elders.

In 1842 the society learned that the English-speaking Second Congregational Church in Rome was for sale. It was located on the west side of North Washington Street between Court and Liberty Streets. In 1847 this frame building was formally dedicated and in 1848 the church officially incorporated. By the 1850s the church had 70 members.

During those early years Rev. John H. Jones conducted the weekly services. He began to preach in 1858 but was not officially ordained until 1867. He spent his entire career preaching in the Oneida Presbytery circuits. His death occurred in 1920. During those early years of Bethel's history, Rev. Richard W. Jones and Rev. Thomas Williams served as supply pastors. Rev. James Lamb came to Rome in 1864 and supplied at Bethel and other area churches. He had been a pastor in Cattaragus County, then returned to Wales for a period of time before coming to Rome. Rev. Lamb died in Liverpool, England in 1889.

In 1883 the church moved to the corner of Turin and Washington Streets where a new brick building was constructed. The old structure was sold to E. C. Griddel and George Scott for $3,500. In 1889 the church called its first regular pastor, Robert Williams, from Wales and he served until 1897.

Bethel Presbyterian Church.
A fine steeple once graced the front of this former church which was built in 1883. Unfortunately, a fire destroyed much of the structure in 1971.

Bethel was always full of activity with three services on Sundays. Prayer meetings were held every Tuesday evening, Bible class was every Thursday, and there was a missionary meeting on the first Monday of every month. One of the outstanding features of the church was the "Seiat y Wlad" ("the County Class Meeting") which was held at two o'clock in the afternoon on the last Thursday of each month. The purpose of this meeting was to allow members who lived at too great a distance to attend regular Sunday services to have the opportunity to participate in a monthly prayer meeting. This practice was followed for over half a century.

The church used the "call and answer" method for raising funds. Under this system, when a member's name was called by the "collector," he would answer with the amount of his pledge. The amount would then be entered in the account book by the "recorder." Although this specific practice was eventually abandoned, a pamphlet was printed yearly with the amount of each member's donation until the end of the church's existence.

One of the most important members of the church was the leader of the singing. For many years Meredith Pugh, a well-known and respected person in the area, filled this position. He later selected William G. Jones to succeed him. Mr. Jones, a local mason known affectionately by the children as Uncle Bill, led the singing until he was a very old man.

Rev. Robert Williams was followed by Rev. John Rhiwen Williams who served from 1898 until 1904. Like his predecessor he came directly from Wales. He also served Camroden during his tenure. His other pastorates included Providence, Kingston, Wind Gap, Olyphant, and Wilkes-Barre in Pennsylvania and Fair Haven in Vermont. He died in 1928.

Rev. Edward Lewis Hughes followed and was pastor from 1904 until 1912. It was during his pastorate that the church first introduced English at one service per month. The decision to introduce English was a hard one and caused heated debates among the members. One of the reasons for introducing English was to help retain the younger members, many of whom were not fluent in Welsh. The more conservative members argued that if English were introduced the children would lose the language.

The Sunday School was the place where the Welsh language was passed on to the younger generation. In fact, Welsh was the language used in Sunday School until the second decade of the twentieth century. Children were given Welsh primers in the same manner as they were given English ones at school during the week.

Children were immersed in Welsh and in the activities of the church. During the year children were expected to observe strictly the Sabbath, with play on Sundays prohibited. Children, however, had little time for themselves on Sundays. They not only would attend Sunday School but often went to two services at 10:30 a.m. and 7:00 p.m. In addition they were involved throughout the year in rehearsals for various pageants and events. The high point of the Sunday School year was rally day when recitations were performed, prizes were given and Bibles were awarded.

E. L. Hughes left Rome in 1912 and moved to Detroit, Michigan where he became a probation officer. From time to time he returned to Rome and preached.

Dr. Robert Thomas Roberts arrived in Rome in 1913. Like many Welsh in the area he came from Aberdaron in North Wales. He had served in Racine, Wisconsin and Wilkes-Barre, Pennsylvania before coming to Rome. Mary Downing, a former member of Bethel, has said that, to the children who spent their lives at the church, Dr. Roberts with his beautiful white hair and forceful presence in the pulpit must have seemed a perfect vision of the Almighty. He continued in the pulpit until his death in 1927.

In the 1920s, when the Calvinistic Methodist Church merged with the Presbyterian Church, the Rome church became known as Bethel Presbyterian Church. Prior to this time the church was known first as the Welsh Calvinistic Methodist Church and then as the Welsh Presbyterian Church. At the time the church had one English service each week. The morning and evening services alternated weekly between Welsh and English.

The elders of the church held a position of importance that was even more elevated than that of the minister. They were the decision makers and soul of the church. As such, they commanded great respect from the congregation. The elders also looked after the individual members of the congregation in a spiritual sense which would be unthinkable today. Mary Downing tells the story of her mother's final illness when she was only ten years old. Her mother, dying of cancer, lay on a couch in the front parlor. One night the elders, including my great-grandfather, called at the door. Dressed in their dark suits, the elders entered one by one and knelt by the dying woman's side and prayed for God to return her to health. Such a powerful image conveys the spirit and faith of the Welsh and the position of the elders in a Welsh church.

Rev. Caradoc Phillips Williams came to Rome from Wales to succeed Dr. Roberts. He remained as pastor until he returned to Wales in 1931. In that year the church officially incorporated as Bethel Presbyterian Church. During the 1920s or 1930s the frosted glass windows were replaced with stained-glass windows. One of those windows was dedicated to my great-grandparents, John S. and Elizabeth Williams. The window depicted the Lord as the Good Shepherd. At the dedication of the windows Rev. Richard J. Williams of Scranton, Pennsylvania, son of Rev. J. Rhiwen Williams spoke and likened John S. Williams' beginnings as a farmer to the nurturing of the Shepherd. He also spoke about the window with Christ Knocking on the Door, indicating that Christ knocks on all our doors but it is up to us to accept him.

After Rev. Williams left in 1931, Rev. Walter H. Jones became the next pastor. He was the last moderator of the Oneida (Welsh) Presbytery. In turn, he was succeeded in the pulpit by Rev. William Eilian Davies.

In 1950 Caradoc Williams returned to Rome from Wales and once again was called to lead Bethel. He was to be its last Welsh minister. In the 1940s the Sunday morning services in Welsh had given way to services in English. Rev. Caradoc Williams, however, continued the tradition of holding Sunday evening services in Welsh and did so until his departure in 1964. In that year he returned to Wales.

Bethel struggled to survive during the next few years and was served by Rev. Wilford Hasbrouck on an interim basis. It was also supplied by many lay preachers. The Presbytery worked hard to care for the church and to see that preachers attended to it.

Finally, in 1971, the church's 70 to 75 members decided it was time to close Bethel's doors. Mary Williams, as President of the Trustees, led negotiations with the Rome Masonic Temple for the sale of the building.

While final legal arrangements were being made for the transfer, the church was damaged by a severe fire. The fire destroyed much of the church's sanctuary and the Good Shepherd window was shattered in the blaze.

The congregation met at the Masonic Temple while the final dissolution arrangements were made. The pews in the undamaged Sunday School were sold to another church, the three pulpit chairs made their way to Mary Downing's shed. At last the church disbanded, but the official dissolution did not come until 1972.

The Welsh church did not officially merge with the First Presbyterian Church but about 50 of Bethel's members joined the church. Bethel's communion set and Bibles were placed in a glass case in the First Presbyterian Church, near its small chapel.

When the Bethel Church finally dissolved, its endowment and the proceeds from its fire insurance settlement and sale of its building were transferred to the First Presbyterian Church. This formed the seed for the Presbyterian Church's own endowment fund. In recognition of this contribution, the church renamed its chapel "Bethel Chapel" and allowed the Welsh to meet there.

For many years the chapel was unused, opened only for showing films. I do recall an occasion in the late 1970s when I attended a Gymanfa Ganu there with my grandmother. At that occasion my father preached and an organ was dedicated in honor of my step-grandfather, Luther E. Olson, who was a pillar of the First Presbyterian Church, but did not have a drop of Welsh blood in him.

In 1984 the Bethel Chapel became the home for a mission of the Korean Church in Syracuse. This group uses the chapel for Sunday morning services and for a weekday prayer meeting. Most of the members are wives of Air Force personnel stationed at Griffiss Air Force Base. In 1993 it applied for admission to the Utica Presbytery as Immanuel Presbyterian Church.

Since 1971 an annual Welsh Heritage Sunday has been held at Rome's First Presbyterian Church to honor the former Bethel Church. Daffodils are placed on the communion table, Welsh hymns are sung, and the Welsh flag is displayed prominently. In 1992 I had the pleasure of preaching at the Welsh Heritage service. As I looked out at the congregation I wondered how many people were actually of Welsh descent. Over tea and Welsh cakes after the service everyone seemed to have a story to tell about their Welsh heritage or about some Welsh person they remembered. Indeed, as I left the church that Sunday, it seemed that the entire congregation had felt Welsh, even if just for that morning.

Rehobeth

There were always good relations between the two Welsh churches in Rome. The Calvinistic Methodist Church was referred to as the Upper Church. This was ostensibly a geographical designation, though some in the older and larger church may have felt the term to be a sign of superiority. In contrast, the Congregational Church was known as "Capel Bach" or the Small Church.

The Welsh Congregationalists in Rome originally worshiped with the Calvinistic Methodists. However, in 1850 they began to meet in a school they had purchased from the First Presbyterian Church. On August 10, 1851, 19 persons gathered to form the Welsh Congregational Church with Rev. Thomas Jones as their first pastor. Soon thereafter they moved from the schoolhouse to a more convenient location on the north side of Liberty Street between George and Madison Streets.

During 1856 and 1857 the church shared its pastor, R. D. Thomas, with the Camroden Congregational Church. He later published *Hanes Cymry America*, one of the most complete histories of Welsh-Americans ever written.

During the 1860s, the church had become very weak and nearly closed. With the arrival of Rev. David E. Pritchard as the new pastor in 1864, the church's situation improved considerably. Rev. Pritchard had served the Welsh Congregational Church in Turin before being called to Rome. Under his guidance the Rome church slowly recovered its vitality so that by 1878 it had 48 members. Rev. Pritchard remained in the pulpit until 1893. Throughout the three decades in which he served the congregation, Rev. Pritchard had definitely been the church's driving force.

In 1879 the church exchanged its building on Liberty Street with the then Court Street Methodist Church. The Court Street Methodist Church became known as the Liberty Street Methodist Church until it moved again and became Calvary Methodist. The Court Street structure had been erected in 1863. It served the Welsh Congregational Church for the remainder of its history.

The next person to serve the congregation of Capel Bach was Rev. Morien Mon Hughes. He had been born in 1857 in Anglesey, North Wales, and assumed the position at Rome in 1894. At that time services at the church were being conducted in both English and Welsh. Rev. Hughes also preached at many of the rural Welsh churches before, during, and after his stay in Rome. He, like many of the Welsh clergy, was a staunch supporter of the temperance movement. Twice in the 1890s he ran as the Prohibition Party's candidate for the New York State Assembly.

Rehobeth.
The present Trinity United Church of Christ was once the home of the Welsh Congregational Church. The structure was erected in 1863 and served the Welsh from 1870 to 1927.

Another Hughes, Rev. Richard Hughes, served as pastor from 1900 to 1904. He was followed by R. Eifion Jones. In 1914 Rev. Caradog Jones came to Capel Bach and as it so happened he would be its last minister. During this time the church was known for its great suppers and its joint activities with Bethel. The children of the two churches frequently joined for singing and pageants.

Near the end of its existence, the church underwent a great debate regarding what name should be given the chapel. After much discussion the name Rehobeth was adopted. Shortly thereafter, in 1927, the church disbanded. Many of its members joined Bethel Presbyterian Church.

Over the years Bethel and Rehobeth had been known for their mutual cooperation, a characteristic not found in many Welsh communities. In 1854 a number of Welsh people from the two churches organized the Bible Society of Rome and Vicinity. Its first officers were President Rev. William Rowlands, Secretary William N. Jones, and Treasurer Robert Meredith. The Society lasted well into the twentieth century.

In 1928 the The United German Evangelical Lutheran Church moved from South James and Ridge Street to the 215 West Court Street site. The church was rededicated on April 15, 1928. In 1934 the congregation became part of the Evangelical and Reformed Church which became a part of the United Church of Christ in 1962. The church is now known as Trinity. A picture of the Welsh congregation still hangs in the church.

Delta

Delta was a small village located north of Rome between the towns of Western and Lee. In 1912 it was flooded to create Delta Lake. I had a great-aunt who was raised in Delta and I was always intrigued to think that her house and the entire village lay under the lake, swept away as if by the Great Flood.

It is said that very dangerous whirlpools and currents exist over those places where the houses once stood. When the lake was drained in the 1980s during the repair of the dam, the outlines of Delta's streets were plainly visible, the tree stumps and the foundations still remaining.

For a brief time in the early 1840s Delta had a Calvinistic Methodist church which held services and a Sunday School. In 1843 the Sunday School had eight officers and 35 pupils. Humphrey Jones moved to Delta in 1847 and shortly thereafter worship services were held for a season at his house. The next year these "house" services were discontinued, and Mr. Jones and the other members of the small congregation decided to attend services in Rome.

Oriskany

In 1840 a Welsh Calvinistic Methodist church was formed in the village of Oriskany. Eleven years later the congregation erected a church on the corner of Charlotte and Main Streets. In the early 1860s the Welsh purchased the old Methodist Episcopal Church located on Utica Street, one lot north of the intersection with Dexter Street.

Oriskany Welsh Church.
This two-family house was once Oriskany's Welsh church.
This was the second structure used by the society.

The church was small with only about 30 members. It was served by supply pastors and was part of the circuit which at times included Rome and Camroden. The association with Camroden lasted from 1867 to 1904. Services were held in Oriskany in the morning and Camroden in the afternoon. Thomas T. Evans was the first pastor to minister to both churches. Rev. Benjamin D. Davies, who came to the county in 1887, was one of the ministers who preached in Oriskany and is the pastor most often associated with the church. The Oriskany church was later yoked with Bethel in Rome during the tenure of Rev. E. L. Hughes.

In 1909 the church had 36 members. Within a few years, however, the society dissolved and the property was transferred to the Waterbury Presbyterian Church in Oriskany. In 1936 the structure was sold to Leonard Pugh. Today, the church has been converted into a two-family house.

Quaker Hill

Quaker Hill is one of the most beautiful areas of Oneida County. It is located among the hills in the northwest corner of the town of Western and at one time had both a church and a small school. While the church has been gone for nearly ninety years, the District 7 school stood until December 1968 when it was destroyed by fire. The nearest hamlet to Quaker Hill is West Branch in the town of Lee. Since West Branch is located on Turin Road, it was there that the early settlers went to get supplies, to collect their mail and to exchange gossip. My great-great-grandfather, Peter Ruff (a German Quaker), moved to Quaker Hill from West Branch in 1860 to escape the corrupting influences and crowding of the latter. Anyone familiar with the size of West Branch should find his reasons for moving amusing.

A society of "Friends" had been in existence on Quaker Hill since before 1810, and it was this small congregation which gave the area its name. In the early 1800s a Quaker meeting house was constructed on the corner of what are today known as Quaker Hill Road and Krzewinski Road. Some years later when a new meeting hall was constructed in West Branch, the old meeting house was sold to a small society of Welsh Calvinistic Methodists. Because it was constructed as a meeting house it looked more like a school than a church.

The Welsh society was formed when Thomas V. Jones came to the Hill from the area of the Penygraig Church in Remsen in 1844. Its first elder was Edward Lewis who lived on the now abandoned portion of Krzewinski Road. Edward Roberts followed Mr. Lewis in the position of elder.

In 1850 the society purchased the old meeting house and shortly thereafter began using the rear of the property as a small cemetery. At the chapel's dedication there were to have been two services, but a tremendous thunderstorm forced the cancellation of the second afternoon service.

Soon after the church opened, many of the farms surrounding the church were purchased by Welsh settlers. By 1872 the church had 24 members.

One of the leaders of the church was John E. Jones, known as John Jones "pumpkin hook." He was given that name because he lost one hand which was replaced by a hook. The story goes that he used that hook to pick pumpkins which grew on his farm, hence the name. The area where he lived, immediately behind the church on what is now Krzewinski Road, became known as "pumpkin hook." The last will and testament of Peter Ruff, who had been the original owner of the present Krzewinski farm, was witnessed by John E. Jones and another John Jones.

During its history, the Quaker Hill church was served by local circuit ministers representing various denominations. The church was the focus of the area's social life for both Welsh and non-Welsh. On Sunday evenings the little church would invite the neighborhood families to share supper and have a community meeting. In the summer these community suppers were often held on the lawn. My grandmother, Mary Craig Olson, was one of the non-Welsh neighbors who shared in those gatherings.

Quaker Hill Cemetery.
This cemetery is located on Krzewinski Road, near Quaker Hill Road.
The first burial was in 1851 and the last in 1902.

In the early 1900s membership at the Welsh church had greatly declined. Edward Lewis passed away on January 7, 1899 at the age of 88. John Jones, "pumpkin hook," also passed away in 1899 at the age of 77 and his wife followed in 1902. With the death of its leaders the church building was abandoned and eventually fell down. Today the cemetery remains as the sole reminder of this small isolated community. Though more than 50 people are buried in the cemetery, only a dozen or so headstones remain, many in memory of infant children of the church's members.

Webster Hill

In the northwesternmost section of the town of Western is Webster Hill. At the corner of Sage Road and Webster Hill Road is a lush green field overlooking the hills of the township and this is where the Webster Hill church is located.

Webster Hill Church.
This former church is located on Sage Road in the town of Western. Constructed in 1877, it served as a church until 1920.

In 1832 John T. Jones immigrated from Anglesey, North Wales where he had been an elder of a Calvinistic Methodist church. This prior experience made him a good candidate for helping organize the Webster Hill society. Many years passed, however, before the society actually built its church structure, which was done in 1877.

It is not clear who served as pastor for the church from that date until the turn of the century. What is known is that Rev. David Jones was received as pastor at another church, at which occasion it was said that he came from Webster Hill.

At one time the church shared its minister, Rev. J. W. Roberts, with the Methodist churches at North Steuben and North Western. Rev. Morien Mon Hughes, who had been the Congregational minister in Rome, became a Calvinistic Methodist minister from 1899 to 1911. During that time he preached at Webster Hill.

In 1905 the church changed its services from Welsh to English to attract members. However, the church was located in such a remote area that the membership continued to decline. In 1920 the church was dissolved and the property turned over to the New York Gymanfa. For years the church building has been used as a farm storage shed. The interior is still covered with wallpaper and the hole which once led to a stovepipe can be seen. From the outside only an active imagination can picture the structure as it was when it served Webster Hill, Ava, and the surrounding area.

Mullen Hill

Richard R. Roberts and his wife came to the town of Western in 1865 and settled on Quaker Hill. Later they moved to Mullen Hill, which is in the southern portion of the town of Western, just north of Delta Lake. Mr. Roberts' home was located immediately to the east of where Mullen Hill Road takes a 90 degree turn toward the east.

Roberts Farm.
The farm of Richard R. Roberts was the meeting place for a Calvinistic Methodist society in the late nineteenth century.

The road up Mullen Hill is rough, but the ride is worth the effort. From the top of the hill one has a beautiful view of the lake. For many years a small community existed on the hill and there was a schoolhouse which served the children of the nearby farmers.

In 1878 the Roberts organized a Calvinistic Methodist society in their home. One year later, in February, it was received into the Oneida (Welsh) Presbytery. At this time there were a number of Welsh farmers on the hill. As the road to Quaker Hill was rough and Rome was too far away, it was very convenient for the Welsh to have a place to worship in their own neighborhood.

In 1907 Mr. Roberts was still living on the same farm and had formed a partnership in a cheese factory known as Evans and Roberts. When Mr. Roberts passed away the church did as well. It never had a structure and probably shared its minister with Quaker Hill, Webster Hill and Rome. By 1920 the farm had passed out of Welsh hands as new ethnic groups came to farm the land overlooking the valley.

Western Hill

In the 1840s the Congregationalists met on Western Hill in the town of Western, just north of Floyd. Little is known about this group but it appears that there never was an actual church structure associated with it.

Chapter VIII

Lewis County and Beyond

NORTHERN ONEIDA COUNTY AND ABOVE is affectionately known as the snow belt. As one travels north from Utica, up Deerfield Hill, through Steuben and Remsen and on towards Boonville, the population thins and the terrain becomes more rugged. Immediately above Boonville is Lewis County where winter comes early and stays late. The Tug Hill Plateau which occupies the southwestern side of the county is well known for its harsh weather. Because of its isolation it remains today much as the early settlers found it.

It took rugged individuals to farm the stony fields, log the thick woods, and work on the Black River. Among those early settlers were many Welsh. In fact, Lewis County was named in 1805 for a Welshman, New York's governor, General Morgan Lewis. He was the son of Francis Lewis, a signer of the Declaration of Independence.

While a few Welsh families settled in Lewis County in the early nineteenth century, the largest immigration occurred between 1835 and 1860. In 1842 a large number of Welsh families made the six-week journey from North Wales to New York on the sailing ship, "The Queen." Once they landed they headed north with the dream of establishing a Welsh community in Lewis County. They settled in the towns of West Turin, Leyden and Greig.

Gomer Flats

The first Welsh service in the county was held at the home of Robert Williams on the east side of the Black River, not far from Lyons Falls. There the Welsh established their own community known as "the far off woods." It was more commonly known as Gwastadedd Gomer or Gomer Flats. The name Gomer refers to one of Noah's grandsons (Genesis 10:2). An eighteenth-century Welshman theorized that the Gomer, from whom "the coastland people spread" (Genesis 10:5), was in fact the "father" of the Welsh, the Cymraig. The name Gomer was popular among the Welsh as both a personal and place name. For example, Welsh settlements in Iowa and Ohio also bear the name.

Gomer Flats, located four miles from Port Leyden, was settled by about ten families which had come to America on "The Queen" in 1842. On Sunday mornings services in the settlement were held at the home of William Davies. Gomer Flats shared a pastor in a circuit with two other churches. William Davies and John J. Williams were the church's first and only elders.

Unfortunately, there was "nothing congenial in the soil or surroundings" to induce people to locate at the settlement. Because of the adverse conditions, the settlement disbanded within three or four years. William Davies went on to become an elder in the Welsh Prairie Church at Lake Emily in Dodge County, Wisconsin.

Collinsville

The center for Welsh activities in Lewis County was the tiny hamlet of Collinsville. Even before a church was established there, Collinsville was where the Welsh of Lewis County convened to discuss matters of common concern regarding the welfare of the county's Welsh churches. The hamlet was important in the mid-nineteenth century because it was located on the route from Lyons Falls to Turin. On September 29, 1836 a Union Worship Society was formed by the English Congregationalists, Episcopalians and Baptists and in the same year the Society built a stone church.

In 1839 a number of Welsh families immigrated to Collinsville, formerly known as High Falls Village. Soon the area became so populated by the Welsh that one preacher stated Collinsville "was the Wales of Lewis County with its beautiful scenery, its climatic location unsurpassed, where the sun is always shining and the sky is always blue, the city built on the hill cannot be hid." That Welsh preacher truly had the gift of hyperbole.

When the first Welsh families arrived in Collinsville they worshiped in the stone church, but within a year these families organized their own

Calvinistic Methodist church in a schoolhouse which stood at a crossroads between Constableville and Collinsville. The Welsh from the two villages met together until 1846 when the Constableville society, at the urging of the Oneida Presbytery, constructed its own church.

Collinsville Union Church
This old stone church was the site of Welsh
worship in Collinsville in 1839.

The Welsh population of the area greatly increased in 1842 with the arrival of settlers on "The Queen." Many of the immigrants on that ship settled within a six-mile radius of Collinsville. During the years 1843 to 1845 the joint congregation worshiped both at Thomas Lewis' home located between Lyons Falls and Port Leyden and in a shop owned by William Davies. Evan Evans of Constableville was the church's first elder and Rev. Edward Rees was the preacher.

On March 13, 1848 two Calvinistic Methodist churches were officially organized: one for Collinsville and one for Constableville. The 24 members of the Collinsville church continued to worship in private homes from 1848 until a place for worship was built seven years later. During this time Rev. Thomas Williams served as pastor. In 1855 a chapel was constructed in Collinsville by Evan Jones of Remsen and was dedicated on January 1, 1856. At the same time the society was officially reorganized.

Collinsville's stone church was located on East Road, north of Route 12D. The Welsh Church was located on the same side of the road, south of the four corners, on the edge of the hamlet. Unlike many Welsh churches, it was constructed with a steeple. It was white with two tall windows flanking the central entrance. A large horse shed stood behind the church. Unfortunately, the steeple was struck by lightning and had to be removed.

By the time the chapel was completed the congregation had grown to 170 members and Collinsville had become the center for Welsh activities north of Oneida County. Like the other Lewis County Calvinistic Methodist churches it was part of the Oneida (Welsh) Presbytery. Because of Lewis County's remoteness, however, the Presbytery did not regularly travel to those churches for its meetings or Gymanfas. Therefore, as early as 1843 a Cyfarfod Pregethu or preaching festival was held in Collinsville. Every June this "big meeting" would attract Welsh from great distances. It was held in the field adjoining the church and crowds of 5,000 to 30,000 would attend the weekend's festivities and hear the great Welsh preachers.

The church's first pastor, Rev. Thomas Williams had come to America in 1845 and preached at Collinsville from 1849 to 1857. He was followed by Rev. Richard Isaac who had come to America in 1842 at the age of 22 and began preaching in 1852. He had once been a presenter, or a hymn leader, in Utica. After that he was ordained at South Trenton. Rev. Isaac served in Collinsville from 1858 to 1861 and again from 1867 to 1873. During that time he also had charge of Seion Church on Welsh Hill and the Welsh Church in Constableville. He moved to Iowa in 1874 where he died in 1892.

Rev. Daniel T. Rowlands preached at Collinsville from 1865 to 1867. Rev. Rowlands later left the Calvinistic Methodist Church and joined the Presbyterian Church. He was followed by Rev. James Jarrett from 1876 to 1881. Rev. Jarrett had immigrated to Central New York in 1870 from Pwllheli and had preached in Utica until 1875, when he began his work in Collinsville. In 1881 Rev. Jarret moved to Plymouth, Pennsylvania where he died in 1901.

After 1881 the church had numerous supply pastors including E. C. Evans of Remsen. Richard Jones, who had worked in the local blacksmith shop, began preaching in Collinsville during this time, and then went on to serve as a minister in Pennsylvania.

Until the 1880s the church's membership had been strong, but as immigration from Wales ceased and the second generation became Americanized, its ranks dwindled. At the same time, Collinsville's commercial importance vanished when the main highway was relocated, by-passing the hamlet.

As with all Welsh churches, singing was an important part of every service at Collinsville. In the early years singing schools were held by H. J. Hughes, who also compiled a book of chants. Hugh D. Jones led the singing in the church for 50 years and was known as a colorful member of the Welsh community.

By the turn of the century the church only had a dozen members. In 1903 the church dissolved and in 1904 the structure was sold to Frank Hoskin of Lyons Falls who dismantled the church and rebuilt it as a sawmill.

The old stone Union Church, where the Welsh had once met, continued as a church until the 1940s. In 1948 it was converted into a community theater for the Lyons Falls Players Guild. Then it ceased to be used at all.

Today Collinsville is a quiet collection of homes along East Road. The old stone church is hidden behind two great pine trees. A warning sign hangs on one of the front doors barring entry by Order of the Lewis County Sheriff's Department. A faded realtor's sign hangs on the other door. Inside, the interior has been gutted with a lone pew remaining along the rear wall. The pulpit has been removed to Constable Hall where it can be seen by visitors. In its place a large hole has been dug in the church's floor.

The days of Collinsville as a center of commerce and as the center of Welsh activities in Lewis County are now past, but this small hamlet's rich Welsh heritage should not be forgotten.

Constableville

Just five miles south of Collinsville on Route 26 is the village of Constableville. In 1839 a number of Welsh families from Denbighshire, North Wales, settled in Constableville, and in 1840 a Calvinistic Methodist church was formed there. As stated previously, the church was comprised of members from both Constableville and Collinsville. In 1846 Constableville formed its own society and on March 13, 1848 its church was erected on the east side of North Main Street. It was a small white frame structure with separate entrances for men and women. Though its church was erected earlier than that of its neighbor to the north, Constableville always lacked the stature of the Collinsville society.

Evan Evans was the church's first elder and was a loyal Calvinist with little tolerance for other denominations. Shortly after a Methodist-Episcopalian minister in the county had had his home destroyed by fire, he chanced to meet Mr. Evans and informed him of his misfortune. He told Evans that "the greatest loss to me was the burning of three hundred of my sermons." To this Mr. Evans replied, "Very good, very good, for they were full of errors."

In 1872 the church had only 30 members. Because of its small membership it never could support its own minister. Constableville always had to share its minister with Collinsville and the other Calvinistic Methodist churches in the county. However, Ellis R. Roberts of the Constableville Church, was received as a preacher by the Oneida Presbytery and he was ordained in 1893. Although Constableville was small, it lasted longer than any other Welsh church in Lewis County. It finally fell into disuse in the early part of this century. In 1917 it was taken down and the lumber was used to construct a cheese factory in High Market.

Turin

North of the town of West Turin, where Collinsville and Constableville are located, is the town of Turin. Today Turin is best known for the Snow Ridge ski slope. The skiing is as good as the farming is hard.

The first Welsh settlers in Turin were Baptists who came to the area in 1818. Thomas Morgan of Steuben came to Turin to minister to both the Welsh and English Baptists. The Welsh at that time were few in number and no permanent church was established.

In 1843 a Congregational church was organized by Rev. Samuel A. Williams of Deerfield and services were held at the home of Griffith Jones, located not far from the village, as well as at the house of Evan Owens. The church was officially organized on May 1, 1848 with Rev. David E. Pritchard as pastor and Robert Williams and John O. Jones as deacons. By that date it had grown to 37 members. This church was associated with the Nebo Congregational Church on nearby Welsh Hill. For a time the Turin Congregationalists met in the Old Stone School House located on the "West Road" between Turin and Constableville. Later they relocated to the "Old Academy" in the village. By 1851 services were held in the Baptist Church on State Street.

In 1864 Rev. Pritchard, who had led the church for 17 years, left to take the pulpit at the Welsh Congregational Church in Rome. In that same year the church purchased the English-speaking Baptist Church, where they had been worshiping. After Rev. Pritchard came Rev. Hugh R. Williams, followed by Rev. Owen Pitcon Jones, a young minister from Treleck, South Wales. When Rev. Jones arrived in 1872 the church had 20 members and a congregation of 60. It also had the same deacons who had served the church for almost a quarter of a century: Robert Williams and John O. Jones.

Turin Welsh Church.
This was originally Turin's Baptist Church. It was purchased by the Welsh and used by them from 1851 until the 1880s. Today it is a storage shed.

Rev. Thomas M. Owen and Rev. Thomas M. Griffith, later of Sharon, Pennsylvania continued the succession of ministers who preached at the Turin Welsh Church. As ministers came and went, one person remained a stalwart figure of the congregation: Deacon Robert Williams remained and was always the soul of the church. Not only did he travel five miles to attend. He also led the singing and was the composer of a number of hymns.

By the 1880s the church was meeting only every other Sunday. In 1885 the Turin Welsh Church closed and its members joined the area's English-speaking churches. Today the old church is used as a storage shed.

Welsh Hill

A mile outside of Turin, Gomer Hill rises into the Tug Hill Plateau. Gomer Hill is the highest point in Lewis County: 2265 feet. Although the Hill is so high that it disrupts radio signals, it is the perfect site for the Civil Aeronautic Radar Division's station which sits at its summit. The area's elevation and location make its Lewis County winters even harsher than in the surrounding towns.

The area, known both as Welsh Hill and Gomer Hill, was first settled by the Irish and Germans. They, in turn, yielded to the Welsh settlers. Eventually the Welsh gave way to the Polish and the Polish left the Hill to the woodchucks. During the years when the Welsh lived on the Hill, namely the 1840s to the 1880s, there was a sawmill, a schoolhouse and three churches (two of which were Welsh) in this remote place.

Welsh Hill Cemetery.
This cemetery served the Welsh Hill community from the 1840s to the 1880s. Rev. David E. Pritchard is buried here.

Nebo

In 1843 the Congregationalists established their church on Welsh Hill. Although it was often referred to as the Tug Hill Church its official name was Nebo. Mount Nebo was the mountain where the Lord showed Moses all the lands he would give to his descendants (Deuteronomy 34:11). The view from Welsh Hill is similarly grand and may have inspired the selection of the name. The Nebo Congregational Church was located on Lyman Road near its intersection with Gomer Hill Road. The structure was 20 x 32 and built at a cost $800.

The church's first pastor was Rev. David E. Pritchard who also served the Welsh Congregational Church in the village of Turin. Although he spent most of his career as pastor in Rome (1864-1893), Rev. Pritchard chose this area as his final resting place. He is buried in the Welsh Hill cemetery. In 1846 Rev. William D. Roberts, formerly of Bryncoch, Cemaes, Montgomeryshire, North Wales was appointed as pastor. He was paid only $20 per year in 1855 while a Presbyterian minister at a similarly sized church in the village of Turin was paid $375.

Rev. Roberts remained as the church's minister for 20 years and it is hoped that during that period his salary increased. When he died in January 1869 he was buried in the Welsh Hill cemetery. His eldest son, David W. Roberts, was deacon in the church. Another son, Rev. Thomas W. Roberts, who had been the pastor of Salem Church in New York Mills, is also buried in the cemetery. After Rev. William Roberts' death, the church shared its pastor with the Welsh Congregational Church in Turin.

The Nebo Congregational Church was more successful than its Turin counterpart and in 1872 had a congregation of 125. Nevertheless, the poor farming on the Hill forced the Welsh settlers to leave the area and by 1880 the church was disbanded.

Seion

In 1846, 14 Calvinistic Methodists formed their own church in the Welsh Hill schoolhouse. That schoolhouse still stands today and is one of the few buildings that has survived on Welsh Hill. Shortly after the society was organized, it erected a small chapel named Seion (Zion) on Gomer Hill Road, across from the cemetery. The Methodists, like the Congregationalists, named their church after a biblical hill. A local shoemaker, William D. Roberts, was one of the principal leaders of the church for many years.

Seion was always small in membership. Furthermore, its structure could not accommodate as many as Nebo. The 1855 census reports 15 members. The membership reached its peak at 40 in 1865.

The church never had its own minister. When the Valley Church closed in 1849 Seion began to share its pastor with Collinsville and Constableville. Those ministers were as follows: Rev. Thomas Williams (1849-1857), Rev. Richard Isaac (1859-1862 and 1867-73), Rev. Daniel T. Rowlands (1865-1867) and Rev. James Jarrett (1876-1881). In the 1850s the church also shared a minister with the Calvinistic Methodist Church in Holland Patent. During that period Rev. Thomas R. Roberts served the two churches. In

1881 the small church closed its doors and the congregation united with the church in Constableville.

The Welsh Hill settlement is now quiet. To get to the area of the former settlement, one takes Gomer Hill Road to Lyman Road. Lyman Road eventually intersects again with Gomer Hill Road, somewhere near the top of the world. There are few houses; the churches and sawmill are gone. The abandoned schoolhouse is one of the few buildings which remains. It closed in 1956 and sits vacant today. The only reason the road remains open is for access to the radar station and the few farms which sit on the top of the Hill.

Welsh Hill School.
It was in this schoolhouse that the Calvinistic Methodists of Welsh Hill first met. The building was used as a school until 1956.

There also remains a Welsh cemetery which is small and neatly kept. There is a gate to the cemetery but there is no reason to lock it. In the summer the lonely flower pots, left by relatives, are blown over by the Hill's fierce winds. In the winter, the snow drifts high over the stones.

Bob Williams of Lee Center is a descendant of the earliest settlers on Welsh Hill. The bell from the old schoolhouse sits on his living room shelf. Mr. Williams, now in his nineties, has tended his relatives' graves on Welsh Hill for years. Each time he visited the cemetery he noticed that the graves immediately adjoining his relatives were uncared for. After years of wondering why the unkept graves were not properly maintained, he translated the Welsh inscription on the tombstones only to find that the graves belonged to other relatives of his.

The Valley Church

Rev. Edward Rees came to Lewis County with several other Welsh families from the vicinity of Bala, Merionethshire and they settled there in 1842. A Calvinistic Methodist society was organized in the same year, not far from Port Leyden in the log home of Thomas Lewis, "Y-Glyn" ("the valley"). The church was therefore called the Valley Church or Eglwys y Glyn. The services were first held in the homes of John Lloyd and Owen Lewis who lived nearby. In 1846 the latter two gentlemen left the area. Services were held, thereafter, in the homes of Pierce Owen and Rev. Edward Rees until the church disbanded in 1849. Its members united with the Collinsville Church. During its existence Rev. Edward Rees was the church's only minister and elder. Rev. Rees was a shoemaker by trade as he could not support himself on money earned from preaching alone. When he would walk to Remsen to preach he would only be paid 50 cents.

Lowville

Lowville is the county seat for Lewis County and is its largest village. For a brief period of time a small society of Calvinistic Methodists worshiped there. In 1845 and for a few years thereafter, services were held in and around Lowville. Edward Rees was frequently the congregation's pastor. Sometimes services were held on a nearby hill in Martinsburg and other times they were held in a local school. The church in Lowville did not flourish and by the 1850s services were discontinued.

Port Leyden

On March 9, 1855 the Calvinistic Methodists of Port Leyden formed a society. Its trustees were Rev. Edward Rees, Pierce Owens, David Roberts, Richard Roberts, Evan Evans, and John Hughes.

Shortly thereafter a church building was erected which could seat 150. The congregation was ministered to by Rev. Edward Rees of the village. This church had only 15 members and therefore its existence was short lived. When it closed its members joined with the church in Collinsville.

Boonville

The town of Boonville is immediately north of the town of Remsen. There was never a large Welsh population in the town: in 1855 there were 67 Welsh-born and in 1865 there were only 46. While no Welsh church was ever erected in Boonville, during the 1840s and 1850s a Calvinistic Methodist society existed in the township. An 1844 issue of *Y Cyfail* reports that the society had 26 children in its Sunday School.

Sandy Creek

On the west side of the Tug Hill Plateau are the town and village of Sandy Creek. The small community is located just five miles north of Pulaski, overlooking Lake Ontario. Because of its location, it attracts many tourists and sportsmen who come to the area to fish and enjoy the lake.

A check of the phone book reveals only a few Welsh names, and the local cemetery has only a few stones bearing Welsh surnames. The local historian had never heard of any Welsh church in the town; a librarian could find no information about a local Welsh community, though she was a Davis (descended from a "Davies" in Prospect); and the local native Welshman, a well-known singer, had no knowledge of there ever having been any Welsh organizations in the area.

While it is now forgotten, the Oneida (Welsh) Presbytery did establish a church in Sandy Creek early in the twentieth century. No church building was ever constructed and the small group of Calvinistic Methodists may have met in homes.

From 1882 to 1937 two Welshmen, Rev. Joseph K. Griffith and Rev. Thomas T. Davies, were pastors of the local English-speaking Congregational Church. Being Welsh they may have ministered to the Welsh church too. If so, the Welsh Presbyterians may have been connected with or worshiped at the Congregational Church.

J. K. Griffith, born in Llanegryn, North Wales in 1843, had immigrated to America at the age of 14. At that time he began to work at Dr. Robert Everett's printing business in Steuben. He was ordained in 1873 in Canada. He came to Sandy Creek in 1882 and served the Congregational Church. When he departed he was replaced by Rev. Davies, with whom he was already well acquainted.

Rev. Davies was pastor of the Congregational Church from 1893 until the church closed in 1935. He was born at Towyn, North Wales on St. David's day in 1860, the son of a Congregational lay preacher. At the age of 21 he came to Utica, and later attended the Holland Patent Academy. In

1887 he was ordained as minister of Capel Ucha where he remained for two years. During his stay he was married to Winifred Jones of Remsen.

Rev. Davies left Remsen to become pastor of the Welsh church in Richville. He then came to Sandy Creek in 1893. Soon Rev. Davies became very active in the town's affairs, including serving as chaplain for the Masonic Lodge for 40 years. For 28 years he also was the pastor for the church in Orwell. It is said that in Sandy Creek he performed 1,300 funerals and married 500 couples. One woman, who was at the town library on the day I visited Sandy Creek, had been among those he married.

After the Congregational Church closed, Davies continued to teach a class at the Baptist Church until shortly before his death in 1937. Although he was a Congregationalist, it would not be unreasonable to believe he presided over the small Welsh society of Calvinistic Methodists, based upon his history of community involvement.

One can only speculate as to the Welsh Society's activities and duration. The Congregational Church today has become the village's Masonic Temple. As Rev. Davies' church itself was very small, the Welsh society was surely only a handful of Christians who wished to worship in their own tongue. Today, while even the memory of the Welsh Church seems to have faded, it is memorialized here as the only Welsh church in Oswego County.

Richville

I had heard of the Welsh settlement in Richville in St. Lawrence County, but had never taken the time to investigate where it was located. Then one day as I was traveling north on Route 11 just north of the village of Gouverneur, I came over a hill and saw a small white church on the right. As I came closer, I read the inscription across the front of the church. It read "Welsh Society of Richville." My curiosity was peeked but as I was late for court in Canton I had to delay any investigation. On my way home, I stopped and peered through the windows and read a marker in front of the church which lists the community's Welsh settlers.

The first Welsh in St. Lawrence County settled in Gouverneur and DeKalb in the 1840s. In 1850 a James Griffith came to Richville and was the first Welsh settler in that area.

Soon thereafter, the Welsh began to come to the region, mainly from Cardigan in West Wales. Most, if not all, of these initial settlers were farmers who tried to make a living in an area with rocky fields, short growing seasons and long, cold winters. They settled along Welsh Settlement Road which leads out of Richville and intersects with Route 11 near the Welsh Church.

The Welsh initially worshiped at First Church, the Congregational church which still stands on Main Street. The Welsh, however, wished to worship in their own language. Consequently, they began to meet at Ty Cerrig, the home of James Jones. He had erected a great stone house on Welsh Settlement Road, less than 1/10th of a mile west of the present church.

Ty Cerrig.
This stone farm house was built by James Jones, one of the early Welsh settlers. It served as a meeting place for the new immigrants.

In the early years of Welsh settlement (1855-1859) there was a Calvinistic Methodist society in the village but it did not last. It did not have a church building and its members, after dissolving their society, probably worshiped with the Welsh Congregationalists.

In the late 1850s, Rev. Gorham Cross, the minister at First Church (Congregational) suggested that the Welsh build their own church. This they did.

Thomas Rees was ordained and was to become the first minister for the new church in 1858. Shortly thereafter land was donated to the church by John Humphrey and in 1859 the building was constructed by Ebenezer Griffith. The first deacon was John Davies who served in that capacity until his death in 1882. Rev. Rees served the church until 1864 when he resigned to accept a position in Ashland, Pennsylvania.

In 1864 Rev. David Jones was called to the pulpit from Trewne in Cardiganshire, which was where many of Richville's Welsh settlers had come from. In that same year, on April 4, the church formally incorporated. Rev. Jones served until his sudden death in 1886. He was followed for a brief two-year period by Rev. George M. Rees.

Richville Welsh Church.
This church was used for services from 1858 to 1919.
Today it is maintained by the Richville Welsh Society.

In 1889 Rev. Thomas T. Davies from Steuben came to the church. Rev. Davies suggested that the church would do well to unite with First Church, so that it would not be necessary to share the expense of two ministers. Many of the Welsh "feared the consequences of a merger," but the strong leadership of Rev. Davies brought the two churches together in 1893. When he passed the torch to Rev. John Rosser Jones in May 1894, however, the plan unraveled and the two churches abruptly separated in 1896.

In 1897 a young man named Lewis E. Lewis was ordained in the Welsh Church. He was to be the last minister to serve only the Welsh-speaking church. He remained until 1902.

After 1902, the Congregational churches again joined with the understanding that the minister of First Church would be Welsh-speaking so that he could serve both parishes. While the churches had officially joined, the Welsh continued to worship separately. As time passed, the children of the Welsh Church members were "turned over to the care of the First Church." The Welsh Church continued services completely in Welsh and did nothing to encourage the young to join their church.

Four men served both churches in the early part of the century: John Williams (1902), J. T. Griffith (1904-1908), David L. Williams, formerly of Fair Haven, Vermont (1908-1915), and finally Griffith Evans (1915-1919). After 1919 regular worship services were discontinued and only one sermon per year was preached in the chapel.

In 1925, seeing the church falling into disrepair, Webster Griffith, grandson of the original contractor, undertook to renovate the structure. He erected a stone in front of the church with a tablet on it listing the ministers of the church and the early settlers in the Richville area. His daughter in turn left $400 in a bank account in Gouverneur to the "Welsh Church."

Historical Marker.
This marker was erected in 1925 in honor of the pastors of Richville's Welsh church and the Welsh settlers of the area.

Not much happened with the little church until the early 1970s when the state proposed to build Route 11, bypassing downtown Richville. In Route 11's path stood the Welsh Church, which the state's records listed as abandoned. Some local citizens wanted to preserve the church and they attempted to get the $400 from the bank for renovations. The bank officials took the position that the money had been specifically left to the "Welsh Church" and could only be released to such a corporate entity.

To get the money and to halt the state's plans, the Welsh Society of Richville was incorporated on October 10, 1974. The church building was thus spared and the bequest was released to the society. Route 11 was eventually built so close to the church that the state had to purchase the church's horse sheds, which stood to the west of it, for $500.

Since 1974 the Welsh Society has become active in maintaining the church building and spreading the Welsh heritage. In the past it has entered floats honoring the Welsh of the area in numerous local parades.

One of the persons instrumental in organizing and maintaining the Welsh Society is Mrs. Helen Reed. At 84, she is a granddaughter of one of the area's early Welsh settlers. Her father, although born in Richville, was fluent in Welsh, having been brought to Wales for an extended period of time as a child. Today, Mrs. Reed is the secretary of the Welsh Society and keeps all their records in her house. She also has the Society over for a St. David's Day dinner every year.

Once each year, when the society feels like it, the church is opened up for a service. They have the Welsh song books to assist them in carrying on the tradition. The original organ has been refurbished to accompany the hymns. Of special note concerning the church is the painting which hangs behind the pulpit. It is almost surrealistic and is similar to the painting at the French Road Church in Steuben.

Mrs. Reed explained that she was not fully Welsh and that many of the members of the present society are not Welsh at all. She indicated that a few years ago there were three people who were fully Welsh but that now there is only one in Richville. Some of the Welsh farms on Welsh Settlement Road are still in use and some are still in the hands of the original Welsh families.

Ty Cerrig still stands just west of Route 11. Mrs. Reed just shook her head when describing that old farm. Indeed, when I passed the stone house there were old cars and a trailer parked in front of the house as the cows looked out into the cold, snowy wind. I gazed at the old stone house down its long driveway, through the swirling snow, turned my car around and headed down Route 11 toward home.

Postscript

WHEN REV. STEVEN REES, president of the St. David's Society of Utica, learned that I was writing this book, he asked me if there are still any Welsh churches in Central New York. It was a good question and one that required some thought to answer. If "Welsh church" means a church where the congregation is solely Welsh in ethnic background and which worships in the old tongue, then the answer is "no." There have been no churches in the county using the Welsh language for 25 years. The congregations of the Welsh churches which did not dissolve have all joined with other churches. Nevertheless, the presence of the Welsh immigrants can still be felt in many of those merged churches today.

Plymouth-Bethesda is probably the most vibrant of those Central New York churches which trace their heritage to a Welsh congregation. The merger of Welsh Bethesda with Plymouth strengthened both churches. The Welsh, formerly of Bethesda, have continued to attend and actively participate in the church located at Utica's Oneida Square. While the church has committed itself to remain in downtown Utica and maintains an urban ministry, it draws its congregation from throughout the region.

Moriah-Olivet, located only a few blocks from Plymouth-Bethesda also continues its ministry, though over the last decade its membership has declined even after the merger of the two churches. Unfortunately for Moriah there are a number of other Presbyterian churches in the city including Westminster, First Presbyterian, and Bethany—all looking for members from a shrinking Presbyterian population. Still, the church does carry on the heritage of the Welsh church which began in 1830 and the congregation is hopeful that it will again thrive when a new minister is called.

Central Methodist is also a product of the merger of a Welsh church with English-speaking churches. Central, however, has not retained any of its Welsh heritage. When I asked the church secretary about Coke Memorial's records she told me she had never even heard of the church.

In Nelson, the old Welsh church is opened to the community for services every summer. Even those attending who are not of a Welsh background are very proud of the church's Welsh heritage.

Camroden Presbyterian still maintains its church, though the congregation is now very small and not Welsh. When it recently celebrated its 150th anniversary, however, it was done with a Welsh choir and with a reminiscence of its Welsh history.

The First Baptist Church of Remsen, the church born from the merger of the Second (Capel Isaf) and Third Baptist (Capel Zion) Churches, is now preparing for its centennial. It is the only survivor from the many Welsh churches which once were scattered across Remsen and Steuben. Capel Cerrig, Bethel and Enlli, all inactive, have been purchased by the Remsen-Steuben Historical Society in an effort to preserve a unique portion of Welsh heritage. French Road opens for one service on the third Sunday in July.

Other reminders of the Welsh are less obvious. Churches have been converted into houses. Many cemeteries have been well-maintained while others have been left unattended. Some of these memory stones sit along major highways and are passed by hundreds daily. Others are hidden deep in forest preserves and in sacred groves whose location are only known to a few. Each of these sites would merely be old houses or cracked stones if the memories associated with them were lost.

The living room of Bob Williams of Lee Center, a 94-year-old Welsh-born gentleman and descendant of earlier settlers in the Turin area and at Bethel, is filled with paintings of his hometown of Aberdaron, from which so many Welsh immigrants to Central New York came. There are also paintings of Penymynydd and the school where the Bethel church was founded. In his study are Welsh books published in Oneida County, volumes of *Y Cyfail* and *Y Cenhadwr*, and photographs of churches now gone.

Bob Williams had known my great-grandfather, John S. Williams. He had grown up with my grandmother and was a friend of my grandfather. He had given my father rides to school when he was a boy. He has seen the last century of the Welsh in Central New York, and the changes which have occurred. As he told me stories about the Welsh in Central New York he sat forward in his arm chair, looked carefully at me for a second, and then pointing to his forehead he said in his Welsh accent, "Memories, that's all

I've got." "Memories." "Memories." The stories behind the Welsh sites are slipping away, held only in the memories of the elderly Welsh.

Today, other ethnic groups are following the footsteps of the Welsh as they settle in Central New York. Mennonite families have settled in small groups in rural Oneida, Madison, Lewis, Herkimer, and St. Lawrence counties. Like the Welsh, they are deeply religious and have separated themselves from others by their customs. The Mennonites each year celebrate the Zwanzigstein Fest. Zwanzigstein means "Twenty Stones." The name comes from the time God safely led Joshua and all the Israelites over the Jordan River. The Lord told Joshua that the twelve chosen men, one from each tribe, were to take a stone from the Jordan and pile them up as a monument, to remind their children of God's amazing miracle.

When the Mennonites' forefathers (about twenty families) came to America from Europe, they too realized the power of God's mighty hand. The Zwanzigstein Fest is the Mennonites' "memory stone" held annually so that if their children should ask, they can tell them of their mighty God.

This book, filled with the memories of so many Welsh-Americans, has been written to a similar end. It is hoped that the readers will go out to those forgotten Welsh hills and discover the overgrown and unattended cemeteries, and that when they drive by the converted Welsh churches they will be able to picture the devout Welsh entering the buildings to attend services.

It is hoped that this book will serve as a memory stone, as a memorial to the Welsh in Central New York, so that when our children ask us about the Welsh, they will see the powerful hand of God guiding those Welsh pilgrims into a new land.

Afterword

THIS HISTORY OF THE WELSH in Central New York is by no means complete. Not a week went by this past last year without someone giving me a picture, an article, or an interesting story for inclusion in this book. I hope that people will continue to provide me with information regarding the churches discussed in this book so that those stories can be shared in future editions.

Sources

Welsh Americans

Greenslade, David. *Welsh Fever.* Cowbridge (Wales): D. Brown & Sons, 1986.

Hartmann, Edward George. *Americans From Wales.* Boston: Christopher Publishing House, 1967.

Hartmann, Edward George. *The History of the Welsh Congregational Church of New York.* Swansea (Wales): John Penry Press, 1969.

Morgan, Vyrnwy. *The Cambro-American Pulpit.* New York: Funk & Wagnalls Co., 1898.

Thomas, R. D. *Hanes Cymry America.* Utica (NY): T. J. Griffith, 1872. Trans. as *A History of the Welsh in America* by Phillips G. Davies. Ames (IA): University Press of America, 1983.

Williams, Daniel Jenkins. *One Hundred Years of Welsh Calvinistic Methodism.* Philadelphia: The Westminster Press, 1937.

Herkimer County

History of Herkimer County, N.Y. New York: F. W. Beers & Co., 1879.

Lewis County

Bowen, G. Byron. *History of Lewis County New York 1880-1965.* Lewis County (NY): Willard Press, 1970.

Hough, Franklin B. *History of Lewis County in the State of New York.* Merrick (NY): Richwood Publishing, 1860.

Peel, Bob. "Tug Hill's Collector of Rare Welsh Bits." *Syracuse Herald American* (December 27, 1981).

Schaaf, Ken. "Bob Remembers the Early Welsh Days." *The Utica Daily Press* (October 2, 1982).

Williams, Lewis. "Lewis County, New York." *The Cambrian* XXV (September 1905): 372-378.

Madison County

Hammond, L. M. *History of Madison County.* Syracuse (NY): Truair, Smith & Co., 1872.

Smith, John E. *Our County and People: Madison County.* Boston: The Boston Historical Company, 1896.

Smith, John H. *History of Chenango and Madison Counties.* Syracuse (NY): D. Mason & Co., 1880.

Oneida County

Boyce, John. *Presbytery of Utica 1843-1943.* Centennial Booklet, Utica (NY) 1943.

Canfield, W. W. & J. E. Clark. *Things Worth Knowing About Oneida County.* Utica (NY): Thomas J. Griffith, 1909.

Durant, Samuel W. *History of Oneida County.* Philadelphia: Everts & Fariss, 1878.

Ellis, David Maldwyn. "The Assimilation of the Welsh in Central New York." *New York History* 32 (July 1972): 299.

Evans, Paul DeMund. "The Welsh in Oneida County." Ph.D. diss., Cornell University, 1914.

Jones, Pomeroy. *Annals of Oneida County.* Rome: Published by author, 1851.

Jones, Erasmus W. "The Early Welsh Settlers of Oneida County." *Transactions - Oneida County Historical at Utica* (Delivered December 3, 1892).

Kelly, Virginia B., Merrilyn N. O'Connell, Stephen S. Olney, and Johanna R. Beig. *Wood and Stone.* Utica (NY): Central New York Community Arts Council, 1972.

Smith, Gail, *Sesquicentennial, Presbytery of Utica 1843-1993.* Utica (NY), 1993

Wager, Daniel C. *Our County and its People (Oneida County).* Boston: Boston History Company, 1896.

Atlases

Atlas of the City of Utica New York. Philadelphia: G. M. Hopkins, 1883.

Atlas of Herkimer County, New York. New York: J. Jay Stranahan & Beach Nichols, 1868.

Atlas of Oneida County New York. Philadelphia: D. G. Beers & Co., 1874.

Beers, D. G. *Atlas of Lewis County.* Philadelphia: Pomeroy, Whitman & Co. 1875

Beers, D. G. *Atlas of Madison County New York.* Philadelphia: Pomeroy Whitman & Co., 1874.

Gillette's Map of Oneida County. Philadelphia: John E. Gillette, 1858.
New Century Atlas, Oneida County New York. Philadelphia: Century Mapping Company, 1907.
New York State Atlas and Gazetter. Freeport (ME): Delorme, Mapping Company, 1988.

Chapter I: Remsen and Steuben

Davis, Margaret P. *Honey Out of the Rafters.* Remsen (NY): By author, 1976.
"First Remsen, Then Niagara Falls." *Newyddion Tref Remsen* (1987): 11.
Jones, Maldwyn A. "Welsh-Americans and the Anti-Slavery Movement in the United States." *Transactions of the Honorable Society of Cymmrodorian*, 1985.
Lewis, Audrey. "Where's the Weekend Action? Try Steuben Corners." *The Utica Observer Dispatch* (August 19, 1992).
Mitchell, Cheryl. "Robert Everett, 1797-1875." Washington (DC): by author.
Reynolds, Lorena. "Early Welsh Settlers in Remsen & Steuben." Utica (NY): Oneida County Historical Society, Utica, N.Y., 1968.
Robb, Edna Roberts. *Honey Out of the Rock.* Middlebury (VA): Middlebury Press, 1960.
Roberts, Milard F. *A Narrative History of Remsen.* Remsen (NY): Published by author, 1914.
Thomas, Howard. *The Road to Sixty.* Prospect (NY): Prospect Books, 1966.
Thomas, Howard. *The Singing Hills.* Prospect (NY): Prospect Books, 1964.
Williams, J. Robert. "Welsh Churches in Remsen & Steuben." *Watertown Daily Times* (December 4, 1988): C-1.

Capel Ucha

Everett, Mary H. "An Historical Sketch of the First Welsh Congregational Church of Steuben N.Y." Steuben, (NY): Pamphlet published by author, 1904.
Jersen, Lorena. "Capel Ebenezer, Capel Ucha." *Newyddion Tre Remsen* (1987): 14.
Squire, Dorothy. "Rev. Robert Everett." *Newyddion Tref Remsen-Steuben* (1992): 32.

Bethel

"In Memoriam: John S. Kent, Remsen." Funeral Program, 1912.
Williams, Bernard. "Bethel Church." *Newyddion Tref Remsen-Steuben* (1992): 8.

First Baptist Church of Remsen

Walter, Emogene. "Remsen's New Church." *Newyddion Tref Remsen* (1987): 17.

Penycaerau

Jones, Margaret Ann & Catherine Jones Roberts. "Pen Y Caerau Church." *Newyddion Tref Remsen* (1987): 9.

"Memorial Service at Penycaerau Church." *The Cambrian* XII (1896): 14-15.

"A Welsh Calvinistic Event." *The Rome Daily Sentinel* (1914).

Penygraig

Thomas, Gilbert. "Pen y Graig" *Newyddion Tref Remsen* (1987): 3.

French Road

Jersen, Lorena. "French Road Church and Cemetery Association." *Newyddion Tref Remsen* (1987): 7.

Kovar, Jonas. "Little Welsh Church still has place in community." *The Utica Observer Dispatch* (January 2, 1985): C-3.

Capel Cerrig

"One Hundreth Anniversary of First Presbyterian Church (Stone Church)." Centennial Program. Remsen (NY), 1931.

"Ordination and Installation of Rev. D. C. Davies at Remsen." *The Utica Daily Press*, 1921.

"Remsen Barn Festival of the Arts Gymanfa Ganu." Program, September 27, 1987.

"The 150th Anniversary-First Presbyterian Church (Stone Church)." Sesquicentennial Program, 1981.

Williams, Shirley. "Historic Remsen Church in Center of Controversy." *The Utica Observer Dispatch* (September 1987).

Wynne, Dorothy. "The Old Stone Church-Capel Cerrig." *Newyddion Tref Remsen* (1987): 1.

Enlli

"The Enlli Church." *Newyddion Tref Remsen* (1987): 15.

"Oral History-Oliver Jones & Family." *Newyddion Tref Remsen-Steuben* (1992) 12.

Chapter II: Neighboring Towns

Trenton

Our Churches (Holland Patent Central Schhol District). Holland Patent (NY), 1941.

Prospect

Slusarczyk, Stanley. *Prospect N.Y. — Then and Now*. Mid-York Library System, 1990.

Thomas, Howard. *The Life of a Village*. Prospect (NY): Prospect Books, 1950.

Holland Patent

Hughes, Robert. "Brief History of the Welsh Calvinistic Methodist Church, Holland Patent." Holland Patent (NY), March 18, 1901.

South Trenton
Brainard, Charles W. "Old Welsh Baptist Cemetery, South Trenton, New York." July 1942.

Cale, Barbara. "Old Home Day address" 1992.

South Trenton: Where Memories Abound and History Resounds. South Trenton Community Association, Beacon Publishing, 1976.

Marcy and Deerfield
Humphrey, Lucia. *History of the Town of Marcy, Oneida County 1832-1976*. Marcy (NY): Marcy Town Board, 1976.

"Town of Marcy Centennial History and Program, 1832-1932." Marcy (NY), 1932.

Salem
Ball, Raymond. "Salem Church-Let's Save It." *Marcy Town Newsletter* (November 1990).

Black, Ira D. Correspondence to Robert Bruce, October 16, 1950.

"Records of the Salem Congregational Society in Marcy." 1830-1925.

Pfeiffer, Paul. "The Salem Cemetery, Marcy, New York." Eagle Scout project, November 19, 1990.

Bethania
Brainard, Charles W. "Bethania Cemetery." 1942.

Newport
History of the Town of Newport. Newport: L. B. Tuttle.

Chapter III: Utica

Utica
Bagg, M. M. *Memorial History of Utica*. Utica (NY): D. Mason & Co., 1892.

Clarke, T. Wood. *Utica for a Century and a Half*. Utica (NY): The Widtman Press, 1952.

Ellis, David M. "The Welsh in Utica." *Transactions of the Honourable Society of Cymmrodorian*. Denbigh (Wales): Gee & Son Ltd, 1981.

Koln, S. Joshua. *The Jewish Community of Utica N.Y. 1847-1948*. New York: American Jewish Historical Society, 1953.

Utica City Directories (1817-1992).

First Baptist
"The Baptists in Utica." *The Utica Daily Press* (July 1, 1876).

Fiske, Herve K. *Tabernacle Baptist in Retrospective*.

Risley, Edward H. *Tabernacle Baptist Church, An Historical Sketch*. Utica (NY), 1919.

The Utica Daily Press (April 21, 1904).

Bethesda

"Anniversary of the Welsh Congregational Church of Utica." *The Cambrian* XII (1892): 44-47, 81-83, 99-101.

"The Bethesda Centenial, Congregational Church, Utica." *The Cambrian* XXII (February 1902): 372-378.

Bethesda Church (Congregational) Yearbook. 1962.

Kover, Jonas. "At home in the city." *The Utica Observer Dispatch* (January 18, 1992): C-1

"Rhys Gwesyn Jones." *The Cambrian* XI (October 1891) 473.

"175th Anniversary Banquet." Utica (NY): Plymouth-Bethesda UCC, 1977.

Moriah

A Decade of Achievement (1948-1958). Utica (NY): Moriah Presbyterian Church, 1958.

Griffiths, T. Solomon. *Hanes y Methodistiad Calfinaidd yn* Utica New York Utica (NY): T. J. Griffith, 1896. Trans. as A History of the Calvinistic Methodists in Utica, New York by Phillips G. Davies. Ames (IA): Sigler Printing and Publishing, 1991.

Moriah, Utica, N.Y., U.S.A. 1830-1930. Utica (NY), 1930.

"Rev. J. Hughes Parry." *The Cambrian* XIX (September 1899): 429.

Williams, R. R. "A Welsh Church in America." *Liverpool Post* (December 10, 1959).

Coke Memorial

Burdick, A. J. "Central United Methodist Church." Utica (NY), 1969.

"William W. Jones." *The Cambrian* XXV (1905): 39-40.

Chapter IV: Utica's Suburbs

New York Mills

"An Appeal on behalf of the Salem Congregational Church." New York Mills (NY), 1926. (Pamphlet at New York Mills Historical Society.)

History of Whitesboro. Whitesboro (NY): The Recreational Committee of Greater Whitesboro, 1977.

Hughes, David John. "Welsh Congregational Church—New York Mills." *The Utica Observer Dispatch* (1925).

"Tablet Unveiled in Salem Church, New York Mills." *The Utica Daily Press* (May 18, 1931).

New Hartford

Smith, George H. *Rambling Tale of a Rambling Town.* New Hartford (NY): New Hartford Central School, 1955.

Clinton

"Welsh Donation." *Clinton Courier* (February 9, 1887)

"Welsh Donation." *Clinton Courier* (February 16, 1887)

"Welsh Donation." *Clinton Courier* (February 23, 1887)

Dever, Mary Bell. *The History of Clinton Square*. Clinton (NY): The Clinton Courier Inc., 1961.

Chapter V: Southern Oneida County
Waterville

"Edward Davies, Waterville N.Y." *The Cambrian* XXV (January 1905): 37.

Waterville Centenial History 1871-1971. Waterville (NY), 1971.

Paris

Kelly, Joe. "Ron Jones: 43 Years in a Country Store." *The Utica Observer Dispatch* (February 1992)

Plainfield

Hurd, D. Hamilton. *History of Otsego County, New York*. Philadelphia: Everts & Fariss, 1878.

Hawkins, Ethelyn. *Frontier Days, Otsego County, 1776-1976*. Otsego County Bicentenial Frontier Days Committee, 1976.

"Moses Davies." *The Cambrian* XII (1892): 179-180.

Chapter VI: Madison County
Nelson

Jones, David. "Nelson." *Country Roads Revisited*. Oneida (NY): Madison County Historical Society, 1981.

Jones, David J. *A Note on the Tractor*. Published by author, 1981.

Capel Bach

Hughes, May. Letter to Owen Evans, Morrisville, New York, (February 10, 1954) Madison County Historical Society, Oneida, New York.

Peniel Church

Bowden, Ramona E. "Music Will Ring Hills at Annual Welsh Day." *Syracuse Post-Standard* (September 21, 1967)

Draheim, H. Paul. "History to 1848, Nelson Parish 105 Years Old." *The Utica Daily Press* (January 10, 1953)

Evans, Owen. "Nelson Old Welsh Church, History is Delineated on the 'Eve of Welsh Day Ceremony, September 12." *Mid York Weekly* (September 9, 1954).

Jones, Mrs. Theodore. "Welsh Church Society 95 Years Old." *Cazenovia Republican* (August 16, 1945).

Jones, Mrs. Theodore. "Welsh Congregational Church." *Cazenovia Republican* (August 1934).

Pennel[sic] *Church*. Information Sheet, Madison County Historical Society, Oneida, New York, 1906.

"Sherrill Pastor to speak at Welsh Church Services." *The Utica Observer Dispatch* (August 6, 1970).

"Welsh Colony Now Remnant of Years Ago." *Syracuse Post Standard* (July 13, 1930).

Chapter VII: Rome
Camroden
Boyle, Timothy. "Centenary of the Death of John Edwards (Eos Glan Twrch) A Great Welsh American." *Ninnau* (1987).

Evans, Edwin C. *Floyd: 180 Years*. Floyd (NY): published by author, 1974.

Herrmann, Virginia V. "Faith Endures in Congregation of Camroden Presbyterian Church." *The Rome Daily Sentinel* (October 1988).

Herrmann, Virginia V. "Service will unite folks apart for 50 years." *The Rome Daily Sentinel* (October 1988).

Jones, Gwawr. Letter to Mrs. Plail. Bangor, Wales (February 25, 1993).

Kovar, Jonas. "Camroden's 'little white church on the corner' is 150." *The Utica Observer Dispatch* (October 15, 1988).

"The Little White Church on the Corner." Program from the 125th Anniversary of Camroden Church, Camroden (NY), 1962.

"One Hundred Fifty Years of Camroden Presbyterian Church." *County News* (October 1988).

Rome
Rome City Directories (1850-1927).

Rome New York, Centenial History, 1870-1970. Rome (NY): Rome Historical Society, 1970.

"The Welsh Bible Society of Rome." *The Rome Daily Sentinel* (1916).

Wager, Daniel E. *Our City and its People: The City of Rome*. Boston: The Boston Historical Company, 1896.

Bethel
"Welsh Heritage Sunday." First Presbyterian Church, bulletin insert, 1990.

Year Book and Church Directory. Rome (NY): Bethel Presbyterian Church, 1931.

Western
Moccasin Tracks to Ski Trails. Western (NY): Town of Western Bicentenial Book Committee, 1976.

Chapter VIII: Lewis County and Beyond
Collinsville
Drew, Hazel C. *Tales from Little Lewis*. Lyons Falls (NY): Published by author, 1961.

Constableville
Traxel, Mary E. *History of Constableville*. Published by author, 1973.

Turin
Williams, Emily and Ethel Evans Markham. *A History of Turin, Lewis County New York*. Lakemont (NY): North Country Books, 1974.

Sandy Creek
Centennial Souvenier History, Sandy Creek, NY. Sandy Creek (NY), 1925.

"Centennial Anniversary, October 28-29, 1917, Congregational Church." Sandy Creek (NY).

"Mrs T. T. Davies." Obituary, *Sandy Creek News.*

"Pastor Completes 35 Years of Service." *Sandy Creek News.*

"Rev. Davies Passes After Long Illness." *Sandy Creek News* (July 27, 1937).

"Rev. Joseph K. Griffith." Obituary, *Sandy Creek News.*

Wart, Arthur H. *Sesquicentennial History of the Town of Sandy Creek 1825-1975.* Sandy Creek (NY): Town of Sandy Creek Service Club, 1975.

Richville

Williams, David L. *Congregational Churches of Richville N.Y.* Remsen (NY): Thomas J. Griffith.

Postscript

"Mennonites Celebrate Zwanzigstein." *The Utica Observer Dispatch* (1992).

Index

Aberdaron (N. Wales) 29,54,55,77, 78,172
Aberystwyth (Wales) 45
Abolition 32,95,114
Ackley-Barry Funeral Home 41
Adams, Jeff 128
Adams, John S. 150,157
Adams Pond Road 150
Albany (NY) 26,148,156
Alder Creek (NY) 37,50
All Saints Episcopal Church (Utica, NY) 109
Allegheny County (NY) 41
Alliance (OH) 72
American Dawn, The; see *Wawr Americanaidd, Y*
Ames, David 59
Anglesey (N. Wales) 122,131,160, 176,181
Anglican Communion 132
Annals of Oneida County 43
Anthony, David 123
Anti-abolitionist 32,
Anti-slavery movement 32,114
Arminian theology 45
Armory (Utica, NY) 131
Ashforth, William 141
Ashland (PA) 198
Auburn (NY) 148
Auburn College 135
Ava (NY) 182
Ava United Methodist Church 68

Bacon's Hill 164; see also Camroden
Bagg, Albert 90
Bagg Square 109
Bala (N. Wales) 165,194
Ball, Raymond 99
Baltimore (MD) 94
Bangor (N. Wales) 165

Bangor Episcopal Church (Churchtown, PA) 132
Bantham, Howland 39,50
Baptist Church (Camroden, NY) 164
Baptist Church (East Nelson, NY) 158
Baptist Church (Holland Patent, NY) 45,87,93
Baptist Church (Newport, NY) 106
Baptist Church (Sandy Creek, NY) 196
Baptist Church (Turin, NY) 189
Baptist Churches; see also Welsh Baptist Churches
Baptist Gymanfa of Oneida County, New York and Eastern Pennsylvania 111
Bardsey Island; see Ynys Enlli
Bardwell Baptist Church (Bardwell Mill, NY) 18, 49,**50-52**
Bardwell Mill (NY) 49, **50-52**
Barnam (Mr.) 122
Barneveld (NY) 26,83,**91-92**
Bathkey, Gus 98
Bartlett, Curry M. Jr. 74
Baxter, Owen 135,165
Baxter, Richard 135
Beaumaris, (Anglesey, N.Wales) 157
Bell Hill Road (Newport, NY) 104
Bellevue (PA) 122
Bellis, R. Wynne 62,65,73
Best, I. A. 141
Beth Israel (synagogue) 115
Bethania Cemetery 102-103
Bethania Church **101-103**
Bethany Church (Paris, NY) **146**
Bethany Church (Utica, NY) 201
Bethel Cemetery Association 39
Bethel Chapel (First Presbyterian Church, Rome, NY) 174

Bethel Church (Bridgewater, NY) 146,**147-148**
Bethel Congregational Church (Remsen, NY) 18,23,33,**37-41**, 43,61,71,85,91,202
Bethel Presbyterian Church (Rome, NY) 73,166-168,**170-175**,176-177,183
Bethel Road (Steuben, NY) 37
Bethesda Church (Steuben, NY); see Capel Isaf
Bethesda Church (Utica, NY) 43,90,**113-119**,122-124,135,161
Bethesda Congregational Church (Merthyr Tydvil, Wales) 116
Bible Society of Rome and Vicinity 177
Big Meeting; see Gymanfa Mawr
Birmingham (England) 121
Birney, James W. 32
Black, Hazel 75
Black, Hugh 75
Black River 184-185
Bleecker Street (Utica, NY) 119
Blunt, Edward 165
Board of Home Missions of the Congregational Church 99
Boonville (NY) 37,66,184,**195**
Boy Scouts 95,99
Bridgewater (NY) 143,146-148
Broad Street Baptist Church (Utica, NY) 110; see also Tabernacle Baptist Church
Broadway (Utica, NY) 111
Brooklyn (NY) 88
Bryn Mawr Cemetery 100-101
Bryn Mawr Church (Deerfield, NY) **100-101**,103
Bryn Seion Cemetery 104
Bryn Seion Church (Newport, NY) **104-105**
Bryncoch (N. Wales) 192
Buffalo (NY) 128
Burton, Richard 127

Cadwalader, John 89,91
Caernarvonshire (N. Wales) 29,48, 123
Calvary Methodist Church (Rome, NY) 175
Calvin, John 44,45,53
Calvinistic Methodists (denomination) 26, 27,53,54,74,111,175
Calvinistic Methodist Church (national) 73, 120
Calvinistic Methodist Church (Barneveld, NY) **91**
Calvinistic Methodist Church (Boonville, NY) **195**
Calvinistic Methodist Church (Camroden, NY) 72,**165-170**; see also Camroden Presbyterian Church
Calvinistic Methodist Church (Collinsville, NY) **185-188**,192,194
Calvinistic Methodist Church (Constableville, NY) 187, **188-189**,192,193
Calvinistic Methodist Church (Delta, NY) **177**
Calvinistic Methodist Church (Gomer Flats, NY) **185**
Calvinistic Methodist Church (Holland Patent, NY) **88-89**,120; see also Zion Church (Holland Patent, NY)
Calvinistic Methodist Church (Marcy, NY) 88,101,102,120; see also Rehobeth (Marcy, NY)
Calvinistic Methodist Church (Mullen Hill) **182-183**
Calvinistic Methodist Church (Nelson, NY); see Capel Bach (Nelson, NY)
Calvinistic Methodist Church (Newport, NY); see Salem Church (Newport,NY)
Calvinistic Methodist Church (New York, NY) 120,125
Calvinistic Methodist Church (Oriskany, NY) **177-178**

Calvinistic Methodist Church (Paris, NY); see Whitefield Calvinistic Methodist Church
Calvinistic Methodist Church (Port Leyden, NY) **194**
Calvinistic Methodist Church (Plainfield, NY) **149-150**
Calvinistic Methodist Church (Prospect, NY) 58,59,85,**86-87**
Calvinistic Methodist Church (Quaker Hill, NY) **179-180**
Calvinistic Methodist Church (Richville, NY) **197**
Calvinistic Methodist Church (Rome, NY) 166-167,175; see also Bethel Presbyterian Church (Rome, NY)
Calvinistic Methodist Church (Sandy Creek, NY) **195-196**
Calvinistic Methodist Church (South Trenton, NY) **93**
Calvinistic Methodist Church (Utica NY) 88,101,103,187; see also Moriah (Utica)
Calvinistic Methodist Church (Webster Hill) **181-182**
Calvinistic Methodist Societies; see Calvinistic Methodist Churches
Cambrian, The 72,132
Cambrian Hall (Utica, NY) 130
Campbellites, Society of 80
Camroden (NY) 72.73,89,102,163-166,167, 170,172,178,202
"Camroden" (hymn) 169
Camroden Presbyterian Church 164,**165-170**,202
Canary family 106
Caniadu y Cysger (*Songs of the Sanctuary*) 33
Canning Factory Road (Paris, NY) 145-146
Capel Bach (Nelson, NY) **156-158**,162
Capel Bach (Rome, NY) 175; see also Rehobeth (Rome,NY)
Capel Bont (Remsen, NY) **52-53**

Capel Bont Cemetery 18,**52-53**,84
Capel Cerrig (Remsen, NY) 18,41, 50,58,60,62,65,**69-77**,80,169,202
Capel Cobin; see Capel Nant
Capel Cymraig, Y (Ilion, NY) 61,**139-141**
Capel Goch (Camroden, NY); see Congregational Church (Camroden, NY)
Capel Goch (Steuben-Remsen, NY) 48; see also Capel Zion
Capel Goch Cemetery (Steuben, NY) 48
Capel Isaf (Steuben, NY) 25,29, **44-47**,48-50,52,84,93-94,202
Capel Isaf Cemetery 18,47
Capel Nant (Steuben, NY) 52,56,58, 62,**63-66**,73,79
Capel Ucha (Steuben, NY) **27-34**,35,38,41,43,44,53-55,58,65,84, 89,91,97,114,196
Capel Ucha Cemetery 18,30,34,37
Capel Zion (Steuben-Remsen, NY) 48,49,84,202; see also Third Baptist Church
Carbondale (PA) 61
Cardigan (Wales) 196
Carmarthenshire (Wales) 114,144,164
Cassville (NY) 145
Catherine Street (Utica, NY) 120
Cattaragus County (NY) 41,104,115,170
Cavanaugh Road (Marcy, NY) 101
Cazenovia (NY) 155
Celtic Church 78
Cenhadwr, Y (The Messenger) 31,32,38, 43,144,202
Central Methodist Church (Utica, NY) 109,132,202
Central United Methodist Church; see Central Methodist Church
Chadwicks (NY) 138
Charlotte Street (Oriskany, NY) 177
Cherry Valley Turnpike 155

"Child's Christmas in Wales, A" 75
Christ Reformed Church (Utica, NY) 126
Christiana, Ed 90
Church in Wales 132
Church of England 132
Church Road (Marcy, NY) 96
Church Street (Prospect, NY) 86,87
Cincinnati (OH) 72,115
Cincinnati Creek (Remsen, NY) 48
City Hall (Utica, NY) 116-117
Cleveland (OH) 152
Clifford (PA) 31
Clinton (NY) 60,133,**141**
Clinton Courier, The 141
Clinton Welsh Quartet 141
Cobin; see Capel Nant
Cobin Cemetery 18,37,64-66
Cockburn, James 24
Coe, Arden 128
Coke, Thomas 131
Coke Memorial Church (Utica, NY) **130-132**,157,202
Coleman, Howard 37
Collinsville (NY) 185-189, 192
Columbia Street (Utica, NY) 115
Columbus (OH) 165
Columbus (WI) 61,89
Colwyn Bay (N. Wales) 116
Commercial Lyceum (Utica, NY) 130
Congregational Church (Deansboro, NY) 144
Congregational Church (Oriskany Falls, NY) 144
Congregational Church (Plainfield, NY); see Shiloh Congregational Church
Congregational Church (Prospect, NY) **85**, 151
Congregational Church (Richville, NY) 197-199
Congregational Church (Sandy Creek, NY) 195-196

Congregational Church (West Winfied, NY) 31,114,154
Congregational Churches; see also Welsh Congregational Churches
Congregationalists (denomination) 26,31, 99,111
Constable Hall (Constableville, NY) 188
Constableville (NY) 186,188,189, 192,193
Coombs Road (South Trenton, NY) 95
Corn Hill (Utica, NY) 109,122,128
Corn Hill School, The 122
Corwen (N. Wales) 124
Cotter, John 103
Cotter, Kate 103
County Class Meeting 136,171
Court Street (Rome, NY) 175,177
Court Street (Utica, NY) 109
Court Street Methodist Church (Rome, NY); see Calvary Methodist
Creedel, Edward 68
Creedel, Paul 68,76
Cross, Gorham 197
Crumb Hill Road (Plainfield, NY) 154
Cyfail, Y (The Friend) 120,123,195, 202
Cyfarfod Pregethu 187

Davies, Benjamin 55,56,57,61,67, 71,119,120
Davies, Benjamin D. 157,167,178
Davies, Caleb E. 152
Davies, David 131
Davies, David C. 61,65,73,168
Davies, David E. (d.1848) 57,120
Davies, David E. (Nelson) 158
Davies, David J. 146
Davies, David T. 130,157
Davies, Donald 150
Davies, Edward 33,38,43,90,91,135, 144
Davies, Evan 26,

Davies, Hugh 138-139
Davies, Isaac 88
Davies, James 89,91
Davies, John (Bridgewater) 147
Davies, John (Penygraig) 61,150
Davies, John (Richville) 197
Davies, John (Utica) 125
Davies, John T. 123
Davies, Joseph 152
Davies, Margaret 35
Davies, Morris 119,120
Davies, Moses 145,149,150,152
Davies, Nathanial 164
Davies, Owen 139
Davies, Reese 130
Davies, Richard 65
Davies, Robert H. 152
Davies, Thomas T. 33,195,198
Davies, William (early settler) 26
Davies, William (Lewis County) 185
Davies, William (Utica) 132
Davies, William Eilian 173
Davies, William H. 139
Davis, John (Penygraig) 61
Davis, John (Penymynydd) 35,37
Davis, Ray 37
Dayton, Daniel 50
Deansboro (NY) 144
Declaration of Independence 163, 184
Deerfield (NY) 96,97,100,104,189
Deerfield, Town of 96
Deerfield Hill 26,93,100,184
Dekalb (NY) 196
Delta (NY) 163,177
Delta Lake (NY) 35,177,182
Democrats 103
Denbigh (N. Wales) 114
Denbighshire (N. Wales) 88,93,94, 188
Detroit (MI) 172
Dexter Street (Oriskany, NY) 178
DiAngelis, Pasqual 89
Dick, James 80

District 7 School (Western, NY) 179
District 9 School (Remsen, NY) 38,39
District 26 School (Deerfield, NY) 97
Dizer, John T. 99
Dobson's Hall (Utica, NY) 117
Donovan, James 34
Downing, Mary 173-174
Draig Goch (Red Dragon) 23
Dustin, Samuel 48
Dustin Road (Remsen, NY) 37
Dyffryn Mawr (Great Valley, PA) 44

East Davis Road (Deerfield, NY) 100
East Nelson (NY) 155,158
East Road (Collinsville, NY) 187,188
Eaton, Town of 162
"Ebenezer" (Ton-Y-Botel) 29
Ebenezer Church (Steuben NY) 29; see also Capel Ucha
Ebensburg (PA) 27,97
Edwards, D. Charles 136
Edwards, David 103
Edwards, Hugh 88
Edwards, John (Eos Glan Twrch) 166
Edwards, John 165
Edwards, William 61
Eglwys y Glyn; see Valley Church, The
Eisteddfod 78,131,151,161
Ellis, Ellis 134
Ellis, Humphrey 65
Ellis, John (Capel Isaf) 46
Ellis, John (Marcy) 101
Ellis, Morris 45
Ellis, Thomas 134
Ellis Road (Steuben, NY) 64-66
Enlli Church (Remsen, NY) 18,33, 58,62,65,73,**77-80**,87,202
Enlii Cemetery 78

Episcopal Church 132
Episcopalians 143,185
Erie Canal 109,111,122
Evans, Arthur 58,66
Evans, Christmas 72
Evans, David 112
Evans, Edward C. 58,65,72,79, 87,187
Evans, Edwin 169
Evans, Elizabeth 96
Evans, Ethel A. (Jones) 66
Evans, Evan (Constableville) 186,188,194
Evans, Evan (Steuben) 31
Evans, Evan (Utica) 131
Evans, Griffith 199
Evans, John 95-96
Evans, John R. 61,67,136,140
Evans, Owen (Camroden) 164,169
Evans, Owen (Frankfort Hill) 138
Evans, Philip 58,66
Evans, Robert (Togwy) 38,43,85,91
Evans, Robert 99
(Evans), Skip 168
Evans, Spencer 66
Evans, Sylvanus 66
Evans, T. J. 88
Evans, Thomas T. 71,88-89,103, 148,167,178
Evans, William M. 112
Evans and Roberts Cheese Factory 183
Evans, Bankert, Cohen, Lutz and Panzone 66
Evans family (Camroden) 168
Evans Road 23
Everett, Mary H. 33
Everett, Robert 31,32,33,35,97,104, 114,195
Everett Hymnal 33
Ewing, John 89

Fair Haven (VT) 130,139,172,199
Fairchild Cemetery 56
Fairchild Road (Remsen, NY) 43,56,77

Faxton Street (Utica, NY) 109
Federated Church (Remsen, NY) 50
Federated Churches of Prospect (Propect, NY) 86
Fellowship Meeting of the County; see Seiat y Wlad
Ferrell Corners (Newport, NY) 106
Festival of the Arts (Remsen, NY) 75,92
Ffestiniog (Wales) 88
First Baptist Church (Remsen, NY) 25,46, 47,**49-50**,74,75,202
First Baptist Church (Steuben Corners, NY) 44
First Baptist Church (Utica, NY) 44,94,**109-113**,114,118
First Calvinistic Methodist Society of Steuben 31,63; see also Capel Nant
First Calvinistic Methodist Society of Trenton 87
First (Congregational) Church (Richville, NY) 197-199
First Congregational Church of Marcy; see Bethania Church
First Free Baptist Union Society, The (East Nelson) 158
First Methodist Church (Utica, NY) 132
First Methodist Society of Steuben 63
First National Bank (New Hartford, NY) 136
First Particular Baptist Church (Steuben, NY) 45
First Presbyterian Church (Remsen, NY); see Capel Cerrig
First Presbyterian Church (Rome, NY) 168,173-175
First Presbyterian Church (Utica, NY) 117, 201
First Society of the Welsh Methodist Episcopal Church at Steu-

ben; see Sixty Church (Steuben, NY)
First Welsh Congregational Society of Marcy 101,103; see also Bethania (Marcy, NY)
First Welsh Congregational Society of the Town of Steuben 31; see also Capel Ucha
First Welsh Methodist Society of Steuben 28
First Welsh Whitefield Methodist Society of Remsen; see Capel Cerrig (Remsen, NY)
Flintshire (Wales) 31
Floyd (NY) 71,164,166,183
Floyd, William 163
Floyd Corners (NY) 164
Fort Schuyler 26
Fox Road (Marcy, NY) 101,103
Foulkes, Thomas 120
Francis, Francis 95
Francis, James 60
Frankfort Hill (NY) 133,138-139
Frankfort Hill Church (Frankfort, NY) 107, **138-139**
Free Baptists 84
Free Methodist Church (Nelson) 158
Free Soil Party 32,95
Free Will Baptiost Church (Prospect, NY) 86
Friend, The, see *Y Cyfail*
French Road (Steuben, NY) 34
French Road Cemetery Association 68,76
French Road Church (Steuben, NY) 18,39,56,58,**66-69**,73,75, 200,202
Fuller Road (Steuben, NY) 27, 29,64,66

Garn (Wales) 46
Garrett, Cheney 92
Garrett, John 92
Garrett, Peter 92
Gates, Phyllis 101

Genesee Street (Utica, NY) 132
Genesee Wesleyan Seminary (Lima, NY) 131
George, David 66
Glass Factory Road (Marcy, NY) 103
Globe Mills (Utica, NY) 110
Godwin, George 141
Gomer Flats (NY) 185
Gomer Hill (Turin, NY) 190-191
Gomer Hill Road (Turin, NY) 191-193
Gorney, Edna Williams 140
Gouverneur (NY) 196
Grace Episcopal Church (Utica, NY) 115,132
Grace Episcopal Church (Waterville, NY) 143-144
Graffenburg Road (Frankfort, NY) 138
Grange Road (Marcy, NY) 102
Grant, Ernest 73,79
Granville (NY) 139
Great Britain 53
Greig (NY) 184
Griddel, E. C. 171
Griffith, Bill 169
Griffith, D. P. 49
Griffith, David 45,111
Griffith, Ebenezer 197
Griffith, Ellen 153
Griffith, Emlyn 41,168,169
Griffith, Evan (Llanegryn) 115
Griffith, Evan 153
Griffith, Francis 153
Griffith, Griffith 84
Griffith, Griffith (Ffestiniog) 115
Griffith, Gwen 102
Griffith, J. T. 199
Griffith, James (Esq.) 169
Griffith, James (Rev.) 89,91,102, 114,115
Griffith, James (Richville) 196
Griffith, John 153
Griffith, John R. 89,102,135,165
Griffith, Joseph K. 195

Griffith, Margaret 60
Griffith, Nicodemus 28
Griffith, Owen (early settler) 26
Griffith, Owen (New York Mills) 134
Griffith, Owen (Rev.) 111
Griffith, Owen (undertaker) 34
Griffith, Rhys 27
Griffith, Robert 27
Griffith, Rowland 114
Griffith, T. H. 150
Griffith, Thomas M. 190
Griffith, Walter A. 27
Griffith, Webster 199
Griffith, William R. 130
Griffith, William T. 130,168-169
Griffiths, Mary 105
Griffiths, Nathaniel 105
Griffiths, T. Solomon 57,122-123, 129
Gwastadedd Gomer; see Gomer Flats
Gymanfa Ganu 75,76,117,138,161, 174,187
Gymanfa Mawr 43,151,187
Gymanfa of New York and Vermont 73

Hackney College (England) 115
Haggard, Cedric 73
Hamilton College (Clinton, NY) 114,127, 141,164,167
Hanes Cymry America 175
Hanover Green (NY) 141
Hardscrabble Road (Bridgewater, NY) 147-148
Harris, A. 131
Harris, Howell 53
Harris, James 27,44,48,110
Harris, John 75
Hasbrouck, Wilford 74,174
Hebron Church (Chicago, IL) 72
Hebron Church (Steuben, NY); see French Road Church
Helmer family 86

Helping Hands Society (Camroden) 168
Henry, William K. 168
Herbert, R. L. 130
Herkimer County (NY) 104,107, 148,203
Hicks, Thomas 92
Higby Road (New Hartford, NY) 138
High Falls Village 185; see also Collinsville
High Market (NY) 189
History of Remsen 71
Holland Land Company 93
Holland Patent (NY) 45,64,83,87-91,93,95,103,131,135,160,167,192
Holland Patent Academy 88,195
Holland Patent Larger Parish 73
Holland Patent Presbyterian Church 73
Holmes, (Rev.) 151
Holyhead (N. Wales) 124
Honey Out of the Rafters 35
Hopper Street (Utica, NY) 130
Hops 141,143,144,149
Hoskin, Frank 188
Hotel Street (Utica, NY) 110,115, 130
House of David, The (synagogue) 112
House of God: Church of the Living Christ 121,123
House of Israel, The (synagogue) 115
House of Jacob, The (synagogue) 121,123
Howell, Stephen 48
Hugh Davies' Church; see Frankfort Hill Church
Hughes (Rev.) (Episcopal priest) 143
Hughes, Charles Evans 68
Hughes, David (Rev.) 97,104,130
Hughes, David (d. 1902) 157
Hughes, David D. Jr. 157
Hughes, E. J. 150

Hughes, E. R. 33
Hughes, Edward 92-93
Hughes, Edward Lewis 172
Hughes, H. J. 188
Hughes, Henry 90,151
Hughes, Hugh (Nant) 65
Hughes, Hugh (Remsen) 69
Hughes, Hugh (Rev.) 101,111
Hughes, John (Baptist) 46,94
Hughes, John (Deerfield) 101
Hughes, John (Port Leyden) 194
Hughes, John (Remsen) 69
Hughes, John H. 103
Hughes, John Isaac 61,89
Hughes, Joseph 103
Hughes, May 157
Hughes, Morien Mon 43,151,176, 181
Hughes, R. W. 117-118,161
Hughes, Richard 89-91,135,160, 176
Hughes, Richard H. 65,123
Hughes, Robert 64
Hughes, Thomas (Paris) 146
Hughes, Thomas (Rev.) 46
Hughes, Thomas (Utica) 130
Hughes, William (Llanwrst) 121
Hughes Road (Nelson, NY) 158
Hughes, Rounds & Schurman 68
Hummel's Office Supply Co. 132
Humphrey, Catherine 57
Humphrey, Humphrey 130,146
Humphrey, John 197
Humphrey, Olwen 136
Humphreys, (Rev.) 132
Humphreys, Edward 46
Humphreys, Hugh G. 136-137
Humphries, Bertram 74
Hutchinson Road (Marcy, NY) 101

Ice cream socials 51,61,80
Ilion (NY) 61,107,133,136,139-141
Immanuel Presbyterian Church (Rome, NY) 174

Independents (denomination); see Congregationalists (denomination)
Iowa 161,185
Ironton (OH) 130
Isaac, Richard 93,187,192
Ixonia (WI) 115

James, B.F. 56
James, Edward W. 135
James, H. C. 111
James Road (Remsen-Trenton, NY) 55,56
Jarmon, Edward 61
Jarrett, James 121,187,192
Jenkins, David 111
Jenkins, Dewitt 106
Jenkins, Jenkin 31
Jenkins, Thomas (Rev.) 33,43,144
Jersen, Lorena 35
Johnstown (PA) 121
Jones, Abraham 152
Jones, C. D. 160
Jones, Cadwalader 146
Jones, Caradog 176
Jones, David (early settler) 27
Jones, David (New York Mills) 134
Jones, David (Rev.)(Baptist) 111
Jones, David (Rev.) (d. 1886) 198
Jones, David (Webster Hill) 181
Jones, David F. (elder) 123
Jones, David M. 65,71,72,76,167
Jones, David O. 88
Jones, Dinah 69
Jones, E. Eurog 131
Jones, Ebenezer T. 87,121,157
Jones, Edward (Capel Cerrig) 69
Jones, Edward 147
Jones, Edward M. 165
Jones, Evan (Penygraig) 65
Jones, Evan (Remsen) 186
Jones, Evans 123
Jones, George Whitefield 73
Jones, Griffith (Garn) 46
Jones, Griffith (Nelson) 160
Jones, Griffith (Plainfield) 154

Jones, Griffith (Rev.) 45,87
Jones, Griffith (Salem) 97
Jones, Griffith (Turin) 189
Jones, Gwawr 165
Jones, Gwen 30
Jones, Humphrey 177
Jones, Hugh D. 188
Jones, J. Eldred 111
Jones, J. Vincent 43,117
Jones, Jacob D. 95
Jones, James 197
Jones, James T. 160
Jones, Jenkyn 78
Jones, Jennie (Capel Cerrig) 75
Jones, Jennie (Penygraig) 62
Jones, Jesse 45-46
Jones, John, "The Farm" 91
Jones, John (Quaker Hill) 179
Jones, John (Rev., Steuben) 46
Jones, John (Rev., Utica) 130
Jones, John (Tire shop) 84
Jones, John D. (Plainfield) 154
Jones, John E. (Bridgewater) 148
Jones, John E. "Pumpkinhook" 179-180
Jones, John H. 170
Jones, John M. 160-161
Jones, John O. 189
Jones, John R. 78
Jones, John Rosser 198
Jones, John Seth 48
Jones, John T. 181
Jones, John W. 48
Jones, Llewelyn 125-126
Jones, Margaret 60
Jones, Morris 31
Jones, Morris S. 65
Jones, Moses 69
Jones, Oliver 79
Jones, Owen Picton 189
Jones, Pomroy 38,43
Jones, R. Eifion 176
Jones, R. J. 72
Jones, Rhys Gwesyn 115-118,135
Jones, Richard (Rev.) 44,45,50,93
Jones, Richard W. 88,167,170

Jones, Robert F. 88
Jones, Robert G. 60,61
Jones, Robert J. 123
Jones, Robert R. 158
Jones, Robert T. 150
Jones, Samuel 155
Jones, T. I. 85
Jones, Thomas (Rev.) 175
Jones, Thomas (Sixty) 82
Jones, Thomas E. 157
Jones, Thomas R. 88
Jones, Thomas V. 179
Jones, Thomas Z. R. 50
Jones, Tudor 115
Jones, W. Caradoc 117,144
Jones, W. N. 59
Jones, Walter H. 73,173
Jones, William (Capel Isaf) 48
Jones, William (Snowden) 61
Jones, William (Utica) 115
Jones, William C. 27,29,30
Jones, William G. 172
Jones, William J. 141
Jones, William N. 170,177
Jones, William P. 26
Jones, Winifred 196
Jones Road (Remsen, NY) 55
Joseph, Watkyn B. (Y Myfyr) 115, 116,118

Kayuta Drive-In 37
Kelly, Christopher 91
Kelly, Virginia 91
Kemmerer, James W. 74
Kennedy Road (Marcy, NY) 101
Kent, Elizabeth 41
Kent, John S. 41
Kent, Silas 41
Kent, Thomas 41
King of Bardsey 78
Kirkland Art Center (Clinton, NY) 141
Knapp, Robert J. 161
Knoxville (TN) 165
Korean Church (Rome, NY) 174
Koziara, Clarice 169

Krzewinski Road (Quaker Hill, NY) 179

La Banda Rosa 108
La Crosse (WI) 103
Lake Ontario 195
Lally, John 160
Lamb, George 65,72
Lamb, James 170
Landers family 135
Lane, William 101
Larson Road (Nelson, NY) 158
Larson Road (Paris, NY) 146
Lawrence, A. E. 50
Lawrence, Patricia Haddock 119
Lee, Philip 162
Lee, Town of 163,177,179
Lee Center (NY) 202
Leeville (NY) 162
Lent, Paul 129
Leport, Charles 168
Lepper, Gaile Winston 99
Lewis, David 120
Lewis, Edward (Quaker Hill) 179-180
Lewis, Edward (West Eaton) 162
Lewis, Francis 184
Lewis, Hugh 102,165
Lewis, John (Remsen) 27
Lewis, John (Salem) 97
Lewis, Lewis 54
Lewis, Lewis E. 198
Lewis, Morgan 184
Lewis, Owen 194
Lewis, Solomon 146
Lewis, Thomas (Y Glyn) 186,194
Lewis, William E. 99
Lewis County (NY) 65,71,184,185, 187,190,194, 203
Leyden, Town of 184
Liberty Party 32
Liberty Street (Rome, NY) 170,175
Liberty Street (Utica, NY) 111,130
Liberty Street Methodist Church (Rome, NY), see Calvary Methodist Church

Life of Morris Roberts, The 43
Lincoln Davies Store (Paris Station, NY) 146
Little Falls (NY) **107**
Little White Church on the Corner (Camroden NY); see Camroden Presbyterian
Littler, Robert 94-95
Liverpool (England) 126,130,171
Llanberis (N. Wales) 125
LLandudno (Wales) 126
Llanegryn (N. Wales) 115,195
Llanfaircaereinion, (Montgomeryshire, Wales) 135
Llanidloes (Wales) 97
Llanwst (Wales) 135
Llewellyn Road (Remsen, NY) 23
Lleyn Peninsula (N. Wales) 27,54
Lloyd, David 128
Lloyd, John 158,162
Lloyd, John (Lewis County) 194
Lloyd, John D. 132
Lloyd, Mair 76,127
Lloyd, R. Glynne 76,90,126-127, 137,161
Lloyd, Richard 128
London (England) 115,121
Long Creek (ID) 73
Long Island (NY)
Loper, David 169
Loper, Susan 75,169
Lower Chapel, see Capel Isaf
Lowville (NY) **194**
Luke Road (Marcy, NY) 101
Lyman Road (Turin, NY) 193
Lyons Falls (NY) 185-186,188
Lyons Falls Players Guild 188

Madison (NY) 43,155
Madison Baptist Church (Madison, NY) 161
Madison County 41,155,203
Madison Street (Rome,NY) 175
Magee, Morton 79
Mahaffy, Charles 74
Mahan, H. W. 141

Mahanoy City (PA) 165
Main Street (New York Mills) 134
Main Street (Oriskany, NY) 177
Main Street (Remsen, NY) 41,50, 72
Main Street (Utica, NY) 109,113
Mallory Road (Marcy, NY) 97
Mappa Ave. (Barneveld, NY) 91-92
Mappa farm (Barneveld, NY) 91
Mappa Hall (Barneveld, NY) 92
Maple Street (Remsen, NY) 48
Marcy (NY) 83,88,96-97,99-103
Marcy Hill (Marcy, NY) 103
Marcy, Town of 96,99,101,103
Marshall, Ken 95
Marshall, Town of 141
Martin's Corners (Newport, NY) 104
Martinsburg 194
Mason, John 150
Mason Road (Plainfield, NY) 150
Masonic Lodge (New Hartford, NY) 136-137
Masonic Lodge (Sandy Creek, NY) 196
Masonic Temple (Rome, NY) 174
McCauley schoolhouse (Plainfield, NY) 150
Mead Hall (Camroden, NY) 168
Mechem, James L. 129
Meifod, Montgomershire (N. Wales) 148
Mennonites 203
Memory stones 18,19
Meredith family (Holland Patent, NY) 88
Meredith, (Mr.) 35
Meredith, M. J. 88
Meredith, Robert (Rev.) 88
Meredith, Robert 177
Meredith, Robert C. 68
Meredith, Robert G. 67
Meredith, Robert R. 88
Merionethshire (N. Wales) 61,194
Merthyr Tydvil (Wales) 116

Messenger, The; see *Cenhadwr, Y*
Methodist Church (Barneveld, NY) 91
Methodist Church (North Steuben, NY) 181
Methodist Church (North Western, NY) 181
Methodist Episcopal Church (denomination), 53; see also Wesleyan Methodist Church
Methodist Episcopal Church (Clinton, NY) 141
Methodist Episcopal Church (Oriskany, NY) 178
Methodist Episcopal Church (Remsen, NY) 53,72
Michael, David 48,111
Middle Ganville (NY) 139
Mid-state Correctional Facility 99, 129
Miller, Collin 127
Milwaukee (WI) 89
Minnesota 72,152
Morgan (Rev.) 135
Morgan, Evan H. 103
Morgan, Joshua T. 111
Morgan, Thomas 45,189
Morgan, William E. 157
Moriah Church (Caernarvon, N. Wales) 123
Moriah Church (Prospect, NY) 44,**84-86**,87
Moriah Church (Utica, NY) 56,57, 60,73,90,**119-129**,136-138,140, 152
Moriah-Olivet United Presbyterian Church (Utica NY), 18,58,109, 113,121,125,129,201; see also Moriah Church (Utica, NY) and Seneca Street Church (Utica, NY)
Morrau, John W. 119
Morris, Daniel 28,113-114
Morris, David 50
Morris, Edward L. 148
Morris, Elmer 102

Morris, Enoch 136
Morris, Evan 57,58
Morris, Humphrey 170
Morris, Rowland 145-147
Morris, Thomas 112
Morrisville (NY) 155,161
Morton, Allen J. 112
Mount Zion; see Bryn Seion
Mullen Hill (Western, NY) 163, 182-183
Mullen Hill Road (Western, NY) 182
Murdock, George 74

Nant Church; see Capel Nant (Steuben)
National Welsh American Foundation 168
Nebo Congregational Church (Welsh Hill, NY) 189,**191-192**
Neenan, Garth 118
Neenan, Norma Roberts 118
Nelli, Barnhardt 101
Nelson (NY) 150,155,158-161,202
Nelson Cemetery Association 161
New Cambria (MO) 115
New Forest Cemetery 111
New Hartford (NY) 61,101,133, 136,138,148
New York City (NY) 26,31-33,94, 114-115,120,122,125,165-166,184
New York Gymanfa (Baptist) 111
New York Gymanfa of the Calvinistic Methodist Church 56,166,182
New York Gymanfa of Welsh Congregational Churches 115
New York Home Mission Society 116
New York Mills (NY) 133,192
New York Mills Cotton Manufacturing Company 134
New York State 25,41,46
New York State Forest Preserve 37,149
Newfoundland (Canada) 160
Newport (NY) 83,104-105

Newport, Town of 105
Newport Road (Newport, NY) 104
Nichols, John 113
Nine Mile Creek (South Trenton, NY) 93
Ninety-Six (NY) 43,77,80,82
Ninety-Six (Calvinistic Methodist) Church 58,**80**
Ninety-Six (Congregational) Church **43-44**,71,80,85
Ninety-Six (Wesleyan) Church 80, **82**,95
Noah's Rump (Plainfield, NY) 149-150
North Main Street (Constableville, NY) 188
North Park Row (Clinton, NY) 141
North Utica Arts Center 99
North Washington Street (Rome, NY) 170

Ohio 41,185
Old Home Day (Bethel) 39,40
Old Home Day (Camroden Presbyterian Church) 164,168-169
Old Home Day (French Road Church) 68
Old Home Day (Nelson, NY) 161
Old Home Day (Salem) 98
"Old Morris"; see Morris Roberts
Old Stage Road (Marcy, NY) 97
Old Stage Road (Prospect, NY) 54
Old State Road (Nelson, NY) 158
Old State Route 12 61
Olden Barneveld; see Barneveld
Olivet Presbyterian Church (Utica, NY) 124,128,129
Olson, Luther E. 174
Olson, Mary Craig 174,180
Olyphant (PA) 172
Oneida County (NY) 24,50,61,66, 84,104,141,143,148,163,165,169, 179,184,187,202,203
Oneida Square (Utica, NY) 117, 201

Oneida Street (New Hartford, NY) 138
Oneida (Welsh) Presbytery 59,60, 68,73,103,125,141,157,173,183, 186,189,195
Order of American True Ivorites 163
Oriskany (NY) 163,167,177
Oriskany Boulevard (Utica, NY) 109,110, 122
Oriskany Falls (NY) 144
Orwell (NY) 196
Oswego (NY) 118
Oswego County (NY) 196
Oswego Street (Ilion, NY) 139-140
Otsego County (NY) 143 148
Owen Ap Iago; see James Owen
Owen, Hugh H. 54,69
Owen, James 30,53,54,57,58,83
Owen, James (home of) 54,55
Owen, John 144
Owen, Pierce 194
Owen, Richard J. 39,61,67,79
Owens, Evan 189
Owens, Owen 101
Owens, Robert 65
Owens, Thomas M. 135,190
Owens. William 165
Owens, William J. 72
Oxford (England) 53

Palmyra (OH) 114,160
Paris (NY) 143,145-148
Paris Hill (NY) 145
Paris Station (NY) 145-147
Paris Union Welsh Church (Paris, NY) **145-147**
Park Avenue (Utica, NY) 123,125
Park Avenue Baptist Church (Utica, NY) 50
Park Place (Holland Patent, NY) 88
Parry, David 146
Parry, John Hughes 124
Parry, Moses 165
Payne, Kim 118

Payne, Sandra Griffith 118
Peabody, Alan B. 74
Pearl Street (New Hartford, NY) 136-137
Pearl Street (Utica, NY) 111
Pen Mount (Steuben, NY) 34,35,37
Pen Mount Church; see Penymynydd
Pen Mountain Cemetery Association 35,37
Penarth farm 135
Peniel Chapel (Utica, NY) 124
Peniel Congregational Church (Nelson, NY) 91,155,157,**158-161**,202
Peniel Congregational Church (Remsen, NY) 33,38,**41-43**,71,85
Peniel School (Utica, NY) 124,126
Penmachno (N. Wales) 138
Penn Mountain Inn 23
Pennsylvania 26,27,44,73,85,111
Pentacostal House of Prayer (Utica, NY) 124
Pen-y-caerau; see Penycaerau
Penycaerau (Remsen, NY) 18,31, **53-60**,63,64,69,70,79,83,87,119
Penycaerau Cemetery 46,56,57
Penygraig 39,56,58,**60-63**,65,66,67, 73,79,106,179
Penygraig Cemetery Association 62
Penygraig Monument 18,63
Penymynydd (Steuben, NY) 18,32,**34-37**
Penymyndd Cemetery Association; see Pen Mount Cemetery Association
Penymynydd Monument 35,36
Perry, Evan 66,67
Perry, Owen F. 50
Petaluma (CA) 116
Pfeiffer, Paul 99
Phelps, George O. 86
Philadelphia (PA) 26,44,113,114
Phillips, David 111
Phillips, Sem 33

Index

Phillips, Sem 33
Phillips, William T. 111
Pierce, William G. 29-31,55,58,64-66,114
Pirnie, Alexander 58
Pirsons, Philetus 50
Pittsburg (PA) 71
Plainfield, Town of 148,150-152, 157
Plainfield Center (NY) 143,145, 148-152
Plainfield Center Cemetery 153
Plank Road (Marcy, NY) 97
Plant Street (Utica, NY) 117,119
Plymouth (PA) 187
Plymouth Bethesda Church (Utica, NY) 17, 18,99,116,118-119,201
Port Leyden (NY) 185-186,194
Posher family 97
Pottsville (PA) 31,130
Poultney (VT) 73,139
Powell, Benjamin 114
Powell, Howell R. (Powell Bach) 114
Powell, Lewis 161
"Powell of Palmyra"; see Howell R. Powell
Preaching festival; see Cyfarfod Pregethu
Plymouth Congregational Church (Utica, NY) 117-119
Presbyterian Church (denomination) 53,73,120,122,125,173
Presbyterian Church (Camroden, NY); see Camroden Presbyterian Church
Presbyterian Church (East Nelson) 158
Presbyterian Church (Ilion, NY) 141
Presbyterian Church (New Hartford, NY) 138
Presbyterian Church (Nelson, NY) 158
Presbyterian Church (North Gage, NY) 170

Presbyterian Church (Westernville, NY) 31, 168
Price, David (Dewi Dinorwig) 115
Price, William 141
Price Road (Floyd, NY) 164
Prichard, David 46
Prichard, John W. 78
Prichard, Love 78
Prichard, R. W. 132
Prichard, W. S. 61
Pritchard, David E. 175,189,192
Pritchard, John M. 161
Pritchard, William 69
Pitchard Road (Steuben, NY) 23, 27
Prohibition Party 144,176
Prospect (NY) 43,44,46,50,52,54, 58,81,83-84,94,151
Prospect Books 84
Prospect Library 84
Prospect Street (Remsen, NY) 69
Providence (PA) 172
Pugh, Gardner 62
Pugh, Leonard 178
Pugh, Meredith 172
Pugh, Myfanwy 62
Pulaski (NY) 195
Pwllheli (N. Wales) 78,121,187

Quaker Hill (NY) 163,179-180,183
Quaker Hill Cemetery 180
Quaker Hill Church (Quaker, NY) **179-180**
Quaker Hill Road (Western, NY) 180
"Queen, The" (ship) 184-186

Racine (WI) 121,125,172
Radnor (OH) 45,46,166
Rahn, Jeffery 118
Rahn, Marilyn Williams 118
Rainbow Circle (Moriah-Olivet) 129
Rees, D. Ben 17-19
Reed, David 110
Reed, Helen 200

Rees, Edward 65,71,186,194
Rees, George M. 198
Rees, Henry 165
Rees, Stephen 201
Rees, Thomas 197
Rehobeth Church (Marcy, NY) **103-104**, 120
Rehobeth Church (Rome, NY) 165,**175-177**
Remington Arms (Ilion, NY) 139
Remsen (NY) 23,24,27,28,32,37,39, 41,43,48,50,53-56,58,60,65,67,69, 71,72,75-77,82,83,84,95,100,108, 117,119,120,142-144,167,179,184, 186,187,202
Remsen Baptist Church (Remsen, NY) 39, 46,50,202 see also First and Third Baptist Church
Remsen Fortnightly Club 75,76
Remsen Gymanfa 61,69
'Remsen Prebyterian Parish 62,65, 73
Remsen-Steuben Historical Society 34,37,41,53,76,77,80
Republicans 95
Reynolds, Gertrude 94
Rhos (Wales) 29
Richards, Augustus Loring 68
Richards, Cadwalader 96,97,99
Richards, D. Morgan 125
Richards, David 99
Richards, Edward 157
Richards, G. J. 118
Richards, John 111
Richards, John E. 157
Richards, Joseph 45,93
Richards, Lizzie 72
Richards, T. 65
Richville (NY) 33,75,196-200
Rickard family 87
Ridge Street (Rome, NY) 177
Roach, Kenneth 118-119
Road to Sixty, The 81,84
Robert ap Gwilym Ddw 123
Roberts, (Mr.) 114
Roberts, Catherine Jones 60

Roberts, D. C. 131
Roberts, David 194
Roberts, David W. 192
Roberts, Edward 179
Roberts, Ellen 128
Roberts, Ellis 96,97
Roberts, Ellis R. (Hon.) 123
Roberts, Ellis R. (Rev.) 189
Roberts, Evan (Rev.) 29,31,35,114
Roberts, Evan (Utica) 119,123
Roberts, Evan Gwyndaf 75,129
Roberts, Griffith W. 33
Roberts, Hugh (early settler) 26
Roberts, Hugh (Rev.) 88,166
Roberts, Humphrey D. 123
Roberts, Idwald 157
Roberts, J. W. 181
Roberts, James 59
Roberts, John (Bethesda) 113
Roberts, John (Nelson) 161
Roberts, (Mrs.) John 158
Roberts, John D. 112
Roberts, John G. 27-30
Roberts, John O. 67
Roberts, Kim 118
Roberts, Mary 56
Roberts, Millard 71,86
Roberts, Morris 31,33,37,38,41-43, 56,71,85,120
Roberts, Richard 194
Roberts, Richard (Rev.) 45,48,50, 111
Roberts, Richard R. 182-183
Roberts, Robert 62
Roberts, Robert E. 123
Roberts, Robert Thomas 59,167-168,172
Roberts, Robert W. 46
Roberts, Sarah Davies 152
Roberts, Thomas 87
Roberts, Thomas R. 88,192
Roberts, Thomas W. 135,192
Roberts, W. Alun 161
Roberts, William (Holland Patent) 88

Roberts, William (New York Mills) 134
Roberts, William D. (Rev.) 192
Roberts William D. (shoemaker) 192
Roberts, William Henry 122
Robinson, Davis 128-129
Rome (NY) 44,89,110,152,163,164, 166,168,170-172,174-178,181, 183,192
"Round Heads" 54
Route 8 148
Route 11 196,200
Route 12 23,28,37,93,96
Route 12D 187
Route 20 148,155
Rowlands, Daniel T. 187,192
Rowlands, Griffith 26
Rowlands, Hugh 65,73
Rowlands, William 88,103,120,121, 166,170,177
Ruff, Peter 179
Rutger Street (Utica, NY) 131

Sacred Grove (Steuben, NY) 24,44, 46
Sage Road (Webster Hill, NY) 181
St. Andrew's Episcopal Church (Barneveld, NY) 91-92
St. Anne's Roman Catholic Church (Hinckley, NY) 42,43
St. David 78
St. David's Choir (Utica, NY) 69,138,161, 169
St. David's Day 128,195,200
St. David's Episcopal Church (Barneveld, NY) 92
St. David's Episcopal Church (Radnor, OH) 132
St. David's Society of Rome 163
St. David's Society of Utica 138, 164,201
St. James Episcopal Church (Perkiomen, PA) 132
St. Joseph and St. Patrick's Church (Utica, NY) 108

St. Louis (MO) 130
St. Lawrence County (NY) 196,203
St. Paul's Episipcal Church (Holland Patent, NY) 92
St. Peter's Episcopal Church (Great Valley, PA) 132
St. Thomas Episcopal Church (Morgantown, PA) 132
Salem Church (Deerfield, NY); see Salem Church (Marcy, NY)
Salem Church (Marcy, NY) **96-100**, 102
Salem Church (New York Mills, NY) **133-135**,192
Salem Church (Newport, NY) **105-107**
Salem Church Cemetery (Marcy, NY) 99
Salem Church Cemetery (Newport, NY) 106
Salisbury (NY) **107**
Salisbury, Ebenezer 61,101
Salisbury Academy (Salisbury, NY) 107
Samuel, Enoch 120,121
Samuels, Mr. (Nelson, NY) 156
Samuels, Samuel 138
Sandy Creek (NY) **195-196**
Sangerfield, Town of 144,155
Sayre Memorial Presbyterian Church (Utica, NY) 118
Schuyler (NY) 104
Scott, George 171
Scott, Willard 23
Scranton (PA) 48,173
Second Avenue (Ilion, NY) 139
Second Baptist Church (Steuben, NY); see Capel Isaf
Second Baptist Church (Utica, NY) 110; see also Tabernacle Baptist Church (Utica, NY)
Second Calvinistic Methodist Society of Trenton (Prospect, NY) 87
Second Congregational Church (Rome, NY) 170

Second Congregational Church (Utica, NY) 115,122
Second Independent Congregational Church of Remsen; see Bethel Congregational Church
Second Presbyterian Church (Utica, NY) 31
Second Ward (Utica, NY) 109,112, 122
Second Welsh Congregational Church (Utica, NY) 91
Seiaty Wlad; see County Class Metting
Seion Church (Turin, NY) 88,187, **192-194**
Senchyna, Alex 68
Senchyna, Myron 37
Seneca Street (Utica, NY) 120-123,130
Seneca Street Church (Utica, NY) 120-123, 130; see also Moriah
Seren Orllewinol, Y (The Western Star) 111
Set Fawr (large pew) 126
Sharon (PA) 190
Shenandoah (PA) 72
Shiloh 151
Shilioh Congregational Church (Plainfield, NY) 150,**151-154**
Shiloh Monument 153
Shiloh parsonage 151,152
Shufelf, Ola 25,34,47
Singing Hills, The 84
Siop Fellon 23,27
Sixty Cemetery 18
Sixty Corners (NY) 64,81
Sixty Road 18,81
Sixty Wesleyan Church (Steuben, NY) **81**,95
Skaneateles Turnpike 148,151
Slatington (PA) 152
Slavery 32
Smith Hill (Deerfield, NY) 96
Snowden (N. Wales) 61
Snow Ridge 189

Society of Friends (Quaker Hill, NY) 179
Society of Friends (West Branch, NY) 179
Sons of Temperance 93
South Church (Utica,NY) 119
South Dakota 73
South James Street (Rome, NY) 177
South Poultney 139
South Street Methodist Church (Utica, NY) 132
South Trenton (NY) 26,45,83,92-95,187
South Trenton Baptist Cemetery 94-95
South Trenton Wesleyan Cemetery 95-96
South Trenton Wesleyan Church 82,**95**
Starr Hill Road (Steuben, NY) 24, 27,29,44, 47,81
State Road (Remsen, NY) 61
State Street (Prospect, NY) 84
State Street (Turin, NY) 189
State Street (Utica, NY) 117
State Street Methodist Church (Utica, NY) 130
Stephens, David 57,71,119,120
Stephens, John 44,94,101,110
Stephens, Thomas 45,46,50
Steuben (NY) 23,24,26-29,31-34,37,39,43-45,47,48,53,56,63-66, 71,83,84,92,94,95,97,111,114,119, 143,144,184,189,195,198,200
Steuben, Baron de 23,24,44,46,47, 60,81
Steuben, Town of 37,47
Steuben Cabin 24,25
Steuben Corners (NY) 44
Steuben Memorial 25,81
Steuben Road (Newport, NY) 104
Steuben Road East (Newport, NY) 105-106
Stittville (NY) 103

Stone Church (Remsen, NY); see Capel Cerrig (Remsen, NY)
Stratonville (PA) 73
Sullivan, John L. 95-96
Summit Street (Prospect, NY) 86
Swansea (MA) 109
Swamp Road (Remsen, NY) 43
Swope, Jean Anne 129
Synagogues; see House of David, House of Israel, House of Jacob
Syracuse (NY) 154,155

Tabernacle Baptist Church (Utica, NY) 109, 110,112,113
Tanner Road (Newport, NY) 104, 105
Taylor, Rev. Dr. 50
Taylor, Edward 116
Taylor, Elizabeth 127
Taylor, John 109
Temperance 32,114,144,176
Third Baptist Church (Steuben and Remsen, NY) 46,**47-49**,95,202
Thomas, (Mrs.) E. H. 141
Thomas, Edward 72
Thomas, Gilbert 62,63
Thomas, Henry 48
Thomas, Howard 81,84
Thomas, Hugh 92-93
Thomas, Isaac 130-131
Thomas, Leola 62
Thomas, Nadine 63
Thomas, R. D. (Iorthryn Gwynedd) 165,175
Thomas, Robert 47
Thomas, Sarah Roberts 165
Thomas, Thomas (Rev.) 82,95,130
Thomas, Thomas 104-105
Thomas, Thomas B. 121
Thomas, William H. 48,111
Thorn Memorial Chapel (Utcia, NY) 112
Tibbits, Evelyn 62
Tibbitts Road (New Hartford, NY) 137
Today Show 23

Town of Marcy Democratic Club 103
Towyn (N. Wales) 195
Trefecca (S. Wales) 53
Treleck (S. Wales) 189
Trenton (NY) 26,44,45,56,83,87, 93,96,160
Trenton, Town of 91
Trenton Falls (NY) 50,94
Trewne (Cardiganshire, Wales) 198
Trinity Episcopal Church (Oxford, Pa) 132
Trinity Episcopal Church (Utica, NY) 109,113
Trinity United Church of Christ (Rome, NY) 176-177
Tug Hill Church; see Nebo Congregational Church
Tug Hill Plateau 184,195
Turin (NY) 185,189-190,192,202
Turin Road 179
Turin Street (Rome, NY) 171
Turin Welsh Church (Turin, NY); see Welsh Congregational Church (Turin, NY)
Twitchell, Frank W. 73
Ty Cerrig (Remsen, NY) 27
Ty Cerrig (Richville, NY) 197,200
Ty Goch Corners (Steuben, NY) 27
Ty Goch Hill (Steuben, NY) 47
Ty Howel (Remsen, NY) 61

Unadilla Forks (NY) 148,153
Uncle Tom's Cabin 31
Union Church (Collinsville, NY) 185-187
Union Street (Utica, NY) 130
Union Welsh Church (New York, NY) 114
United Church of Christ (denomination) 177
United German Evangelical Lutheren Church 177
United Methodist Church (denomination) 53

United Methodist Church (Morrisvillle, NY) 161
United Methodist Church (Prospect, NY) 79
United Methodist Church (Remsen, NY) 76,79
University of Wrexham 114
Upper Chapel (Steuben, NY); see Capel Ucha (Steuben, NY)
Upper Church (Camroden, NY), see Congregational Church (Camroden, NY)
Upper Church (Rome, NY); see Bethel Presbyterian Church (Rome, NY)
Upper Mills (Whitestown, NY) 113
Utica (NY) 26,28,31,32,44,56,64,75, 94,96,99,100-102,107-109,111, 113-116,118-123,130-133,135- 136,138,140-143,148,151,152, 157,161,164, 166,184,187-188,201
Utica Daily Press 112
Utica Presbytery 66,75,76,125, 168,174
Utica Rescue Mission 75
Utica Street (Oriskany, NY) 178

Valley Church, The 192,**194**
Varick Street (Utica, NY) 110
Van Buren, Martin 32
Vaughan, John J. 167
Vermont 139
Vincent, William 104

Wakely, Clarence 157
Walcott, Benjamin 134
Walker, Benjamin 24
Wall, Ceinwen Davies 131
Washington (D.C.) 34
Washington, George 24
Washington Court (Utica, NY) 123
Washington County (NY) 139
Washington Mills (NY) 138
Washington Street (Utica, NY) 113-116,130

Waterbury Presbyterian Church (Oriskany, NY) 178
Waterville (NY) 43,135,143-146, 152
Waterville Cemetery 144
Waterville Village Hall 144
Watford (Glamorganshire, Wales) 53
Watkins, John 101
Watson, JoAnn 169
Wawr Americanaidd, Y 111
Weaver, Allison 128
Webster Hill (Western, NY) 163, 181-183
Webster Hill Church **181-182**
Weeks, Ebenezer 27
Weld, Richard 128
Wells, William A. 50
Welsh Anti-Slavery Society of Steuben, Remsen, Trenton and Vicinities 32
Welsh Association of New York State 90
Welsh Baptist Church (denomination) 109-112
Welsh Baptist Church (Bardwell Mill, NY); see Bardwell Baptist Church
Welsh Baptist Church (Holland Patent, NY) **87**
Welsh Baptist Church (Marcy, NY) **101**
Welsh Baptist Church (New York, NY) 94
Welsh Baptist Church (Prospect, NY) 46, 52,**84**
Welsh Baptist Church (South Trenton, NY) 45,**93-95**
Welsh Baptist Church (Swansea, MA) 109
Welsh Bible Society 89
Welsh Bush (NY) 107
Welsh Calvinistic Methodist Church (Rome, NY); see Bethel Presbyterian Church (Rome, NY)

Welsh Church, The (Clinton, NY) **141-142**
Welsh Church, The (Ilion, NY) **139-141**
Welsh Church, The (Turin, NY); see Turin Welsh Church
Welsh Church Road (Nelson, NY) 155
Welsh Congregational Church (Barneveld, NY) 89,90,**91-92**
Welsh Congregational Church (Camroden, NY) **164-165**,175
Welsh Congregational Church (Holland Patent, NY) **89-91**,135
Welsh Congregational Church (Nelson, NY); see Peniel Church (Nelson, NY)
Welsh Congregational Church (New York Mills, NY); see Salem Church (New York Mills, NY)
Welsh Congregational Church (Paris, NY) **145**
Welsh Congregational Church (Richville, NY) **196-200**
Welsh Congregational Church (Rome, NY); see Rehobeth (Rome, NY)
Welsh Congregational Church (Turin, NY) 175,**189-190**,192
Welsh Congregational Church (Utica, NY), 28,31,97,114,119; see also Bethesda (Utica, NY)
Welsh Congregational Church (Waterville, NY) 135,**143-144**,145
Welsh Congregational Church (West Eaton, NY) **162**
Welsh Congregationalists (denomination) 111,113
Welsh Day (Camroden, NY) 164, 168-169
Welsh District Road (Remsen, NY) 52
Welsh Episcopal Church **132**
Welsh Heritage Sunday 113,174-175
Welsh Hill (Plainfield, NY); see Noah's Rump (Plainfield, NY)
Welsh Hill (Turin, NY) 189,190-193
Welsh Hill Cemetery 191-193
Welsh Hill Church (Clifford, PA) 31
Welsh Hill School (Turin, NY) 192-193
Welsh Independent Church (Utica, NY) 115
Welsh National Gymanfa Ganu Association 41,60,128
Welsh Prairie Church (Lake Emily, WI) 185
Welsh Presbyterian (denomination) 53,139; see also Calvinistic Methodist (denomination)
Welsh Presbyterian Church (Rome, NY); see Bethel Presbyterian Church (Rome, NY)
Welsh Settlement Road (Richville, NY) 196, 197,200
Welsh Society of Richville 196
Welsh Temperance Society of Utica 32
Welsh Union Church (New York, NY) 30
Wesley, John 45,53
Wesleyan Methodist Church (Paris, NY); see Bethany Church
Wesleyan Methodists (denomination) 26,82
West Branch (NY) 179
West Davis Road (Deerfield, NY) 100
West Eaton (NY) 155,**162**
West Exeter (NY) 150,154
West Pawlet (VT) 139
West Road (Turin, NY) 189
West Turin, Town of 184,189
West Winfield, (NY) 31,114,154
Western, Town of 35,163,177,179, 181-183

Western Hill (Western, NY) 163, **183**
Western Star, The; see *Seren Orllewinol, Y*
Westernville (NY) 163,168
Westminster Presbyterian Church (Utica, NY) 117,201
White, L. D. 130
White Birch Inn (Remsen, NY) 77
Whitefield, George 53,70
Whitefield (Calvinistic) Methodist Society (Paris, NY) **145-146**
Whitesboro (NY) 109
Whitesboro Street (Utica, NY) 109,113-116
Whitestown, Town of 133
Wilkes-Barre (PA) 91,172
Williams, Abraham 110
Williams, Alfred 62
Williams, Ambrose 48
Williams, Benjamin H. 160
Williams, Bernard 39,40
Williams, Caradoc Phillips 173
Williams, Daryl 127
Williams, David (Capel Cerrig) 71
Williams, David (Coke) 130
Williams, David (Holland Patent) 88
Williams, David J. 46,57,84
Williams, David L. 199
Williams, David R. 61,106
Williams, Elizabeth Davies 152,173
Williams, Esther 158
Williams, Evan G. 58,79,87
Williams, Henry D. 77,80
Williams, Henry R. 89
Williams, Hermine 80
Williams, Hugh 170
Williams, Hugh R. 85,151,189
Williams, Humphrey 167
Williams, Isaac T. 152
Williams, J. T. 153-154
Williams, James (elder) 78
Williams, James (Rev.) 160
Williams, Jay G. 74,80,127

Williams, Jay G. III 76,80,127-128, 164,169,175
Williams, Jay Gomer 89,167,168, 170
Williams, John (Plainfield: Congregationalist) 153
Williams, John (Plainfield: Methodist) 154
Williams, John (Utica) 109
Williams, John (Richville) 199
Williams, John (King of Bardsey) 78
Williams, John J. (Bridgewater) 147
Williams, John J. (New Hartford) 136
Williams, John J. (Turin) 185
Williams, John R. 82,95
Williams, John Rhiwen 167,172
Williams, John S. 79,170,173,202
Williams, John W. 104
Williams, Lewis 61,117
Williams, Mary (Moriah) 123
Williams, Mary (Rome) 174
Williams, Morgan 44
Williams, Morris J. 48,93,111
Williams, Norman 41
Williams, R. R. 126
Williams, Rees T. 90,118
Williams, Richard 151
Williams, Richard J. 61,173
Williams, Richard M. 167
Williams, Robert (Lee Center) 193,202
Williams, Robert (Lewis County) 185,189
Williams, Robert (Rev.) 124
Williams, Robert (Rome) 171,172
Williams, Robert (South Trenton) 94
Williams, Robert L. 87
Williams, Samuel A. 102,104,189
Williams, Stewart Jr. 113
Williams, Thomas 71,170,186,187, 192
Williams, Thomas J. 29,88

Williams, Thomas O. 128
Williams, Waldo 39
Williams, William (Captain) 26
Williams, William (Holland Patent) 88
Williams, William (Rome) 170
Williams, William D. 31,35,89,91, 97,98,102,134
Williams, William P. 66
Williams, William R. 136,140
Williams, William T. 56,69-71,119
Williams Corners (NY) 162
Willowvale (NY) 138
Wilton Park (England) 130
Wind Gap (PA) 172
Winston, Ann Williams 98
Winston, David 99
Winston, Neal 99
Winston, Samuel 98
Winston, William D. 99
Winston Road (Marcy, NY) 97
Wisconsin 48,61,71,72,115,120,166, 167,185
Wright Settlement Cemetery 163, 165,166
Wright Settlement Road 163
Wynne, Dorothy 23,75,76
Wynne, Leonard 23,74,76

Ynys Enlli (Bardsey Island, Wales) 77,78
Yorkers 95

Zion Baptist Church (Remsen, NY); see Capel Zion
Zion Church (Holland Patent, NY) 73,**88-89**,103,120
Zion Church (New Hartford, NY) 73,126, **136-138**
Zion Church (Steuben, NY); see Capel Zion and Third Baptist Church
Zion Church (Welsh Hill, NY); see Seion
Zion Lutheren (Utica, NY) 109

Zion Welsh Presbyterian Church (New Hartford, NY); see Zion Church (New Hartford, NY)
Zwanzigstein Fest 203

APPENDIX

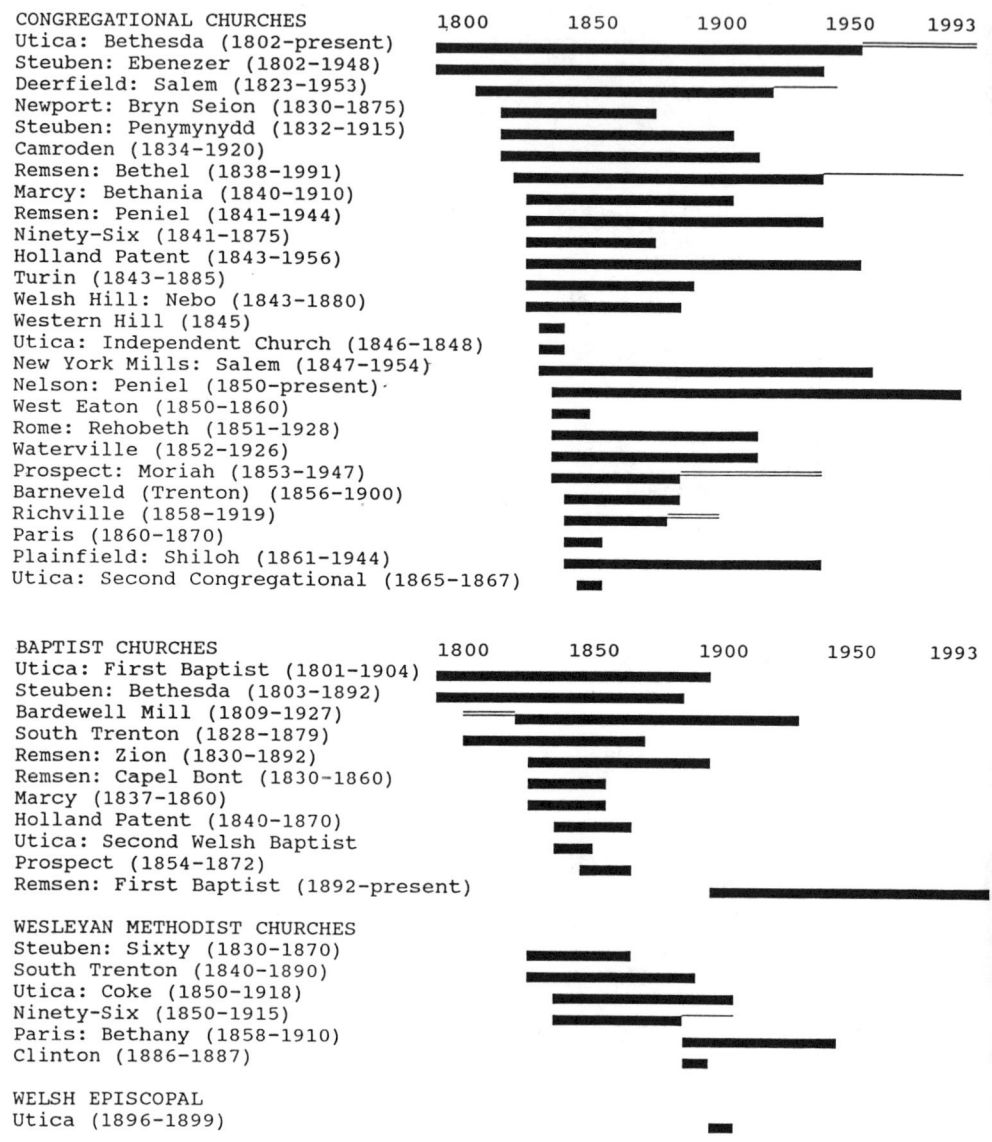

CONGREGATIONAL CHURCHES
Utica: Bethesda (1802-present)
Steuben: Ebenezer (1802-1948)
Deerfield: Salem (1823-1953)
Newport: Bryn Seion (1830-1875)
Steuben: Penymynydd (1832-1915)
Camroden (1834-1920)
Remsen: Bethel (1838-1991)
Marcy: Bethania (1840-1910)
Remsen: Peniel (1841-1944)
Ninety-Six (1841-1875)
Holland Patent (1843-1956)
Turin (1843-1885)
Welsh Hill: Nebo (1843-1880)
Western Hill (1845)
Utica: Independent Church (1846-1848)
New York Mills: Salem (1847-1954)
Nelson: Peniel (1850-present)
West Eaton (1850-1860)
Rome: Rehobeth (1851-1928)
Waterville (1852-1926)
Prospect: Moriah (1853-1947)
Barneveld (Trenton) (1856-1900)
Richville (1858-1919)
Paris (1860-1870)
Plainfield: Shiloh (1861-1944)
Utica: Second Congregational (1865-1867)

BAPTIST CHURCHES
Utica: First Baptist (1801-1904)
Steuben: Bethesda (1803-1892)
Bardewell Mill (1809-1927)
South Trenton (1828-1879)
Remsen: Zion (1830-1892)
Remsen: Capel Bont (1830-1860)
Marcy (1837-1860)
Holland Patent (1840-1870)
Utica: Second Welsh Baptist
Prospect (1854-1872)
Remsen: First Baptist (1892-present)

WESLEYAN METHODIST CHURCHES
Steuben: Sixty (1830-1870)
South Trenton (1840-1890)
Utica: Coke (1850-1918)
Ninety-Six (1850-1915)
Paris: Bethany (1858-1910)
Clinton (1886-1887)

WELSH EPISCOPAL
Utica (1896-1899)

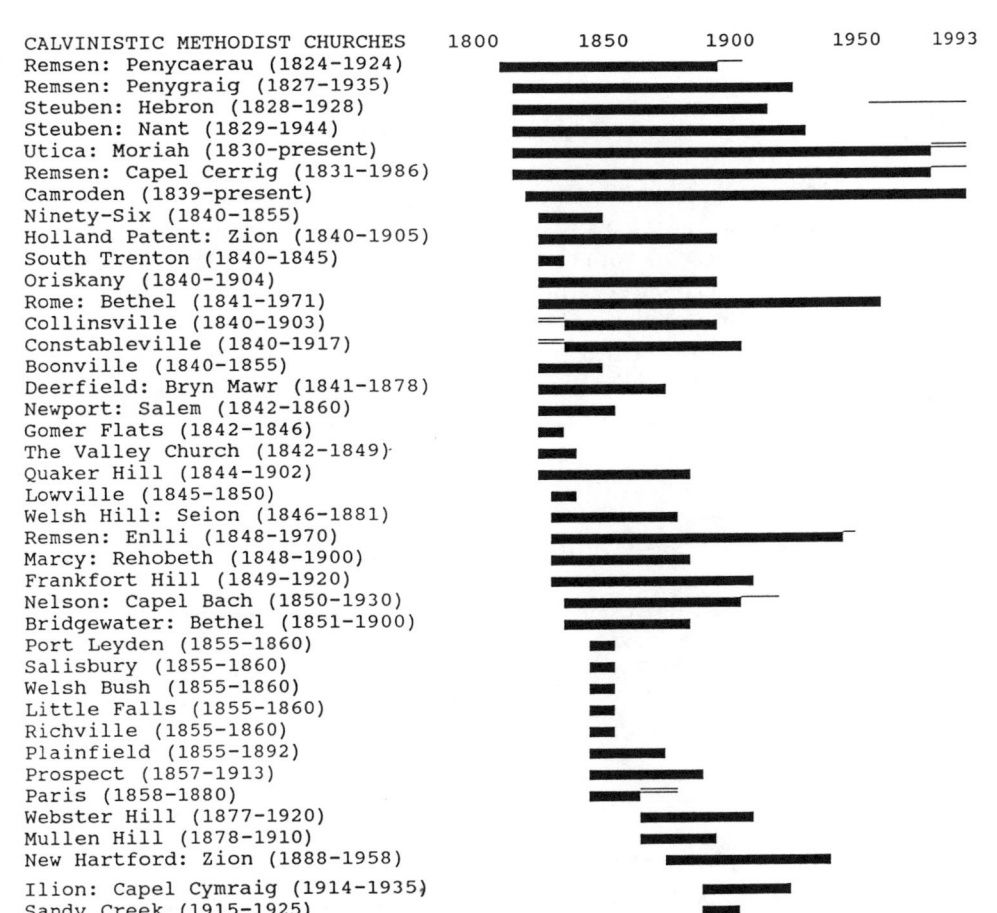

| CALVINISTIC METHODIST CHURCHES | 1800 | 1850 | 1900 | 1950 | 1993 |

Remsen: Penycaerau (1824-1924)
Remsen: Penygraig (1827-1935)
Steuben: Hebron (1828-1928)
Steuben: Nant (1829-1944)
Utica: Moriah (1830-present)
Remsen: Capel Cerrig (1831-1986)
Camroden (1839-present)
Ninety-Six (1840-1855)
Holland Patent: Zion (1840-1905)
South Trenton (1840-1845)
Oriskany (1840-1904)
Rome: Bethel (1841-1971)
Collinsville (1840-1903)
Constableville (1840-1917)
Boonville (1840-1855)
Deerfield: Bryn Mawr (1841-1878)
Newport: Salem (1842-1860)
Gomer Flats (1842-1846)
The Valley Church (1842-1849)
Quaker Hill (1844-1902)
Lowville (1845-1850)
Welsh Hill: Seion (1846-1881)
Remsen: Enlli (1848-1970)
Marcy: Rehobeth (1848-1900)
Frankfort Hill (1849-1920)
Nelson: Capel Bach (1850-1930)
Bridgewater: Bethel (1851-1900)
Port Leyden (1855-1860)
Salisbury (1855-1860)
Welsh Bush (1855-1860)
Little Falls (1855-1860)
Richville (1855-1860)
Plainfield (1855-1892)
Prospect (1857-1913)
Paris (1858-1880)
Webster Hill (1877-1920)
Mullen Hill (1878-1910)
New Hartford: Zion (1888-1958)

Ilion: Capel Cymraig (1914-1935)
Sandy Creek (1915-1925)

LEGEND
▬▬▬ : denotes the years when the church was active.
═══ : denotes the years when the church had merged with another.
──── : denotes the years when the church was only opened for an annual service.

About the Author

JAY G. WILLIAMS III is an attorney in Utica, New York. He is a graduate of Hamilton College and Albany Law School and presently resides in Clinton, New York with his wife Lilly and their children Thomas Emrys and Elizabeth Caitlin. As a fifth generation Welsh-American he has been active in Welsh activities in Central New York. He is a fomer director of the St. David's Society of Utica and the National Welsh American Foundation. He is a life member of the Welsh National Gymanfa Ganu Association and is a frequent conductor in New York and Pennsylvania.

About the Photographer

DR. JAY G. WILLIAMS has been a professor of religion at Hamilton College in Clinton, New York since 1960. He is the author of a number of books including *The Riddle of the Sphinx* and *Along the Silk Route*.

About the Publisher

PURPLE MOUNTAIN PRESS is a publishing company committed to producing the best original books of regional interest as well as bringing back into print significant older works. For a catalog write: P.O. Box E3, Fleischmanns, NY 12430 or call 914-254-4062.